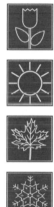

JEWISH COOKING

for All Seasons

JEWISH COOKING

for All Seasons

FRESH, FLAVORFUL KOSHER RECIPES FOR HOLIDAYS AND EVERY DAY

Laura Frankel

PHOTOGRAPHS BY BEN FINK

WILEY

John Wiley & Sons, Inc.

Photographs © Ben Fink Photography
Interior design and layout: Joel Avirom, Jason Snyder, and Meghan Day Healey
Cover design: Suzanne Sunwoo

Published by Wiley Publishing, Inc., Hoboken, New Jersey
Published simultaneously in Canada

For general information about our other products and services, please contact our Customer Care Department within the United States at (800) 762-2974, outside the United States at (317) 572-3993 or fax (317) 572-4002.

Wiley also publishes its books in a variety of electronic formats. Some content that appears in print may not be available in electronic books. For more information about Wiley products, visit our Web site at www.wiley.com.

Library of Congress Cataloging-in-Publication Data:

Frankel, Laura.
    Jewish cooking for all seasons : fresh, flavorful kosher recipes for holidays and every day / Laura Frankel ; photographs by Ben Fink.
        p. cm.
    Includes index.
    ISBN-13 978-0-7645-7184-8 (cloth)
    ISBN-10 0-7645-7184-2 (cloth)
 1 Cookery, Jewish. 2 Kosher food. I. Title.
    TX724.F64 2006
    641.5'676—dc22   2005032323

Printed in the United States of America

10 9 8 7 6 5 4 3 2 1

This book is lovingly dedicated to the memory of my father
Gunnard H. Johnson (1935–2004).

He was a generous host and loved to entertain friends and family.
He taught me to "at least try a taste of everything."

We miss you, Dad!

ACKNOWLEDGMENTS

WHILE WRITING, TESTING, AND EATING every recipe in this book, I had friends, family, and customers in mind. Like shopping for presents, I wrote every recipe considering favorite ingredients or techniques of people I know and love. Here is my chance to name the people who keep me cooking and "playing" with ingredients.

Zachary, Ari, and Jonah Frankel—for eating just about everything I make. For encouragement, love, support, and humor. Without you three, I would be incomplete.

My mother—for never doubting that I could do it. For love, encouragement, and showing me the way in all things.

Dennis Wasko—I lift a glass to you for all your help in the Shallots® kitchens, for your undying enthusiasm, and artistic sensibility. Thank you for your friendship and trust. We have cooked thousands of meals together. Here's to the next thousand!

Norm Finkel—you have been my friend and supporter through thick and thin. Something great is bound to happen, right?

Judith Weber—my literary agent who patiently waited for me to get it right. Thank you for you wisdom and steadfastness.

Beth Bassman—you always have the right words at the right time. You are a life raft on a stormy sea.

Stuart Dick—you seem to always call just when I need you. Thank you for reminding me about cauliflower.

Rabbi Samuel Fraint, Rabbi Steven Denker, Rabbi Dovid Jenkins, Rabbi Chaim Goldsweig, Rabbi Simcha Smolensky— thank you and L'chayim to all of you!

Peter Stern—your brilliance is inspirational.

David and Nathan Herzog—without your wines, the kosher consumer cannot feast.

Chefs Jacquy Pfeiffer and Sebastian Cannone—thank you for constant advice and instruction. You opened my eyes in the "pastry boot camp."

Dr. Ron and Cathy Silver—thank you for your support and friendship. I love feeding your family!

Gershon Bassman, Debbie and Robert Hartman—for your vision and love of the Chicago Jewish community, and for helping to make sure there is somewhere to eat.

Karen and Hal Sider, Edie and Murray Salzman, Julia and Donald Aaronson, Jeffrey and Sherri Bressman, Joan and Alan Sohn, Kim and Alan Frankel, Karen Walanka, Chani and Mordechai Tessler, Dr. Michael and Susie Friedman, Dr. Roy and Faye Weiss, Ira Kirsch, Rob Solomon, Aaron and Jennifer Minkus, Jeffrey Stein, Dr. Julian and Sarah Unger, Eric Rothner, Pam and Lenny Cohen, and the kosher community of Chicago—I love seeing you in the dining room.

Linda Ingroia, my editor—thank you for your support and for orchestrating this book.

I appreciate all the efforts that many other people at Wiley made to help make this book special and to spread the word, including production editor Ava Wilder and the publicity and marketing team of Gypsy Lovett, Todd Fries, and Michael Friedberg.

To cover designer Suzanne Sunwoo, interior designer Joel Avirom, photographer Ben Fink, food stylist Megan Fawn Schlow, and prop stylist Barb Fritz—thank you for your talented work and for helping to make this book beautiful.

Caroline Schleifer—thank you for helping me find my voice. Your focus and direction were essential for this book.

CONTENTS

INTRODUCTION

Comfort me with apples, for I am sick of love.

SONG OF SOLOMON 2:5

I HAVE THE BEST JOB IN THE world. As a chef, I cook nearly every day, and there's nothing I love more. I enjoy the whole experience of taking piles of vegetables and cutting them into interesting shapes and seasoning them with herbs, olive oil, salt, and pepper. I love scraping a vanilla bean and marveling at the amount of seeds and fragrance packed into the tiny, wrinkly pod. My heart skips a beat every time I pull a cake from the oven and add the fillings and flourishes that turn it into a luscious dessert. Making food from scratch is essential to me—I want to work only with the freshest and best ingredients.

The thrill of working with great ingredients keeps me cooking year after year, no matter how tired I am and no matter how many times I do it. At home, where I cook for my three sons, it isn't much different. Dinner is usually faster, but not always, especially on Shabbat. I cook the same kinds of foods for my family, with the same attention to ingredients and techniques, that I make at the restaurant. In my kitchens, I'm not just the chef or Mom; I am an artist, sculptor, and visionary every time I make a dish. It's a great feeling.

Both of my parents cooked, and like many families, the center of our house was the kitchen. My father liked to try everything and insisted that my brothers and I also try new things. Sometimes I liked it, sometimes not. But now I realize how much that trying affected my curiosity about food and formed my palate. My extended family also cooked. I remember how fascinating it was to watch my aunt make homemade fruit dumplings. I was mesmerized, watching her encase the fruit in a sweet dough. I was maybe five or six years old. Holidays always brought our family together. My grandmother would arrive at our house early in the day and get her marching orders. By the time I was a teenager, I was the one with the labor roster and would give Granners her favorite sit-down job of chopping. We had a great time together in the kitchen and could spend the entire day—sometimes days—laughing and cooking. The eating part was great, but I think the preparation is what I remember best from childhood. Sometimes I can't recall the menus, but I can always recall the jokes and songs.

My mother loved to check out new food trends, and I believe for one solid year we "wokked" chicken several times a week. (It was the thing to do in the 1970s.) To this day, my mother prefers to keep things simple and pure; she will always choose a tried-and-true rustic dish over a fussy, overworked recipe. I learned so much from her about not meddling too much with food.

We have a great family friend whom I would be remiss not to mention. Ina made—and still makes—desserts like no one else. She is a terrific baker and probably wished at times that she had a swanky pastry shop. I always had to know what Ina was bringing for dessert. When we went to her home, I would eventually have to be shooed out of the kitchen. I guess I don't blame the adults for trying to get rid of me. I was very young and very chatty, but I really just wanted to watch the "show" in the kitchen.

My love of music and of food have always gone hand in hand. I don't think that music and food are so different from one another. To truly enjoy both requires a higher sense of awareness. Everyone eats, but with a discerning palate you can dine— or even better, feast. You can have on some background music, or you can listen to music that chills your spine and moves your soul. Sometimes I get lucky and feast while listening to my favorite musicians. That is just about as good as it gets. Again, my parents influenced me greatly—they both appreciated classical and jazz music. I guess that is the approach I take with food as well. I use classical techniques to create new ritts. I try not to view strawberries as just a fruit for dessert. I sauté them and liberally sprinkle them with pepper. Cucumbers can be for salad or pureed with lemongrass and frozen into sorbet. Why limit yourself? I have to credit my parents with encouraging me to always think for myself. That has helped me adapt to new circumstances, as it did when I became kosher. I have never viewed the kashrut laws as a hindrance. I accept the list of shalls and shalt nots and move on from there.

One of the things that makes me different from countless other talented chefs is that I have kept kosher for almost thirteen years. Deciding to keep kosher, like many other life-changing decisions, stemmed from such a small incident that looking back I find it almost funny. When my eldest son, Zachary, turned three, my husband and I (we're now divorced, but we still raise our sons together) decided to enroll him in the local Jewish preschool. The first time one of his school friends came over to play, I realized that snack time had to be kosher. I, a chef and foodie, had to serve potato chips out of a snack bag on a paper napkin. No home-baked cookies, no sandwiches, no fruits and vegetables . . . just because my home wasn't kosher. The decision to go kosher was an easy one to make; I wanted all of my kids' friends to feel welcome in my home. We also realized that neither one of us really knew much about the incredibly rich history and traditions of Judaism. But we wanted our kids to have that grounding. Committing to observance of the laws and traditions was the natural choice for us.

When I started reading about what it takes to keep kosher, I immediately began to wonder how it would affect my cooking. The decision would change one of the most important parts of my life. But the more I read, the more I relaxed. By the time I met with my rabbi to get the lowdown on which items I could continue to use and which I could not, I didn't view kashrut as an obstacle to preparing great meals. I knew that if I started with great

ingredients, I could still make the same great food. For that you need only two things: top-notch ingredients and the desire to eat well.

The recipes in this book are all about using the best ingredients to their advantage. You don't need TV chef skills or flashy equipment. All that you need is to become a sleuth to locate the best ingredients and to accept no substitutes. What do I mean? You need to find local sources for the highest quality foodstuffs and then choose to cook only with those ingredients. This is the secret of all good cooks, but as kosher cooks we have even greater challenges. If you're not already best friends with your butcher, you should start today; your butcher can make your life easier and so much more interesting! Find the fishmonger who has the freshest and most beautiful fish (look at the whole fish—do they look like they're alive? Are their eyes moist and shiny?) Even if it's a bit out of the way, go to the local farmers' market and always buy what's in season. After all, you're cooking for your friends and loved ones and for yourself, so it's worth it.

Some kosher-certified ingredients are wonderful, but many are not, and some may not be to your taste. Invest some time in trying and tasting all the ingredients you use: If a recipe calls for chocolate, purchase the best chocolate possible, even if it means sampling several brands (a tough job, but someone has to do it!), and then use the one you think is fabulous. Similarly, if a favorite dessert recipe calls for butter and cream, don't substitute nondairy whipped topping and margarine. No amount of kitchen time and added ingredients will ever make them taste great. Butter is simply the best; cream has no substitute. If that means you can't have the main course you were planning, then be flexible and make something different.

I propose that as kosher-observant Jews we should always put our best on our tables. For me, that intention starts with seasonal produce; so purchase the most in-season, deeply flavored fruits and vegetables and turn them into natural, healthy treats. The same is true of any ingredients you buy. When you invest in the best bittersweet chocolate and most fragrant vanilla beans, don't spoil their beautiful flavors with fake products like shortening.

At work, where I'm surrounded by meat at least twelve hours a day, an employee sometimes asks me when I eat dairy products. My response is that I spend my weekends going full-on dairy. At home we eat fish all the time; fortunately my kids love fish, especially salmon, so it's a staple for us. Then I do not kid around with fake crème brûlée or soy cheesecake. I eat the best butter, cheeses, and ice cream I can find or make. I do not mess around with margarine cookies—I am in the trenches with my butter! I don't think kosher-observant Jews should ever have to put up with compromised food.

And we don't need to eat boring food either. Life is a daily adventure, and one of the ways to bring zest to life is with an adventurous meal. That's the premise of Shallots. We opened our first restaurant in Chicago in 1999, and we opened in New York one year later. My co-chef Dennis Wasco and I didn't want to cook kosher-observant food that was just as good as any regular restaurant—we wanted it to be much better! We set out to create the kind of place you could just drop into for a night out or plan to come to for the most elegant special occasion. We have always had signature dishes, from our lamb tagine to gorgeous steaks and chops. Currently, we are at home in Shallots Bistro, where our menu has plenty of French and American bistro favorites, from steak frites to homemade pâtés, but we also explore the cuisines of the world with our "passport menus" to bring the most exciting foods to our customers.

While I shop locally, I hate to have to limit myself to one kind of cuisine. There's a whole world of cooking out there, and I look to the Mediterranean, the Middle

East, the small towns of Italy, southern France, and Mexico, and many other regions for inspiration. After cooking, my greatest passion is travel. I bring something back from every place I visit, whether it's a particular spice mix or the memory of a fantastic flavor combination. I remember gingerly carrying a large jar of date confit with me all around the Middle East. I was so obsessed with keeping that jar intact that I planned all my other purchases around it. When I finally got home, it was the first thing I unpacked.

I adore trips to Israel, and it only takes a whiff of *za'atar* to bring back all my memories. I can recall a great dish just by grinding some spices together; then I am instantly transported to that place, half a world away. I think that is why I am so wild about Sephardic cooking. The food is filled with spices, fragrance, and the occasional spicy kick of hot peppers. I am Ashkenazi, and just didn't have that kind of food growing up. I read cookbooks more avidly than novels, so when I'm not on the road, I can still revisit the places I've been or plan for future trips. In this book, I hope to open your eyes to some of the flavors of the world that I particularly love.

While this book is not meant to be a kosher primer, it is important to state the basics. The laws of kashrut come from the Bible in the book of Leviticus. Leviticus lists the animals that are considered kosher and those that are not. In order for an animal to be kosher, it must have split hooves and chew its cud. Animals must be raised in a kind and cruelty-free environment and then must be slaughtered in a ritual manner by a *shochet* (a specially trained observant individual who performs the slaughter). The "life" blood must be drained from the animal and then the meat is salted to remove any traces of blood. Poultry—mainly chicken and duck—follows similar laws. Domesticated fowl are kosher when slaughtered and salted in the same manner as meat. Only eggs and milk from a kosher animal are permitted. Fish with scales and fins are permitted. Some fish have scales that they shed at a later stage of development; those fish are prohibited. Shellfish are never kosher. Fish can be purchased from any fishmonger or grocery store, but many people who keep kosher buy their meat, chicken, eggs, and milk from a kosher market.

There are three categories of food in kashrut: dairy, meat, and pareve. A passage in Deuteronomy states that you may not cook a kid in its mother's milk, so it is forbidden to eat milk and meat at the same time or to cook them in the same meal. Pareve refers to foods that are neutral and can be eaten with both meat and dairy. Eggs, fish, grains, fruits, and vegetables are pareve, although it is not acceptable to eat fish and meat off the same plate. For an in-depth description of kashrut, I suggest *How to Keep Kosher* by Lisë Stern (New York: Morrow, 2004). There are also many online sources, and your rabbi can offer direction and guidance. Also keep in mind that the kosher industry is ever evolving and companies often change their kashrut supervision. It is wise to stay current about your favorite products—frequently check product labels and check with local rabbis.

All the recipes in this book follow kashrut guidelines, and they are annotated with symbols identifying what part of a kosher meal they fit into: *D* for dairy, *M* for meat, and *P* for pareve (can be eaten with either dairy or meat dishes). I've tried to offer many pareve desserts and starters, to give you plenty of options for making menus that work for you. In several recipes, the addition of dairy (usually cream) is optional—it's strictly up to you. There are suggestions about which dishes will be good for Passover as well as for all other holidays when food is important (and that's all of them, isn't it?). I think one of the first things you'll notice is that you won't find any of the recipes considered typically Jewish here. In other words, don't look for a brisket recipe—nor gefilte fish, kugel, tsimmes, and such. I find the traditional Ashkenazic Eastern European recipes to be too heavy and not what I enjoy eating.

Also, I can't compete with family traditions and your Bubbe's recipes, so I don't serve those dishes at Shallots Bistro either. That's not to say you shouldn't have them if they are part of your family tradition, but as I've said to friends who are considering becoming kosher: Mix things up, make your kosher kitchen yours; you need to find your "inner cholent." That's the modern way to keep tradition

If you already follow or are considering adopting a kosher lifestyle, you and your family can—and should—enjoy the best foods that the world has to offer. The dinner table in the kosher home is the center of family life, and there's nothing more important than that. Religiously, the dinner table is supposed to be identified with the altar in the Temple, and the food that goes on it is sanctified through blessings and prayers. I think that some of the essence of kashrut is the conviviality of the table, and I love to sit with my family to enjoy a slow-paced meal. After all, I didn't go through all that trouble just to have the meal wolfed down. In order to be relaxed when I eat, I always prepare things ahead, so I've included as much make-ahead information as I could to help you get started. I love Shabbat dinners when everyone gathers eagerly to sit, feast, and share the adventures of the day or week together. Cooking with great ingredients takes me back to that Shabbat table every time I prepare a meal, even on a Tuesday!

As you start looking over this book, some of the recipes may appear to be complex or even a bit difficult at first. I suggest taking recipes in steps and making just the parts that suit you. As with any kind of cooking, things will go more smoothly if you take the time with your *mise en place*, that is, having ingredients measured and prepped well ahead of time. Life is infinitely better and easier when you have a well-stocked pantry filled with ingredients that already taste good. My "pantry" refers to my kitchen cabinets, freezer, and refrigerator, so take a look at the Basic Recipes chapter (pages 13–30) for some suggestions. The less you have to do before getting started, the better. Then, just buy your fresh ingredients and get cooking! If I had to summarize one essential that I teach young staffers at the restaurant and cooking students, it's that each ingredient that goes into the pot should be delicious unto itself. The end result will be a great dish.

KITCHEN EQUIPMENT

IT IS BETTER TO OWN FEWER PIECES OF high-quality, versatile equipment that you use often than to stock up on dozens of items you never use. This is especially true in a kosher kitchen, where you are required to have two or three sets of most everything: one for meat, one for dairy, and one for Passover if you wish. So you must be extra careful about not overstocking your kitchen with useless items. That said, having the right tool for the task makes cooking easier and more fun. When you can, try to purchase a high-quality item instead of a cheaper, flimsier one. This is especially important for knives, pots, and pans. There are plenty of relatively inexpensive and useful gadgets, too, so when you find one that you know you'll use, go ahead. I recommend the following items and have outfitted my kitchens with them.

KNIVES Every cook needs several high-quality knives. There are many brands on the market; look for knives that are full tang (made of one piece of metal from blade to handle) with rivets to hold the handle to the tang. High-quality knives last a lifetime and sharpen easily. They also hold an edge longer than a cheaper knife. In short, you get what you pay for with knives. As a woman chef, I actually prefer a heavy knife. I am not as big as some male chefs, so I need the extra weight of a big knife to help me cut through hard, large vegetables, like squash or celery root. The kosher cook needs to own two sets of knives. However, I do not recommend purchasing knife block sets that come with many knives you may never use. Instead, purchase several utility knives that can do double duty for everything you need to cut. I recommend:

Paring knives Buy several for peeling and fine cutting.

Santoku This is my favorite new knife. Although I've used a chef's knife for years, I find that now I reach for my stainless steel Japanese-style santoku for just about every task in the kitchen. A true Japanese santoku tends to have a carbon blade, which is difficult to take care of, but most European and American knife companies now make a version using stainless steel, which is sturdy and easy to care for.

French or chef's knife The workhorse of the kitchen, it's standard to buy one with a 10-inch blade. If your hands are particularly big, you may prefer a 12-inch blade. Once you get used to working with this knife, it will be your best friend in the kitchen!

French slicer This knife should only be used for cutting cooked meats. It is handy for roasts and large cuts, and I also use it to slice Gravlax (page 50).

Serrated bread slicer This knife is best used for cutting breads but can be helpful for cutting tomatoes as well.

HIGH-QUALITY SAUTÉ PANS AND SAUCEPANS I suggest purchasing a few basic pans and then building from there. Most essential are 10-inch and 12-inch sauté pans and a 3- to 4-quart saucepan for everyday meals. Several companies make pans with different finishes, which make it easy to

Sauté

I was once asked in a survey of chefs what I considered the tool I could not live without on a desert isle. I really did not have to think at all before I replied "my sauté pan!" In French the term *sauté* means "jump." To sauté means to cook the food in a small amount of fat over relatively high heat, while tossing it so that the food jumps and turns over. When you sauté properly, the food cooks evenly on all sides and develops a crisp, browned exterior. If you can't toss the way a restaurant chef does (it's tricky, but if you practice enough you can do it), then stirring occasionally is fine as well.

To sauté properly you have to use high heat and some quality regular (not extra-virgin) olive oil or butter for dairy cooking. It helps to have a heavy-bottomed pan that conducts heat evenly. Place the sauté pan on the burner and allow it to become hot. Then add the olive oil and wait until it also is hot. You should see a whiff of smoke. Gently add food of similar size and type in the sauté pan. (Don't try to sauté mushrooms and chicken at the same time, as the mushrooms cook much more quickly than the chicken.) Lightly salt and pepper the food in the pan and occasionally toss or stir the food in the pan to cook it evenly.

Be careful not to overload the pan, as the food will just steam and not cook quickly or evenly. Your food is done when it is browned on all sides. Simply move the sautéed food to a plate and continue with another batch.

distinguish which pan is for which food item. A good pan will be made of stainless steel with an aluminum or copper core. The handle should have rivets that hold the handle close and firmly to the pan. Make sure the pans you buy can stand up to high heat cooking temperatures. Some high-end pans cook only at low to moderate heat. You want pans that will multitask for you.

NONSTICK PANS I am very protective of my omelet pan. I hide it from my children and never let anyone else use or wash it. I use it only for egg dishes. It never has been scrubbed or scratched and will never see the inside of a dishwasher. My omelets are perfect and never scorch or stick because of my pan. For all egg lovers, I recommend a pan that is used only for cooking eggs. My egg pan is Teflon-coated, heavy gauge with an aluminum core. The handle is fastened with rivets. This pan was expensive, but is over eight years old and still in perfect condition. I also have a special nonstick pan for Roasted Garlic–Potato Galettes (page 178), but that is not as essential unless you fall in love with the recipe!

HIGH-QUALITY STOCKPOT
Canned stocks have little flavor and body. Learning to make stock is essential in any kitchen, and a stockpot can also be used for cooking pasta, simmering soup, and for blanching large amounts of vegetables. Make sure to purchase a stainless-steel pot with a heavy bottom, to ensure even heating and cooking. About 8 quarts is the most useful size. The kosher cook will also find it handy to have a large pot to *re-kasher* (boil) any items that may have become confused.

DUTCH OVEN OR BRAISING PAN I love heavy, enamel-lined Dutch ovens. These pans cook food evenly and are easy to clean. They will probably be heirlooms for my children, as they are crafted to last a lifetime. These pans perform best for long, slow cooking at medium to low temperatures. Some of these pans are very attractive and make great serving pieces. A large size, from five to seven quarts, is most useful.

BAKING DISHES AND OVENPROOF CASSEROLES It's helpful to have several sizes, some small enough to hold just a few fish fillets, and one that's large enough for lasagna.

ROASTING PAN Look for a heavy-duty roasting pan that can go from oven to stovetop. It should have handles that make it easy to move in and out of the oven.

METAL CAKE PANS, JELLY ROLL PANS, AND BAKING SHEETS

Jelly roll pans and baking sheets are good for baking desserts, and also for all-purpose cooking. Reserve your cake pans just for cakes. I recommend 9-inch round and square cake pans in an uncoated heavy gauge metal. They will last a lifetime. A few cake cooling racks are useful as well.

HEAVY-DUTY STAND MIXER

I prefer the large heavy-duty type that comes with whisk and cake paddle attachments. They come in the 4½-, 5-, and 6-quart sizes. They are a true luxury item, but worth saving for. They will last many years and will perform many kitchen tasks.

HANDHELD MIXER FOR PASSOVER
A good handheld mixer is adequate for Passover baking. You probably do not need to invest in an additional heavy-duty mixer for the holiday.

FOOD PROCESSOR
This machine is handy for chopping and blending. Prices range from very expensive to cheap. Because of the needs of the kosher kitchen, I recommend purchasing moderately priced models.

HIGH-SPEED BLENDER
I find the blender almost more useful than a food processor. The blender will puree soups more finely than a food processor. It will also combine ingredients more thoroughly.

Immersion blender This blender is sometimes called a stick blender; it is very useful if you make a lot of soups—you can use it to puree soups right in the pot.

ICE CREAM MAKER
Obviously not an essential, but if you wish to try any of the sorbets in this book, you will need one. The ones with a cannister you must chill in your freezer are much more reasonably priced than the models that both process and freeze the sorbet mixture.

MIXING BOWLS AND STRAINERS

You can't have too many mixing bowls. Make sure you have several sizes in stainless steel as well as some in heatproof glass. It's helpful to have several strainers in different sizes as well, from one small enough to strain lemon juice to one large enough to drain a pot of pasta.

PEPPER MILL
The flavor of freshly ground pepper cannot be duplicated with bottled ground pepper. (See page 5 for more information on salt and pepper).

Salt and Pepper

There are two ingredients that appear in almost every cuisine in the world and in all my savory recipes: salt and pepper. When I cook, I constantly taste and adjust seasoning at every step. It is particularly important to pay close attention to seasoning when cooking with kosher meat and poultry, because they are salty to begin with, due to the koshering process. Food always tastes better if you salt each ingredient as it cooks. It is impossible to season correctly if you wait until the end, and it's also more likely that you will oversalt the dish.

On a recent trip to a specialty food store I counted eleven different types of salt: There was sea salt from several different countries, salt from mountains, salt from quarries in India, salt from volcanoes in Hawaii, and more. I narrowed my choices down to three:

- Most chefs use kosher salt to cook with, as I do. It is a pure salt and has no ingredients added to keep it from clumping. I recommend keeping a small dish next to your stovetop. You can simply pinch the amount of salt you need and add it to your pan. When you pinch the salt you can feel how much is in your hand. When you use a shaker, you have no idea how much is going into the pan.

- For garnishing, I recommend a coarse sea salt from France. These salts have a nice texture and add a sparkly flavor to salads, raw dishes, and vegetable or meat platters.

- For baking, I use finely ground sea salt that dissolves quickly and evenly in liquids. You could use regular table salt, but I find it has an unpleasant and bitter aftertaste, from the additives. Fine sea salt can be used in your salt shakers as well. However, if you've seasoned during cooking, you'll find that you need less at the table.

Pepper—actually peppercorns—is also essential and sometimes confusing. The three main types of peppercorns seen on the market are really the same ingredient, only in different stages of ripeness. The black peppercorn is picked when the berry is slightly unripe. Its flavor is sharp with a touch of sweetness. I recommend Tellicherry peppercorns; they are full-flavored and robust. The white peppercorn is the ripened berry that has the skin removed. Its flavor is less pungent, and I use it when I don't want dark specks of black pepper in my food. The green peppercorn is the underripe berry, and it comes either dried or in brine. It has a very subtle flavor and is best used in combination with white and black peppercorns.

Peppercorns are available whole or ground. There's no question that I prefer to purchase them whole and grind them in a peppermill.

MINI SPICE GRINDER I set aside a coffee grinder just for grinding spices. Freshly ground spices have more flavor and aroma, so they deliver more "bang for your buck."

JAPANESE SLICER OR FRENCH MANDOLINE I have both of these items in my home, and I find I use the Japanese slicer more often than the French mandoline. The more expensive French mandoline is an investment but will give you many years of service. The Japanese slicer is inexpensive, works well, and is easier to set up and clean. Both are safe if used properly. They help you cut thin, delicate slices you could not do with a knife and does it quickly. Both tools are available in specialty cooking supply stores.

WHISKS There are many types, each one with a specific use. I suggest at least two: a large balloon whisk (which helps add volume) for hand-whipping egg whites and whipped cream; and a narrower French whisk, for breaking up eggs, combining dry ingredients, and whisking together vinaigrettes.

POTATO RICER This specialized tool is essential for light and fluffy mashed potatoes and gnocchi. If you don't have one, you can use a potato masher, but the texture won't be as good.

THERMOMETERS A good meat thermometer is essential for testing doneness of meats and poultry. It is also a good idea to have an oven thermometer: Sometimes it is not the cook that is "off," but the oven. While a candy thermometer isn't necessary, it can be very useful if you do a lot of baking.

ROLLING PIN I prefer a French rolling pin; it resembles a tapered dowel. I find that it maneuvers easily, and I can better control the pressure than with a pin that has handles.

PASTRY BRUSHES Brushes are great for applying sauces, marinades, and, of course, egg washes (reserve one for baking only). They also help brush off excess flour that can burn easily or make dough tough.

PARCHMENT PAPER OR SILICONE SHEETS Parchment is a must for baking and for everyday kitchen tasks to prevent sticking. If you want to indulge in a treat, buy a silicone sheet for baking; it prevents even the most delicate cookies and pastry items from sticking and overbrowning.

MISCELLANEOUS PEELERS, SPOONS, AND SPATULAS

Look for high-heat resistant spatulas and spoons made of silicone, tools with soft handles, and tools in different colors, which makes it easier to distinguish your meat and dairy tools. These tools are fairly inexpensive and are constantly being improved.

PASTA MACHINE If you plan to make your own pasta anytime, it's useful to have a pasta machine that you can attach to your countertop. The hand-cranked models work best and take up far less room than any electric pasta machine.

TOOL TIP The hardware store can be a cook's best friend. I have found many useful tools there that work perfectly in the kitchen. For example, I use a spackle knife as a work surface scraper when making bread dough and "pinch nose" pliers for removing fish bones. Sometimes, these inexpensive items are even better than the items marketed to cooks. Explore a good hardware store and see if you can find tools that perform for you in your kitchen.

HOLIDAY AND SEASONAL MEAL IDEAS

THE RECIPES IN THIS BOOK WILL SERVE you well for everyday family meals and special occasions. Below is a list of recipe options to consider when planning Jewish holiday feasts followed by menu suggestions for Shabbat gatherings and special events throughout the year.

HOLIDAY RECIPES

SEASONAL MENUS

SPRING

SHABBAT LUNCHEON

Cream of Celery Soup 43

Asparagus and Goat Cheese Lasagna 57

SHABBAT SUPPER

Gravlax 50

Spring Vegetable Soup with Basil Pistou 45

Roasted Lamb Chops with Fava Beans
and Minted Risotto 73

Strawberry-Rhubarb Crisp 83

Strawberry Sorbet 82

MOTHER'S DAY FEAST

Chilled English Pea and Mint Soup 39

Buckwheat Blini with Gravlax 49

Olive Oil–Poached Halibut with Herbed
Semolina Gnocchi 67

Chocolate Mousse Puffs 84

SUMMER

SHABBAT LUNCHEON

A Quartet of Gazpachos 95

Roasted Baby Carrots with Ginger-Lemon
Vinaigrette 105

Summer Vegetable Cassoulet 112

Shredded Lamb Salad with Mint and
Fig-Balsamic Reduction 108

Granita al Caffè 139

SHABBAT SUPPER

Chilled Cucumber Soup 91

Cucumber-Lemongrass Sorbet 92

Heirloom Tomato Salad 100

Roasted Duck Breasts with Cherry–
Red Wine Reduction 118

Peaches in Moscato with Amaretti 133

FATHER'S DAY BARBECUE

Sumac-Dusted Beef Skewers with Spicy
Mango Chutney 114

Grilled Flatbreads 122

Grilled Rib-Eye Sandwiches with Grilled
Vegetables 124

Bing Cherry Fruit Soup 135

Sour Cherry Sorbet 136

INDEPENDENCE DAY FEAST

Roasted Fig Salad with Honey-Lavender
Vinaigrette 104

My BLT (Bison, Lettuce, and Tomato) 121

Shallots Fried Chicken 116

Blackberry-Lemon Frozen Custard 131

BASIC RECIPES

Worries go down better with soup.

JEWISH PROVERB

HERE ARE THE RECIPES THAT HELP MAKE the others in this book shine from within. When your refrigerator, freezer, and pantry are filled with your own homemade stocks, spice mixes, vinaigrettes, and dessert sauces, you'll never be at a loss for a wonderful meal. Some of these preparations take time and patience. Veal stock, for example, may take you an afternoon to prepare, but most of that time it's simply simmering while you can be doing something else. When it's ready, though, you'll have what I call kitchen gold: It keeps for ages in the freezer, and it's so delicious that a spoonful or two stirred into a pan sauce or into a soup makes all the difference. Some of these recipes are fast—making your own spice mix only takes a few moments, so make a little extra. Then you'll have something special on hand to jazz up a weeknight dinner.

Chicken Stock	Roasted Bell Peppers
Dark Chicken Stock	Garlicky Aioli
Vegetable Stock	Herbes de Provence
Fumet (Fish Stock)	Za'atar
Veal Stock	Harissa
Balsamic Reduction	Chocolate Sauce
Pasta Dough	Raspberry Coulis
Preserved Lemons	Champagne Glaze
Tomato Confit	Champagne Sabayon
Slow-Roasted Tomatoes	Simple Syrup
Muhummarah	

Chicken Stock

M ▪ *Makes 2 to 3 quarts*

If there is one stock worth the time to make, it is this one. It is invaluable in sauces, soups, and reductions. I always recommend that my students make their own stock. The flavor and richness cannot be found in any purchased product. You can add or substitute ingredients as you wish, according to your tastes. For example, if you have fennel or parsnips on hand, use them instead of celery and carrots. If you have some garlic cloves or mushroom stems or chopped fresh tomatoes, it's fine to toss them in as well. Of course, you can also add some leek greens to your stock.

MAKE AHEAD/STORAGE This stock can be stored in the refrigerator, covered, up to 5 days, or frozen for 3 months.

  3 to 4 pounds chicken bones (wings, carcasses, necks)

  Water for blanching

  1 medium Spanish onion, coarsely chopped

  2 medium carrots, peeled and coarsely chopped

  1 celery stalk, coarsely chopped

  1 thyme sprig

  5 flat-leaf parsley sprigs

  1 bay leaf

  1 whole clove

  Approximately 12 cups water

1 Place the chicken bones in a large stockpot and cover with water.

2 Place the stockpot over medium-high heat and bring to a boil. Boil the bones for 3 to 5 minutes. Remove from the heat and drain through a strainer. Discard the water. (Blanching the bones helps to get rid of the scum that forms on top of the stock and can make it cloudy and bitter.)

3 Return the bones to the stockpot and add the onion, carrots, celery, thyme, parsley, bay leaf, and clove. Cover the bones and vegetables with cold water only to the top of the bones. (If you add too much water the flavor will be diluted.)

4 Place the pot back on the heat and bring the mixture to a slow simmer. Continue simmering for 3½ hours.

5 Strain off the stock and discard the bones and vegetables. Cool the stock completely to room temperature before refrigerating, covered. Ladle off the fat from the top of the stock when it has solidified, about 6 hours or overnight. Stock can be transferred to small containers or resealable plastic bags for storing in the refrigerator or freezer.

15

Dark Chicken Stock

M ▪ *Makes 2 to 3 quarts*

This is an incredibly rich stock with full flavor and deep color. It is great for wine sauces and dark-colored soups. We use it in the restaurant when we need an intense flavor but do not want the heaviness of a veal stock.

MAKE AHEAD/STORAGE This stock can be stored in the refrigerator, covered, up to 5 days, or frozen for 3 months.

3 to 4 pounds of chicken bones (wings, carcasses, necks)

1 medium Spanish onion, coarsely chopped

2 medium carrots, peeled and coarsely chopped

1 celery stalk, coarsely chopped

Leek greens (from 1 medium leek)

1 thyme sprig

5 flat-leaf parsley sprigs

1 bay leaf

Approximately 3 quarts water

1 Preheat the oven to 450°F.

2 Spread the chicken bones in a roasting pan and roast until dark brown, about 45 minutes.

3 Transfer the bones from the pan to a large stockpot.

4 Drain off and discard any fat remaining in the pan, and add the onions, carrots, celery, and leek greens. Roast the vegetables until lightly browned, about 30 minutes.

5 Add the vegetables to the stockpot.

6 Place the roasting pan over a medium flame and add a little water to the pan. Scrape off the browned bits (fond) with a rubber spatula. Add the dissolved fond to the stockpot (it is loaded with flavor!).

7 Add the thyme, parsley, and bay leaf to the stockpot. Cover the bones and vegetables with water just to the top of the bones. Place over medium heat and simmer uncovered 3½ hours.

8 Strain off the stock and discard the bones and vegetables. Cool the stock completely to room temperature before refrigerating, covered. Ladle off the fat from the top of the stock when it has solidified, about 6 hours or overnight. Stock can be transferred to small containers or resealable plastic bags for storing in the refrigerator or freezer.

Vegetable Stock

P ▪ *Makes 6 cups*

This is a classic example of "the more you put into it, the more you get out of it." When I make a vegetable stock, I don't use scraps or odds and ends of vegetables I set out with the purpose of making a fragrant, tasty stock. In a kosher kitchen, a vegetable stock can be invaluable for making pareve soups and sauces. In my home, I keep vegetable stock frozen in small quantities in resealable plastic bags. I can thaw the bags and add flavor to any soup or sauce, instead of using water.

MAKE AHEAD/STORAGE The stock can be stored in the refrigerator, covered, up to 1 week or frozen for 3 months.

½ pound cremini mushrooms (caps and stems), coarsely chopped

1 large onion, coarsely chopped

Leek greens (from 1 medium leek)

4 garlic cloves, coarsely chopped

Olive oil

1 medium red bell pepper, seeded and coarsely chopped

1 can (14 ounces) chopped tomatoes

1 large flat-leaf parsley sprig

1 large thyme sprig

1 medium fennel bulb, coarsely chopped

1 medium celery stalk, coarsely chopped

2 medium carrots, peeled and coarsely chopped

1 teaspoon whole black peppercorns

½ cup dry white wine, such as Sauvignon Blanc

About 8 cups water

1 Preheat the oven to 400°F.

2 Place the mushrooms, onions, leek greens, and garlic in a large bowl, and lightly toss with olive oil.

3 Spread mixture on a sheet pan and roast, without stirring, until browned, about 15 minutes.

4 Transfer the roasted vegetables to a large stockpot, and add the bell pepper, tomatoes, parsley, thyme, fennel, celery, carrots, peppercorns, and wine. Cover with water only to the top of the vegetables. Bring to a simmer over medium heat and continue simmering uncovered for 1 hour. (Do not simmer this stock for more than 1 hour. The cellulose fiber in the vegetables will soften and absorb some of the liquid. This will reduce your yield.)

5 Strain the stock through a cheesecloth-lined strainer and discard the vegetables. Cool the stock completely to room temperature before refrigerating, covered. Stock can be transferred to small containers or resealable plastic bags for storing in the refrigerator or freezer.

Fumet (Fish Stock)

P ▪ *Makes 3 to 4 quarts*

I eat a lot of fish. I like simple and exotic preparations, and this stock can be used for both. This stock is easy to make and can be stored in the freezer, ready to be pulled out and put into action. It is an essential ingredient in my favorite fish stew, Bourride (page 172).

MAKE AHEAD/STORAGE The fumet can be stored in the refrigerator, covered, up to 3 days, or frozen for 3 months.

6 pounds fish frames (heads and tails, gills removed; ask your fishmonger for halibut, snapper, or bass and avoid stronger flavored fish such as salmon or bluefish)

Olive oil

2 cups white wine

5 celery stalks, coarsely chopped

3 medium onions, coarsely chopped

Zest of 1 lemon, cut into strips

5 flat-leaf parsley sprigs

2 thyme sprigs

10 whole black peppercorns

1 bay leaf

10 to 12 cups water

1 Rinse the fish frames well.

2 Coat the bottom of a large stockpot lightly with olive oil. Place the fish frames in the pot. Sweat the frames over low heat until the bones appear opaque, about 15 minutes.

3 Add the wine, celery, onions, lemon zest, parsley, thyme, peppercorns, bay leaf, and enough water to just cover the fish bones, and bring to a boil over high heat. (Add only enough water to cover the bones; if too much water is added, the stock will be weak flavored, with no body.) Reduce the heat and simmer uncovered for 30 minutes. Skim the scum during the cooking.

4 Strain the fumet and discard the solids. Cool the fumet completely to room temperature before refrigerating, covered. Fumet can be transferred to small containers or resealable plastic bags for storing in the refrigerator or freezer.

Veal Stock

M ▪ *Makes about 3 quarts*

Veal stock is like kitchen gold! It is an essential component in rich pan sauces and reductions. But it can be hard to find a large quantity of veal bones. I have a standing order with my butcher to save bones for me. I jealously guard them and store them in my freezer until I have a sufficient amount to make this delicious stock. The stock requires a short amount of active cooking time. The magic happens over a long, slow simmer that does not require your attention. You can make beef or venison stock in exactly the same way;

just ask your butcher for beef or venison bones instead.

MAKE AHEAD/STORAGE This stock can be stored in the refrigerator, covered, up to 5 days, or frozen for 3 months.

10 pounds veal knucklebones or shanks

3 medium onions, coarsely chopped

1 whole medium leek, coarsely chopped

3 medium carrots, peeled and coarsely chopped

2 celery stalks, coarsely chopped

2 medium tomatoes, cut in half

2 cups chopped mushroom stems

6 whole garlic cloves

2 small bay leaves

10 flat-leaf parsley sprigs

5 thyme sprigs

About 5 quarts water

1 Preheat the oven to 450°F.

2 Place the veal bones in a large roasting pan. Lightly coat the bones with olive oil. Roast until browned but not scorched, about 1 hour. Transfer the bones to a large stockpot.

3 Add the vegetables to the roasting pan and roast them, stirring occasionally, until browned and caramelized, 30 to 40 minutes. Add the vegetables to the pot. Place the roasting pan over a medium flame, and add a little water to the pan. Scrape off the browned bits (*fond*) with a rubber spatula.

Add the dissolved fond to the stockpot (it is loaded with flavor!). Scrape up any browned bits and juices, and add them to the pot.

4 Cover the ingredients with water. Only use the amount necessary to cover them. (Too much water will result in a weak and flavorless stock.)

5 Simmer the stock over very low heat for about 8 hours, or until the stock is intensely flavored and full-bodied.

6 Strain the stock and discard the bones and vegetables. Cool the stock completely to room temperature before refrigerating, covered. Ladle off the fat from the top of the stock when it has solidified, about 6 hours or overnight. Stock can be transferred to small containers or resealable plastic bags for storing in the refrigerator or freezer.

Balsamic Reduction

P ■ *Makes 1 cup*

This reduction is an essential garnish. It requires only minimum effort and lasts almost forever! We use it the restaurant to add flavor and presentation to a dish. I use it in my home as well to dress up even the simplest plates. Drizzle it over the food or directly on the plate to add a pleasant, palate-opening tartness and attractive, professional look.

Basic Recipes

MAKE AHEAD/STORAGE This reduction can be stored in a ramekin, covered with plastic wrap, at room temperature up to 3 months. Reheat to use. (I reheat it in the microwave at home and in a water bath at the restaurant.)

4 cups balsamic vinegar

¼ cup dark brown sugar

Place a large, nonreactive saucepan over low heat. Add the vinegar and sugar. Stir the mixture until the sugar has dissolved. Continue reducing the mixture, without stirring, until it has the consistency of molasses (I do this over low heat, as it can quickly become almost solid when the liquid is evaporated over high heat), about 45 minutes.

Pasta Dough

P ▪ *Makes about ¾ pound pasta*

Once you've made your own homemade pasta, nothing else will ever taste as good. The texture and flavor are incomparable. It's time consuming, but the dough is fun to work with, and I find it a pleasant and very satisfying task. Kids have fun helping to roll out the pasta. It's easy to give your pasta extra flavor and color: Saffron makes it a perfect match for fish and for vegetables; lemon pasta is also delicious with fish and vegetable dishes, and with chicken and simple butter and herb sauces.

MAKE AHEAD/STORAGE The dough will keep in the refrigerator, wrapped tightly in plastic, up to 2 days. Pasta can be rolled out and cut, then chilled on a parchment-lined baking sheet. I have also hung it on hangers at home and spread it around the house to dry; then it can be kept at room temperature in an airtight container for about 3 months. However, when cooked this will taste slightly different from fresh pasta.

1 pound all-purpose flour (4 to 5 cups), plus more if needed

3 large eggs, lightly beaten

2 tablespoons extra-virgin olive oil

About ½ teaspoon kosher salt and ¼ teaspoon freshly ground black pepper

1 Mound the flour on a clean, dry work surface. Make a well in the center of the flour with your hands and place the eggs, olive oil, salt, and pepper in the well.

2 Gently whisk the wet ingredients until they are combined, then with your fingertips, start to incorporate the flour into the liquid a little bit at a time. When the mixture starts to form a ball, push the excess flour away to the sides and start to knead the dough, adding back some more flour if it is too sticky. Continue kneading the dough with a little vigor until it is smooth and elastic, about 10 minutes.

3 Form the dough into a smooth ball and wrap it in plastic wrap. Let the dough rest at room temperature at least 1 hour, or chill until ready to use.

20

4 Cut off about one-eighth of the ball and flatten it slightly with floured hands on a floured work surface. (Keep the remaining pasta wrapped while rolling out each piece.) Lightly dust the dough with flour and feed the dough into a pasta machine set to its lowest setting. Feed the pasta through again on the second lowest setting, dusting the sheet of dough with flour to prevent sticking, and repeat at progressively higher settings until the pasta reaches the desired thickness. Set aside the rolled-out pasta on a lightly floured baking sheet or dish towel and repeat procedure with remaining dough.

5 Cut pasta into desired shapes. To make fettucine or tagliatelle, cut the pasta sheets in half lengthwise and pass the pasta sheets through the appropriate cutting blades. To make large ravioli, lay the pasta sheets on the work surface and cut them lengthwise with a knife or wheel cutter every 3 inches. If you are not using the cut pasta immediately, dust it with flour and allow it to dry on a floured baking sheet.

6 Cook pasta in a large pot of rapidly boiling salted water until al dente, about 3 minutes, and drain in a colander.

Saffron Pasta (P) Soak 1 teaspoon saffron threads in 3 tablespoons hot water at least 10 minutes, until water is bright yellow. Add the saffron water to the well in the flour with the eggs and olive oil. This dough will be slightly wetter than plain pasta dough, so it may absorb more flour.

Lemon Pasta (P) Add 1 teaspoon freshly grated lemon zest and 1 tablespoon fresh lemon juice to the well in the flour with the eggs and olive oil. This dough will be slightly wetter than plain pasta dough, so it may absorb more flour.

Preserved Lemons

P ■ *Makes about 1 quart*

I always have jars of preserved lemons in the kitchen. They have a silky texture and distinctive flavor. They are an essential ingredient in Moroccan cooking and have found their way into many other foods. I slice them into salads and stews, toss them in pilafs, shake them in vinaigrettes, and use them to garnish countless other recipes.

MAKE AHEAD/STORAGE Preserved lemons keep indefinitely in the refrigerator.

21

10 ripe lemons

½ cup kosher salt

1 cinnamon stick

3 whole black peppercorns

1 bay leaf

3 whole coriander seeds

Pinch of fennel seeds

1 Scrub the lemons and pat them dry. Cut four of the lemons in into quarters from top to bottom about seven-eighths of the way— do not cut all the way through.

2 Sprinkle the lemons heavily with half the salt and place them in a clean, dry preserving jar.

3 Repeat with four more lemons, packing them into the jar. Add the spices to the jar, pushing them down around and under the lemons.

4 Squeeze the juice from the two remaining lemons and pour it into the jar. Cover the jar, and keep it at room temperature for 1 month. Shake it every day to redistribute the juice and salt. (The salt draws out the juices that will eventually completely cover the lemons.)

5 Refrigerate the lemons after one month.

6 To use a lemon, rinse off the salt and separate the peel from the flesh. Discard the flesh and chop the peel or cut it into thin strips, as needed.

Tomato Confit

P ■ *Makes 3 to 4 cups*

This recipe is very useful to remember whenever you have a great big batch of tomatoes, whether they're wonderful or less so. It's a great way to "hold onto" tomatoes when you don't have an immediate use for them. I love to confit heirloom tomatoes and stretch their season for several weeks. This confit is juicy and tender, while the Slow-Roasted Tomatoes (page 23) have a much drier texture.

This recipe can be doubled or tripled, based on the amount of tomatoes you have.

MAKE AHEAD/STORAGE Tomato Confit can be stored in the refrigerator, covered, up to 2 weeks. The oil can be stored separately in the refrigerator, covered, up to 1 month.

12 plum tomatoes or your favorite tomatoes (about 3 pounds), halved and seeded

3 garlic cloves, lightly smashed

1 thyme sprig

½ teaspoon chili flakes

1½ cups extra-virgin olive oil

1 Preheat the oven to 200°F.

2 Stir together all the ingredients in a shallow baking pan, and bake until tomatoes are soft and fragrant but not broken, about 1½ hours. Let tomatoes cool in oil until they can be handled comfortably.

3 Remove the tomatoes and garlic from the olive oil and strain out the remaining ingredients. Store tomatoes and garlic with some of the oil in resealable plastic bags or in small plastic containers. The remaining oil can be stored separately in a plastic or glass container with a lid. The oil is great for sautéing and can also be used for vinaigrettes. Use the garlic for sautéing or rubbed onto toasted bread for croutons.

Slow-Roasted Tomatoes

P ■ *Makes about 6 cups*

Slow roasting infuses tomatoes with the flavors of the herbs and slowly concentrates their rich tomato flavor by evaporating their water. I like to roast a large batch at a time; I refrigerate some for use within the next weeks and freeze the remainder to have when peak tomato season has passed. The flavor of these tomatoes is intense and very fragrant. You can use any kind of tomato—round, plum, heirloom, or any other.

MAKE AHEAD It takes a bit of time as indicated by the name of the recipe, but this delicious summer staple can be stored in extra-virgin olive oil in the refrigerator up to 2 weeks or frozen for 3 months. I like to do a large batch at a time so that I don't have to do it again for some time.

5 pounds tomatoes

½ cup chopped mixed fresh herbs (such as parsley, thyme, basil, and rosemary, or your favorites) or Herbes de Provence (page 27)

Extra-virgin olive oil

1 Preheat oven to 200°F. Line two or three jelly roll pans with parchment paper and fit a cooling rack in each pan.

2 Slice the tomatoes in half crosswise and scoop out the seeds and gel. (Save the insides for a homemade sauce if desired.)

3 In a large bowl, toss the tomatoes with the herbs and enough olive oil to coat them generously. Place the tomatoes cut side down on the racks.

4 Roast the tomatoes for 3 to 4 hours, until they are very fragrant and semidry but still soft, checking after 3 hours and then every 15 or 20 minutes, until they reach the desired texture. Let tomatoes cool to room temperature.

5 Pack the tomatoes into containers with tight-fitting lids and pour in the roasting oil to cover.

23

Spice Mixes

It is said that "variety is the spice of life." I would have to argue that spice is the variety of life! Spices and spice mixes add zest and excitement to food. They also satisfy our creative culinary urges. A simple piece of beef can be transformed into a Persian feast one evening with a sprinkling of Advieh (page 64). The same piece of meat can transport you to the American Southwest with a rub of dried chiles and other spices.

I insist on making my own combinations of spices for each dish. That way I can rely on my own likes and dislikes and customize my mixes. I encourage you to do the same. When I cannot leave Chicago, I often go to the Indian, Persian, or Chinese markets. It is amazing to see how much the cuisines vary just by their use and types of spices.

Whenever I go on a trip I head first not to the museums (though I eventually do get there) but to the open-air markets. My greatest thrills come when I discover an unusual ingredient. I remember shopping in the *souk* in Jerusalem. I went by the stall of a crafty spice merchant and saw that he had "incorrectly" labeled his turmeric as saffron. I pointed out his mistake and asked if I could see his saffron. He smiled and pulled out a large bag filled with beautiful saffron threads. He then became my friend for the remainder of my shopping trip and helped me negotiate my way through the maze that was the market.

Spices come from the seeds, roots, bark, and berries of plants. They are dried and come ground or whole. It is always best to purchase your spices whole and grind them yourself, because their flavor diminishes over time and can even turn rancid due to their volatile oils. Freshly ground spices have a whole different intensity and color than their preground counterparts.

I suggest purchasing a small coffee grinder and using it exclusively for spice grinding. Don't rinse it after each use, simply wipe it out with a damp cloth. (If you feel you really need to remove an aroma, try grinding a few pieces of bread or a handful of sugar in it.)

I buy my spices in small amounts from The Spice House (see Sources, page 257) and grind only what I need for a particular recipe. If I have any ground spices leftover, I store them in a sealed container away from heat and light.

Spice mixes and condiments you'll find here are:

Advieh (page 64)

Harissa (page 28)

Herbes de Provence (page 27)

Moroccan Spices (see Braised Veal Shanks with Moroccan Spices and Mango "Gremolata," page 241)

Muhummarah (page 25)

Poivrade (see Venison Loin Poivrade with Roasted Sweet Potatoes, page 183)

Za'atar (page 28)

Muhummarah

P ■ *Makes about 1½ cups*

This is one of my favorite condiments. It is so versatile that anytime I'm stuck for how to make a dish more special, I look to this fragrant concoction. Muhummarah can be baked as a crust on fish or chicken or even smeared on meats before grilling (try it on lamb chops). When I served Muhummarah with some homemade crackers at Shallots, a Chicago food writer called it the "city's best chips and dip." That's another favorite use: as a dip for vegetable crudités or even dolloped on poached pears. This recipe is based on a traditional Turkish preparation, and there are endless possible variations. I settled on this version, which has become our favorite in the restaurant and at home.

MAKE AHEAD/STORAGE Muhummarah can be stored, covered, in the refrigerator up to 5 days.

2 Roasted Bell Peppers (page 25; use red peppers)

1 cup walnut pieces, toasted

2 tablespoon tomato paste

¼ cup pomegranate molasses (see Sources, page 257, and page 161 for more information)

1 cup fresh untoasted bread crumbs (leftover challah is perfect)

¼ teaspoon chili flakes

1 teaspoon ground allspice

½ teaspoon ground cumin seed

½ teaspoon kosher salt and ¼ teaspoon freshly ground black pepper, or to taste

About ⅓ cup extra-virgin olive oil

Place all the ingredients in a food processor, and pulse until the mixture is fairly smooth. You may need to add more olive oil to adjust the consistency if the mixture is too thick. Transfer to a container and press plastic wrap directly onto the surface of the muhummarah to prevent it from drying out.

Roasted Bell Peppers

P ■ *Makes about 2 cups*

Roasted peppers are useful for tossing into salads or pureeing into vinaigrettes and sauces. They're also delicious on their own, drizzled with some extra-virgin olive oil and Balsamic Reduction (page 19).

MAKE AHEAD/STORAGE Roasted peppers can be stored in olive oil, covered, in the refrigerator up to 5 days.

4 large red, yellow, or orange bell peppers, or some of each

Extra-virgin olive oil (optional)

1 Preheat the oven to 400°F.

2 Place whole peppers on a baking sheet and roast them until their skins are almost black, about 30 minutes.

3 Transfer the peppers to a bowl and cover with plastic wrap. When the peppers have cooled, peel, halve, and seed them.

4 To keep them for a few days, layer the peppers in a small container and pour on enough olive oil to cover them completely.

Garlicky Aioli

P ■ *Makes about ¾ cup*

Fresh aioli is creamy and rich. A famous chef once called it "the butter of Provence." What could I possibly add to that description?

MAKE AHEAD/STORAGE Aioli can be stored in the refrigerator, covered, up to 5 days.

> 2 large and very fresh garlic cloves
>
> Kosher salt
>
> 1 egg yolk
>
> 1 teaspoon Dijon mustard
>
> 1 tablespoon fresh lemon juice
>
> ¼ cup extra-virgin olive oil
>
> ⅓ cup neutral-flavored oil, such as canola oil
>
> 1 tablespoon water
>
> Freshly ground black pepper

1 Place the garlic and 1 teaspoon salt in a mortar and pound it to a paste; or on a cutting board smash and scrape the garlic and 1 teaspoon salt with the side of your knife. Transfer the garlic paste to a food processor or blender or to a mixing bowl.

2 **Using a Food Processor or Blender** In a food processor or blender process the garlic paste, yolk, mustard, and lemon juice until well combined. With the motor running, slowly add the oils, drop by drop, until the mixture thickens. When all the oil has been added, keep motor running and slowly add the water to thin the sauce slightly. Season to taste with salt and pepper.

3 **By Hand** Place the garlic paste, yolk, mustard, and lemon juice in a nonreactive stainless-steel or glass bowl and whisk together until smooth. Slowly drizzle the oils into the bowl, whisking constantly, until the sauce resembles a loose mayonnaise, then whisk in water to thin the sauce slightly. Season to taste with salt and pepper.

VARIATIONS

Harissa Aioli (P) Stir in 1 to 3 tablespoons Harissa (page 28), until the aioli is as spicy as you like.

Serrano Chile Aioli (P) Use the food processor method. Before adding the oils, blend in ½ teaspoon ground cumin, 1 extra teaspoon lemon juice, and 2 halved, seeded serrano chiles. (If you like, also remove the veins from the inside of the chiles; this is where the heat is most intense. Be careful not to get too much of the chile on your hands, as it can burn.)

Herbes de Provence

P ■ *Makes about ½ cup*

This handy herb mixture is a fixture in my home and restaurant kitchens. I sprinkle it on chicken, fish, and even vegetables. It is delicious in braised dishes and with caramelized onions.

MAKE AHEAD/STORAGE This herb mixture can be stored covered at room temperature for several months.

3 tablespoon dried marjoram

3 tablespoon dried thyme

1 tablespoon dried summer savory

1 tablespoon crushed dried basil

1 tablespoon crushed dried lavender

½ teaspoon crushed dried rosemary

½ teaspoon crushed dried sage

½ teaspoon fennel seeds

Mix all the ingredients together. Store covered in a cool, dark place.

Herbs

Although I live in the middle of a city, I am still a gardener. My terrace herb garden provides me with some of my most essential ingredients. My plants are beautifully aromatic, and nothing makes me happier than seeing them from my kitchen window. At any time I might have pots of lavender, basil, rosemary, thyme, and many others going. Taking a moment to brush my hand over the lavender always lifts my spirits. It's not surprising, since herbs are so powerful, that their aroma and flavor can really transform a dish.

Herbs are the stems, leaves, and flowers of plants. They can be found dried or fresh. Dried herbs and fresh ones have different flavors and different uses. The flavor of dried herbs is intensified, so they are best used in long cooking methods such as braising or confit. Because fresh herbs contain more water, their flavor is more delicate. A sprinkling of fresh herbs added during the last few minutes of cooking enhances all the other flavors of a dish. Using dried and fresh herbs in tandem also works wonders. I like to flavor a long-cooking tomato sauce or red wine reduction with dried herbs such as bay leaves, then add chopped fresh herbs such as basil or thyme at the end of cooking to brighten the flavors.

Za'atar

P ▪ *Makes about ¾ cup*

The slightly astringent quality of the sumac combined with the earthy flavors of hyssop and thyme make Za'atar a great spice mix for a vegetable platter or potatoes. A typical way of using Za'atar in the Middle East is to dip bread into olive oil and then into Za'atar. I sprinkle it on everything from my scrambled eggs to the focaccia we make in the restaurant.

MAKE AHEAD/STORAGE Za'atar can be stored, covered, at room temperature for several months.

2 tablespoon sesame seeds

¼ cup sumac (see Sources, page 257)

¼ cup dried thyme

2 tablespoon dried hyssop (see Sources, page 257; put through a fine-mesh sieve or strainer to remove any sticks)

1 Toast the sesame seeds in a small sauté pan over medium-high heat, stirring, until they are toasted and somewhat darker. Do not add oil. Remove the sesame seeds from the pan and allow to them cool completely.

2 Combine the sesame seeds with the sumac, thyme, and hyssop. Store covered in a cool, dark place.

Harissa

P ▪ *Makes about ½ cup*

Harissa, an essential condiment in Moroccan cooking, is fiery hot but has flavor and depth. It is also my son Jonah's favorite hot sauce. We use it in the restaurant whenever food needs a kick— and Jonah uses it on absolutely everything!

MAKE AHEAD/STORAGE Harrisa can be stored, covered, in the refrigerator for months.

½ cup chili flakes

1 cup boiling water

1 cup extra-virgin olive oil

1 garlic clove

¼ teaspoon ground cumin

1 tablespoon fresh lemon juice

1 teaspoon kosher salt

½ teaspoon freshly ground black pepper

Add the chili flakes to 1 cup boiling water off the heat, and let steep for 5 minutes to rehydrate. Drain the flakes in a fine-mesh sieve or strainer set over a bowl and transfer the flakes to a blender. Add the olive oil, garlic, cumin, lemon juice, salt, and pepper, and process to a smooth paste, adding some of the chili soaking water if needed. Adjust seasoning to taste with salt and pepper.

28

Chocolate Sauce

P ▪ *Makes about 3 cups*

Smooth and velvety! There is a theory that says "some people do not know to stop eating until they have had a bit of something chocolate." I am one of those people! A good chocolate sauce drizzled on a simple slice of cake or on fruit is usually the signal I wait for.

MAKE AHEAD/STORAGE Chocolate sauce can be stored in the refrigerator, covered, up to 3 weeks, or frozen for 3 months.

- 2 cups water
- 1¼ cups sugar
- ½ cup light corn syrup
- ¾ cup high-quality cocoa powder (I like Valrhona or Callebaut)
- 1 pound best-quality bittersweet chocolate, chopped (I like Valrhona or Callebaut; see Sources, page 257)

1 Place the water, sugar, and corn syrup in a medium saucepan, and cook over medium heat until boiling. Add the cocoa and stir until combined.

2 Remove the syrup from the heat and pour over the chopped chocolate in a heatproof bowl. Allow the chocolate to melt (3 to 5 minutes), then whisk the mixture together until smooth. Pour into a clean container with a tight-fitting lid.

Raspberry Coulis

P ▪ *Makes about 1 cup*

A coulis is simply a thick puree. It is an embellishment and sometimes can be the "icing on the cake." This is not a typical classical sauce, as it is not cooked. I like it because the vibrant color remains and the flavor is bright.

MAKE AHEAD/STORAGE This sauce can be stored in the refrigerator, covered, up to 1 week, or frozen for several months.

- 3 cups fresh raspberries or frozen, thawed and drained
- 1 cup sugar, plus more if needed
- 2 tablespoon fresh lemon juice, plus more if needed

Place the raspberries, 1 cup sugar, and 2 tablespoons lemon juice in a blender and process until the berries are completely broken up. (Do not overprocess, or the seeds will be crushed.) Strain the sauce through a fine-mesh sieve or strainer to remove the seeds and pulp. Taste and adjust with additional sugar or lemon juice as needed.

Champagne Glaze

P ■ *Makes ¾ cup*

Use the best-quality bittersweet chocolate you can find for this glaze topping. I prefer Valrhona or Callebaut, but you should taste several brands and decide which one you like best. Pour the glaze on top of any simple cake to add a finishing touch.

MAKE AHEAD/STORAGE The glaze can be stored in the refrigerator, tightly covered, up to 5 days, or frozen for 1 month. Rewarm in the microwave, or set heatproof container in a saucepan of simmering water and stir until melted.

¼ cup Champagne or sparkling wine (leftover is fine)

⅔ cup light corn syrup

½ cup sugar

6 ounces best-quality bittersweet chocolate, chopped

Heat the Champagne, corn syrup, and sugar in a small saucepan over medium heat, stirring until the sugar dissolves. Remove from the heat and add the chocolate. Allow the mixture to stand until the chocolate has melted, about 5 minutes. Whisk until smooth. Transfer to a container with a tight-fitting lid if not using immediately.

Champagne Sabayon

P ■ *Makes 4 cups*

I use this simple sauce when I need a really quick pareve dessert. It dresses up everything, and once you get the hang of it, you can customize it to fit your taste and pantry ingredients. As with all pareve recipes, it is important to use the best ingredients possible. Use a good-quality wine and best-quality vanilla. You don't have to spend a fortune on the wine; there are many delicious, inexpensive kosher sparkling wines and Champagnes on the market. Enjoy a glass or two while you're making this sauce, and maybe this will become a regular recipe in your repertoire.

MAKE AHEAD/STORAGE The sabayon can be stored in the refrigerator, covered, up to 1 day.

½ vanilla bean, split lengthwise

½ cup sugar

1 cup Champagne or sparkling wine (leftover is fine)

6 egg yolks

1 Place a heatproof glass or metal bowl over a pan of simmering water. Do not allow the bowl touch the surface of the water.

2 Scrape the seeds from the vanilla bean (save the pod for another use). Place the sugar, vanilla bean seeds, and Champagne in the bowl. Whisk the mixture until the sugar has completely dissolved. Add the egg yolks and whisk constantly until the mixture has tripled in volume and a thermometer reads 140°F.

3 Remove the bowl from the heat and continue whisking until the mixture has cooled slightly, about 3 minutes.

4 If not using immediately, transfer the sabayon to a container with a tight-fitting lid and refrigerate.

VARIATION

Chocolate Sabayon (P)   When the bowl is removed from the heat, add 2 ounces finely chopped bittersweet chocolate and allow the sabayon to sit for a few moments, without whisking, just until the chocolate melts. Then continue whisking until the mixture is completely cooled.

Simple Syrup

P ▪ *Simple syrup made with 1 cup sugar and 1 cup water makes about 1 cup syrup*

This is a versatile tool to have in the kitchen. It is perfect for sweetening sauces and vinaigrettes without adding the grittiness of plain sugar. It is essential for iced tea and is a must for the bar when fancy cocktails need sweetening. It will keep indefinitely if made and stored properly. Make sure that all utensils that come in contact with the syrup are clean and dry; also make sure the storage container is clean and dry.

MAKE AHEAD/STORAGE   Simple syrup can be stored in the refrigerator, covered, indefinitely. Store the syrup in a clean, dry container with a tight-fitting lid.

In a clean saucepan, bring equal parts sugar and water to a boil over medium-high heat, stirring until the sugar dissolves. Boil the syrup for 2 to 3 minutes. Remove from the heat and let cool, uncovered, to room temperature.

31

SPRING

April is the cruelest month, breeding
Lilacs out of the dead land, mixing
Memory and desire, stirring
Dull roots with spring rain

T. S. ELIOT

SPRING IS MY JOY. THE CHANGEABLE
weather may not be agreeable, but I know
it's finally spring when I find myself craving
the first of the season's fresh and delicate
flavors. Spring produce and fresh herbs
enter the market almost spontaneously,
and I find I plan some of my best meals
that way as well.

One of the first signs of spring is
asparagus. I have seen it pushing up through
the snow, sometimes as early as March. This
versatile member of the lily family comes in
a variety of colors and sizes. I generally
use the green variety for most dishes and
garnish with white or purple varieties. I love
serving simple and elegant Asparagus Soup
(page 38) during Passover, garnished with
fresh mint leaves and scattered with bite-
size asparagus pieces. One of my favorite
creations is Asparagus and Goat Cheese
Lasagna (page 57); the tangy goat cheese

and asparagus marry together to make a
creamy and comforting concoction.

As quickly as the asparagus appears, so
do the artichokes. Baby artichokes, a true
celebration of spring, are delicate and
gorgeous on any plate. I am a fanatic for
these little gems and include them in many
recipes and dishes despite the time it
takes to prepare them. Honestly, should
everything we eat be easy? Sometimes the
result is worth the trouble. I love to sliver
the tender artichokes, quickly sauté them,
and pile them on fish, steaks, and chicken. I
also highlight them by slowly poaching them
in extra-virgin olive oil. The artichokes pick
up the fruitiness of the oil and the oil in turn
benefits from the nutty flavored artichokes.
Everyone wins with this dish!

My new favorite spring discovery is
fava beans. Fresh favas are getting easier
to find in farmers' markets and at grocery

stores, so they're appearing more often on menus as well. I love their bright green color and earthy nuttiness. I always try to share my passion for more unusual vegetables with my customers and family, so I've included a few different ways to use these tasty beans. Favas pair wonderfully with fresh herbs, especially mint. Try the Roasted Lamb Chops with Fava Beans and Minted Risotto (page 73) for a dish that's picture perfect, with flavors that sing the praises of spring. Favas also provide a crisp contrast to the tender baby artichokes in the Artichoke Confit and Fava Bean Salad (page 47); and they're wonderful mixed with vibrant spring vegetables in the Spring Pea Salad (page 76).

Another sign of spring I look forward to is the opening of Alaskan salmon season. I can hardly wait for the first boats to go out and come back with my favorite fish. I think that I sometimes take salmon for granted during the latter parts of its season, but in spring it's new again. I have tremendous respect for this fish and go to great lengths to train my staff to cook it properly. I'll even speak to customers about the virtues of wild salmon over the farmed varieties. My fondness for salmon doesn't stop there—Pan-Roasted Wild King Salmon with Mustard-Chive Sabayon (page 69) is a staple in my home and the kids love it.

One of spring's sweetest offerings is strawberries, which are always most luscious at the beginning of the season. I remember bringing some fresh-picked berries to the restaurant several years ago. I organized a side-by-side tasting for my staff of the organic berries and some mass-produced ones. I will never forget the look on one server's face as she ate her first fresh-picked berry and then exclaimed that she had always wondered what a real strawberry tasted like. I'm always anxious to get the berries onto the menu both at home and in the restaurant, so I try to make the most of them with Strawberry Fruit Soup (page 80), Strawberry-Rhubarb Crisp (page 83), and—my favorite—Strawberry Sorbet (page 82), with its bright color and refreshing flavor. The sorbet stretches the relatively short berry season: If you freeze some fresh-picked strawberries, you can save them for making sorbet later in the summer.

Each of my children has his favorite dishes and requests. I suppose I'm lucky because my children have always eaten fruits and vegetables without complaint, but they all truly love berries. My kids can be my toughest critics. They always expect something grand for dinner, and they're actually quite insistent about it.

Spring

Of course, this can work to my advantage, because I use them as a testing ground for my creations. At first, a dish combining pepper and strawberries with duck was met with suspicion until it was eventually tasted and praised. It was a proud "tah dah!" moment for both the Mom and the chef in me. You'll be pleased when you get similar results.

Sometimes spring is hard to pin down. Here in the Midwest, we can't always tell when it has finally sprung. The thing that I know for sure is that a great way to awaken from our winter hibernation is with a trip to the produce market: What refreshing delicious temptations await? Enjoy your exploration as I do mine and your meals and your families will benefit.

SOUPS, STARTERS, AND SALADS

Asparagus Soup

Chilled English Pea and Mint Soup
with Mint Pesto Crostini

Leek-Spinach Soup

Cream of Celery Soup

Spring Vegetable Soup with Basil Pistou

Persian Tomato-Rice Soup

Artichoke Confit and Fava Bean Salad

Buckwheat Blini with Gravlax

Venison Carpaccio with Artichoke Slivers
and Preserved Lemon

Duck Breast Salad with
Peppered Strawberry Vinaigrette

Leek and Onion Tart

MAIN DISHES

Asparagus and Goat Cheese Lasagna

Morel Mushrooms
Stuffed with Ground Veal

Herbed Roasted Chicken
with Quinoa-Mushroom Pilaf

Persian Meatballs (Kufteh)
in Tomato-Saffron Broth

Roasted Red Snapper with Preserved
Lemon Broth and Artichokes

Olive Oil–Poached Halibut with
Herbed Semolina Gnocchi

Pan-Roasted Wild King Salmon with
Mustard-Chive Sabayon

Roasted Lamb Chops with Fava Beans
and Minted Risotto

Ginger-Marinated Venison Loin
with Purple Sticky Rice
and Spring Pea Salad

Standing Rib Roast with
Porcini Mushroom Crust and
Mushroom-Onion Ragout

DESSERTS

Strawberry Fruit Soup with Fresh Mint

Strawberry Sorbet

Strawberry-Rhubarb Crisp

Chocolate Mousse Puffs

Floating Islands with Strawberry Fruit Soup

Asparagus Soup

P ■ *Serves 6 to 8*

Pure and *simple* are the words to describe this soup. Spring and early summer asparagus are sweet and beautifully colored with bright green spears and purple tips. The soup is as versatile as it is delicious, since it can be served cold or hot. This makes it perfect for a Shabbat soup; you can have it hot Friday night and cold Shabbat afternoon. I love it enriched with heavy cream or simply garnished with sour cream or drizzled with olive oil and lemon juice.

MAKE AHEAD/STORAGE This soup can be stored covered in the refrigerator up to 3 days or frozen for 1 month. Stir in cream just before serving, if using.

2 pounds fresh asparagus

Olive oil

2 large Spanish onions, chopped

Kosher salt and freshly ground black pepper

½ cup dry white wine, such as Sauvignon Blanc

5 cups Vegetable Stock (page 17)

2 teaspoons grated lemon zest

2 tablespoons fresh lemon juice

½ cup heavy cream (optional)

1 Trim the tough woody ends of the asparagus spears. Cut the spears into ½-inch pieces. Set aside about 1 cup of pieces.

2 Heat a large saucepan or stockpot over medium heat and lightly coat the bottom of the pan with olive oil. Cook the onions and asparagus, with salt and pepper to taste, until very soft and fragrant, 20 to 30 minutes. Add the wine and continue cooking until the wine has evaporated.

3 Puree the vegetables in batches in a blender or food processor, adding some of the Vegetable Stock, if needed, to make a smooth puree. Return the puree to the saucepan and add the remaining stock, lemon zest and juice, and the reserved asparagus pieces. Simmer the soup until the asparagus pieces are tender and the flavors have melded, about 10 minutes. Adjust the seasoning with salt and pepper. Stir in the cream just before serving, if using.

Chilled English Pea and Mint Soup with Mint Pesto Crostini

P ■ *Serves 4 to 6*

The bright, springy flavor of this soup is dependent upon fresh sweet peas. Just sit down with a large bowl and shell away. Shelled peas can be blanched, shocked, and frozen. (See page 41 for information on blanching and shocking vegetables.) But frozen peas out of the package are no substitute. They won't be as sweet and are often starchy.

MAKE AHEAD/STORAGE This soup can be stored covered in the refrigerator, up to 3 days.

5 pounds fresh English peas in the shell

Olive oil

2 medium leeks, white and light green parts only (save the dark green tops for stock), thinly sliced

2 medium shallots, thinly sliced

Kosher salt and freshly ground black pepper

½ cup packed fresh mint leaves

4 to 5 cups Vegetable Stock (page 17) or water

Mint Pesto Crostini (recipe follows)

1 Bring a large stockpot of lightly salted water to a boil and, while waiting, shell the peas (you should have about 3 cups). Prepare a large bowl of ice water with a strainer that fits inside the bowl. Cook the peas until tender, about 12 minutes, and drain them into the strainer. Immediately shock the peas by submerging the strainer in the ice water (see page 41 for more information on blanching and shocking vegetables). When peas have cooled completely, remove the strainer from the ice water and set the peas aside.

2 Heat a small sauté pan over medium heat, and lightly coat the bottom of the pan with olive oil. Add the leeks, shallots, and salt and pepper to taste and sweat until limp and translucent, 15 to 20 minutes. Remove and set aside 2 tablespoons of the leek mixture for use in the Mint Pesto. Puree the remaining leek mixture with the peas, mint, and 4 cups stock, in batches, in a blender or food processor until completely smooth.

3 Combine all batches of pureed soup, and adjust the seasoning with salt and pepper. If soup is too thick, add more stock to adjust consistency to your liking. Chill the soup, covered, until cold.

4 To serve, ladle the chilled soup into bowls and float several mint pesto crostini, if using, on top.

Mint Pesto Crostini

P ■ *Makes about ½ cup pesto*
and about 15 crostini

These are delicious on their own, but for a special occasion add these little crostini as a floating garnish on the Chilled English Pea and Mint Soup (page 39). I love the bright green color and the unexpected burst of mint in the pesto.

MAKE AHEAD/STORAGE The pesto can be made up to 3 days ahead and stored covered in a small container in the refrigerator. Press plastic wrap directly onto its surface (this keeps it from oxidizing and turning very dark).

¼ cup packed fresh mint leaves

¼ cup packed fresh flat-leaf parsley

2 tablespoons cooked leek and shallot mixture, reserved from Step 2 of the Chilled English Pea and Mint Soup (page 39)

¼ cup fresh, untoasted bread crumbs

2 tablespoons extra-virgin olive oil

1 small baguette, sliced thin (about 15 slices)

1 Process the mint, parsley, reserved leek mixture, bread crumbs, and olive oil in a blender or food processor until smooth.

2 Toast baguette slices until crisp and lightly browned. Spread toasts with pesto.

40

Blanching and Shocking

Blanching and shocking are exactly what they sound like: Vegetables are boiled (blanched) in lots of salted water just until tender, and then they are plunged into ice water (shocked) to stop the cooking.

This technique is essential for cooking vegetables properly. It's a restaurant technique, but any cook will appreciate the results. It allows you to prepare vegetables ahead, then reheat them right before serving, and it is a great way of keeping vegetables longer so they don't spoil or discolor. The technique works so well that you can prepare tender vegetables several hours or even days ahead, and then at the last minute briefly sauté them, toss them in a warm sauce, or add them to another cooked dish.

In the case of green vegetables, blanching releases the chlorophyll as a gas in the cells of the vegetable. Then, the shocking process traps the gas in those cells, giving the vegetable its bright green color. If you have ever boiled or steamed a vegetable until it was bright green and then watched as it turned to an unappealing khaki gray on the plate, that was because it wasn't shocked.

To properly blanch and shock vegetables, prepare a large pot of boiling salted water. Also prepare a large bowl of ice water with a large strainer that fits into the bowl. Peel or trim your vegetables, and add them to the pot of boiling water. Remember that vegetables cook at different rates, depending on size and density. Test for doneness by either checking with a knife or tasting a piece. For the average sugar snap pea or haricot vert, the cooking time may be as little as 1 minute. New potatoes can take as long as 12 to 15 minutes to become tender. Remove the vegetables from the boiling water either by draining them through the strainer or fishing them out with the strainer. Then plunge the strainer into the ice water and allow the veggies to chill completely. Remove the strainer, let the water drain out, and place the vegetables on a separate plate or in a bowl to dry.

By using the strainer you can blanch and shock vegetables in batches without having to change and reheat the water each time. This is a great process to use for a variety of vegetables that require different amounts of time to cook. Start with the lightest color vegetable first and then proceed to the darker ones.

Leek-Spinach Soup

P ▪ *Serves 6*

One of my favorite vegetables, leeks, are available all year long but seem to be at their tender best in the spring and summer. When cooked, they have a soft onion-garlic quality that enhances other vegetables. I think they're the secret ingredient to making deep-flavored soups.

MAKE AHEAD/STORAGE This soup can be stored covered in the refrigerator up to 3 days, or frozen for 1 month. Stir in cream just before serving, if using.

Olive oil

2 large leeks, white and light green parts only (save the dark green tops for stock), chopped

1 garlic clove, chopped

1 medium shallot, chopped

1 medium fennel bulb, trimmed, quartered, cored, and chopped

Kosher salt and freshly ground black pepper

½ cup dry white wine, such as Sauvignon Blanc

5 cups Vegetable Stock (page 17) or water

1 cup roughly chopped fresh spinach

¼ cup chopped fresh flat-leaf parsley

2 teaspoons chopped fresh thyme

2 tablespoons fresh lemon juice

½ cup heavy cream (optional)

1 Heat a large saucepan or stockpot over medium heat and lightly coat the bottom of the pan with olive oil. Slowly cook the leeks, garlic, shallot, and fennel with salt and pepper to taste, until the vegetables are tender and fragrant, about 15 minutes.

2 Add the wine and continue cooking until the wine evaporates. Add the stock and simmer until the vegetables are completely soft, about 15 minutes. Remove the soup from heat and allow it to cool.

3 Add the spinach leaves, parsley, and thyme, and puree the soup in a blender or food processor in batches until it is smooth. Return the soup to the pan and add the lemon juice. Adjust the seasoning with salt and pepper. Simmer the soup 15 minutes longer, to allow the flavors to meld. Stir in the cream just before serving, if using.

Cream of Celery Soup

P ■ *Serves 6*

There comes a time at the end of winter when I begin craving the light tastes of spring, yet the farmers' market is still bare of new crops. This soup heralds spring with its light color and flavor. The ingredients are simple, but the end result is complex and flavorful.

MAKE AHEAD/STORAGE This soup can be stored covered in the refrigerator, up to 3 days, or frozen for 1 month.

1 bunch of celery

Olive oil

2 leeks, white and light green parts only (save the dark green tops for stock), chopped

1 small celery root (celeriac, 6 to 8 ounces), peeled and cut into medium dice

1 medium Yukon gold potato, peeled and cut into small dice

½ cup dry white wine, such as Sauvignon Blanc

5 cups Vegetable Stock (page 17) or water

1 teaspoon celery seeds

Kosher salt and freshly ground black pepper

1 cup heavy cream

Suggested Garnishes celery leaves, additional celery seeds, Porcini Oil (page 148), crème fraîche

1 Peel off the outer stringy part of the celery and discard. Cut the celery into small dice (reserve the inner leaves for garnish). Set aside.

2 Heat a large stockpot or saucepan over medium-low heat and lightly coat the bottom of the pan with olive oil. Add the leeks and sweat them until limp and translucent, 15 to 20 minutes (do not allow them to brown).

3 Add the diced celery. Cook until tender, about 15 minutes.

4 Add the diced celery root and potato to the leek mixture, and continue to slowly cook the vegetables until they are slightly softened and fragrant, about 15 minutes more. Add the wine and continue cooking until the alcohol evaporates, about 2 minutes. Add the stock, celery seeds, and salt and pepper to taste and simmer the vegetables until they are completely soft and falling apart, about 30 minutes.

5 Remove the pan from the heat and allow the soup mixture to cool. Puree the soup in a blender or a food processor in batches until smooth. Return the soup to the pan and add the cream. Bring the soup to a simmer and adjust the seasoning with salt and pepper.

6 To serve, ladle the soup into bowls and top with your choice of garnish.

Spring

Spring Vegetable Soup
with Basil Pistou

P ▪ *Serves 8*

This is my version of the hearty vegetable and bean soup found all over the Mediterranean region, whether it's *soupe au pistou* in the south of France or *minestrone* along the Italian coast. I make sure it's chockful of the best vegetables of the season, but I particularly love it in late spring, when the asparagus is still at its best and the first green and yellow beans begin to appear at the farmers' market. This fresh and healthy soup makes a wonderful light dinner on its own or with a simple salad. Plan to cook the chick peas and cannellini beans the day before or just use canned beans.

Olive oil

1 celery stalk, chopped

1 medium onion, chopped

1 leek, white and light green parts only (save the dark green tops for stock), thinly sliced

2 garlic cloves, finely chopped

2 tablespoons tomato paste

½ pound fresh asparagus, woody ends trimmed off, cut into ½-inch pieces

½ pound yellow wax beans, cut into ½-inch pieces

½ pound French green beans (haricots verts) or tender green beans, cut into ½-inch pieces

2 medium zucchini, cut into ½-inch cubes

1 medium red bell pepper, cut into ½-inch dice

1 medium head of escarole, roughly chopped

2 cups cooked chick peas

2 cups cooked cannellini beans

½ cup dry white wine, such as Sauvignon Blanc

Kosher salt and freshly ground black pepper

One 14- to 15-ounce can whole peeled plum tomatoes

About 8 cups water or Vegetable Stock (page 17)

Basil Pistou (recipe follows)

1 Heat a large stockpot or saucepan over medium heat, and lightly coat the bottom of the pan with olive oil. Slowly cook the celery, onion, leek, and garlic until soft and fragrant, about 15 minutes. Stir in the tomato paste.

2 Add the asparagus, wax and green beans, zucchini, bell pepper, escarole, chick peas, cannellini beans, wine, and salt and pepper, to taste, and cook until the wine has evaporated. Add tomatoes with their juices, breaking up the tomatoes with your hands; add enough water to cover, and simmer the soup until the vegetables are tender and the flavors have melded, about 30 minutes. Adjust the seasoning with salt and pepper.

3 To serve, ladle soup into bowls and stir a spoonful of pistou into each serving.

Basil Pistou

P ■ *Makes about ½ cup*

It's always worthwhile to double the recipe for this basil condiment so you have extra on hand: You can toss it with steamed vegetables, drizzle it on tomato salad, swirl it with pasta, smear it on a sandwich. Just use your imagination, and you'll use it all up.

MAKE AHEAD/STORAGE This pistou can be stored covered in a small container in the refrigerator, up to 2 days, or frozen for 1 month. Press plastic wrap directly onto its surface (this keeps it from oxidizing and turning very dark).

1 cup lightly packed fresh basil leaves

1 garlic clove, chopped

¼ cup extra-virgin olive oil

Kosher salt and freshly ground black pepper

1 Fill a medium saucepan with water and bring to a boil over medium-high heat. Prepare a bowl of ice water with a strainer that fits in the bowl. Place the basil in the strainer and lower it into the boiling water for about 10 seconds or until completely wilted. Immediately transfer the strainer to the ice water and cool the basil completely. (See page 41 for more information on blanching and shocking vegetables.) Transfer the basil to paper towels to dry, and squeeze out all the water.

2 Process the blanched basil and the garlic in a blender or food processor until well blended. With the motor running, drizzle in the olive oil until it forms a thick paste. Season the pistou to taste with salt and pepper.

Persian Tomato-Rice Soup

P ■ *Serves 6 to 8*

This is a perfect dish for the two days of feasting for Purim, which originated in ancient Persia. Purim falls during the spring some years and sometimes at the end of winter. It's a calendar phenomenon, and we are used to it! Canned tomato puree and rice are pantry staples, so this soup is perfect for late winter or early spring, before the new spring crops start to appear at the farmers' market or even in the grocery store.

MAKE AHEAD/STORAGE The soup can be stored in the refrigerator, covered, up to 2 days.

1 cup basmati rice

4 cilantro stems (save leaves for garnish)

4 to 5 cups Chicken Stock (page 15) or Vegetable Stock (page 17)

2 cups tomato puree

1 tablespoon ground allspice

1 tablespoon ground coriander

1 tablespoon fresh lemon juice

Kosher salt and freshly ground black pepper

Suggested Garnishes chopped fresh cilantro, Advieh (page 64)

1 In a large saucepan, bring the rice, cilantro stems, and 4 cups chicken stock to a boil. Reduce the heat to medium-low. Simmer the rice, covered, until it is slightly overcooked and very tender, about 25 minutes.

2 Discard the cilantro stems and stir in the tomato puree, allspice, coriander, lemon juice, and salt and pepper to taste. Simmer the soup for 30 minutes to allow the flavors to combine.

3 Puree the soup in a blender or food processor in batches until smooth. If the soup is too thick, adjust the consistency with more stock and adjust the seasoning with salt and pepper.

4 To serve, ladle the soup into bowls and sprinkle with your choice of garnish.

Artichoke Confit and Fava Bean Salad

P ▪ *Serves 4*

When spring has finally sprung, baby artichokes appear in the market, and I'm quick to grab them. One of my favorite ways to prepare them is to confit them in extra-virgin olive oil, so they absorb the fruity oil flavor and aroma. A big plus to making the confit is that the artichokes keep for up to a week, unlike traditional boiled artichokes. The fava beans can be prepared several days ahead as well, so this salad is perfect for tossing together at the last minute. I always save the extra-flavorful confit olive oil. I use it to confit other vegetables, such as cipollini onions, shallots, fingerling potatoes, garlic, and tomatoes. It's also wonderful whisked into vinaigrettes.

MAKE AHEAD/STORAGE The artichokes can be prepared up to 1 week ahead, the favas can be prepared up to 2 days ahead, and the confit olive oil keeps for several weeks, each stored separately, covered, in the refrigerator.

For the Confit

  1 lemon

  8 baby artichokes or frozen artichoke bottoms, thawed

  2 garlic cloves

  2 thyme sprigs

  1 medium shallot

  About 2 cups extra-virgin olive oil

  1 pound fresh fava beans in the shell

  ¼ cup chopped fresh mint leaves

  2 tablespoons chopped fresh flat-leaf parsley

  2 tablespoons fresh lemon juice

  Sea salt and freshly ground black pepper to taste

  4 cups mixed greens

1 Make the Confit Preheat the oven to 275°F. Cut the lemon in half, squeeze the juice into a medium bowl filled with water, and place the lemon in the water (this will keep the artichoke from discoloring).

2 Snap off the outer leaves at the base of an artichoke. Use a paring knife to trim off the green outer layer of the stem; try to leave the stem attached to the artichoke. Continue to peel off the outer layer of leaves from the artichoke using a paring knife or a vegetable peeler. Continue trimming until the inner leaves are half green and half yellow, then cut off the top half, leaving a cup-shaped artichoke. Scoop out the fuzzy choke in the center using a melon baller or small spoon. Drop the cleaned artichoke into the bowl of lemon water. Clean the remaining artichokes in the same manner.

3 Drain the artichokes and shake of any excess water. Place artichokes (or thawed artichoke bottoms, if using) in a shallow ovenproof casserole or small baking dish and add the garlic, thyme, and shallot. Pour in enough olive oil to completely cover the artichokes. Loosely cover the casserole with a piece of crumpled parchment paper, pressing it right onto the surface of the artichokes to keep them from popping out of the oil too much. Bake the artichokes until they are tender when pricked with a paring knife, about 30 minutes. Carefully transfer the artichokes, garlic, and shallot to a baking sheet to cool. Cool the olive oil.

4 Shell the fava beans. Bring a medium saucepan of salted water to a boil, and prepare a bowl of ice water with a strainer that fits inside the bowl. Cook the fava beans until tender, about 5 minutes, and drain them into the strainer. Immediately shock the favas by submerging the strainer in the ice water (see page 41 for more information on blanching and shocking vegetables). When favas have cooled completely, remove the strainer from the ice water and peel the transparent skin off the beans.

5 To make the salad, slice the artichokes in quarters and toss them with the fava beans, mint, parsley, 2 tablespoons of the reserved confit oil, the lemon juice, and salt and pepper to taste. If desired, chop the confit garlic and shallot and toss with the artichoke mixture. Serve on salad greens, chilled or at room temperature, sprinkled with additional salt and pepper to taste. Extra confit oil can be stored in a container with a tight-fitting lid and used for vinaigrettes or for sautés.

48

*Standing Rib Roast with Porcini Mushroom Crust
and Mushroom-Onion Ragout (Page 78)* ■ SPRING

Asparagus and Goat Cheese Lasagna (Page 57) ▪ SPRING

Roasted Lamb Chops with Fava Beans and Minted Risotto (Page 73) ▪ SPRING

Strawberry–Rhubarb Crisp (Page 83) *with*
Strawberry Sorbet (Page 82) ▪ SPRING

Gazpacho Variations, front to back: Tomato Gazpacho (Page 95),
Shallots Bistro-Style Gazpacho (Page 97), and Green Gazpacho (Page 97) ■ SUMMER

Grilled Rib-Eye Sandwiches with
Grilled Vegetables (Page 124) ■ SUMMER

Shallots Fried Chicken (Page 116) with
Za'atar Spiced Potato Salad (Page 117) ▪ SUMMER

Blackberry–Lemon Frozen Custard (Page 131) ■ SUMMER

Buckwheat Blini with Gravlax

P ■ *Serves 6 as an appetizer (makes about 36 blini)*

This is an elegant starter for a Mother's Day brunch or really any occasion. Buckwheat has an assertively nutty flavor. The blini pair wonderfully with the salmon or can be topped with chutney, cured meat, or grilled vegetables instead.

MAKE AHEAD/STORAGE Blini are best served right away, but extras can be stored, wrapped tightly, at room temperature for 1 day or frozen for 1 month.

2 tablespoons unsalted butter or neutral-flavored oil

1¼ cups whole milk or water

½ cup buckwheat flour

½ cup all-purpose flour

Pinch of kosher salt

2 large eggs

Olive oil

About ½ pound Gravlax (recipe follows)

Suggested Garnishes sour cream, Mixed Olive Tapenade (page 230), Garlicky Aioli (page 26), Muhummarah (page 25), chopped fresh parsley or dill, chopped hard-cooked egg, chopped shallots

1 Heat the butter with the milk in a small saucepan just until butter melts. Alternatively, heat the water and oil together just until warm to the touch.

2 Meanwhile, in a food processor or blender process both flours and salt briefly to combine. With the motor running, pour in the warmed liquid. Add the eggs and process until just combined. Transfer the batter to a bowl and cover with plastic wrap. Let the batter rest for 30 minutes.

3 Preheat the oven to 200°F. Heat a griddle or large sauté pan over medium heat and lightly brush the pan with olive oil. Drop the batter onto the griddle by tablespoonfuls, forming pancakes that are 2 to 3 inches in diameter. Cook the blini until nicely browned on the first side, about 1 to 2 minutes, then turn to brown the other side, about 1 minute more. Transfer the blini to an ovenproof platter and keep them warm in the oven while making remaining blini. Continue until all of the batter is used.

4 To serve the blini, slice the Gravlax very thin on the bias. Mound the salmon onto the blini, and top with your choice of garnishes.

Gravlax (Cured Salmon)

P ■ *Serves 6 as an appetizer*

Homemade cured salmon tastes clean and fresh, without the overwhelming smoky flavor or mushy texture of some commercially prepared smoked or cured salmon. I love the versatility of this dish; it's a perfect match for the blini, but I've also found it's delicious on vegetable slices or toast points. I use any leftovers to dress up salads, to stir into scrambled eggs, and of course to pile on bagels with cream cheese! It's also a great way to take advantage of the wild salmon season, which unfortunately doesn't last all year. I'm not a fan of smoked salmon and much prefer it cured.

MAKE AHEAD/STORAGE Gravlax can be stored, wrapped tightly, in the refrigerator up to 2 weeks or frozen for 3 months.

One 3- to 4-pound wild Alaskan king, Copper River, or other wild salmon, filleted and pin bones removed, skinned

¼ cup vodka

¼ cup coarsely ground black peppercorns (optional)

½ cup coarsely chopped fresh herbs, such as dill, tarragon, basil, parsley, savory, or a mix of favorite herbs

½ cup light brown sugar

½ cup kosher salt

1 Place the fillets on a work surface and sprinkle all over with the vodka, then the pepper, if using, and the herbs.

2 Combine the sugar and salt in a bowl. Pat the fillets all over with a thick layer of the salt mixture, using all of it. Stack the fillets on top of one another, tail to tail with nonskin sides facing, and wrap them together tightly with plastic wrap, leaving the ends open so that the liquid can drain off.

3 Place the salmon in a large container and weighted down with a cutting board with heavy cans on top. Let the salmon cure for 2 days in the refrigerator, draining off any liquid that has accumulated each day.

4 On the second day, unwrap the salmon and separate the fillets. Rinse off the salt mixture under cold running water and pat the fillets dry with paper towels. The gravlax can be served at this point, but for a drier texture, return the salmon to a clean, dry container and refrigerate the fillets, uncovered, for 1 day more. Slice the gravlax very thin on the bias for serving.

Venison Carpaccio with Artichoke Slivers and Preserved Lemon

M ■ *Serves 6 to 8*

If you love beef carpaccio, you'll enjoy this twist, because venison has an even richer, more intense flavor than beef. This is such a refreshing, tasty appetizer that I could easily eat it every day. The pure simple flavors are not complicated by a lot of seasoning—plus the cooking is kept to a minimum.

MAKE AHEAD/STORAGE Carpaccio can be stored, wrapped tightly, in the refrigerator up to 3 hours.

1 pound venison loin, silverskin removed by your butcher*

3 baby artichokes

Juice and grated zest of 1 lemon

1 Preserved Lemon (page 21)

1 medium blood orange, peeled and sectioned (see Step 6, page 152; reserve juice for another use)

1 garlic clove

Extra-virgin olive oil

Coarse sea salt and freshly ground black pepper

*If venison is not available at your butcher, see Sources (page 257).

1 Cut the venison into long, thin pieces. Don't worry if they are not all even. You should have about 16 pieces.

2 Place one piece of venison on a cutting board. Place a large sheet of plastic wrap over the venison. Use a mallet or the bottom of a sauté pan to pound the venison. Start in the center of the venison and pound out to the edges of the piece. The venison should be paper thin when you are finished. If there are holes in the pieces, you can piece together another carpaccio to make a large neat one. Transfer the venison to a platter and cover tightly with plastic wrap to prevent drying out. Continue with remaining venison. Refrigerate venison while preparing remaining ingredients.

3 Snap off the outer leaves at the base of an artichoke. Use a paring knife to trim off the green outer layer of the stem; try to leave the stem attached to the artichoke. Continue to peel off the outer layer of leaves from the artichoke using a paring knife or a vegetable peeler. Continue trimming until the inner leaves are half green and half yellow, then cut off the top half, leaving a cup-shaped artichoke. Scoop out the fuzzy choke in the center using a melon baller or small spoon. Drop the cleaned artichoke into the bowl of lemon water. Clean the remaining artichokes in same manner.

4 Use a vegetable peeler or mandoline to slice the artichokes thinly to create slivers. Place the slivers back in the bowl with the lemon juice and water to prevent discoloration.

5 Remove and discard the flesh from the Preserved Lemon. Rinse the rind. Slice the rind as thin as possible. Set aside.

6 To plate the carpaccio, rub 6 to 8 flat plates or a large platter with the garlic clove. Sprinkle lightly with olive oil. Lay the venison pieces on the plates or platter to completely cover. If there are holes or uneven edges, patch with another piece. Sprinkle with artichoke slivers, preserved lemons, blood orange sections, and additional olive oil. Garnish with coarse salt and freshly cracked pepper. Serve immediately.

Duck Breast Salad with Peppered Strawberry Vinaigrette

M ■ *Serves 4*

Something very interesting happens with this vinaigrette: The pepper makes the berries taste more pungent and bright, and the strawberries make the pepper taste sweet and more complex. Start with the best berries in season that you can find, preferably one of the smaller and more tender varieties that you can find at the farmers' market, and always use freshly ground black pepper. When I demonstrated this dish at a farmers' market in Chicago, the audience was a little doubtful about the combination at first. They were won over by the bright, intense flavor and versatility of the vinaigrette. Try drizzling it on grilled chicken or fish, or even roasted veal.

MAKE AHEAD/STORAGE The vinaigrette can be stored in the refrigerator, covered, up to 3 days or frozen for 1 month.

For the Vinaigrette

2 pints fresh strawberries

2 tablespoons granulated sugar

2 tablespoons dark brown sugar

3 tablespoons balsamic vinegar

2 tablespoons fresh lemon juice

Pinch of kosher salt

1 generous tablespoon freshly ground black pepper

3 tablespoon neutral-flavored oil, such as canola

4 boneless duck breasts, skin on

Freshly ground black pepper

6 cups mesclun or favorite salad mix

Extra-virgin olive oil

Kosher salt

1 Make the Vinaigrette Wash and stem the strawberries, and halve or quarter them if large. Heat the strawberries, sugars, vinegar, lemon juice, and salt and pepper in a medium nonreactive sauté pan over medium heat. Cook the mixture, pressing lightly on the berries, until the strawberries are soft and have released their juices, about 10 minutes. Remove the pan from the heat and transfer the strawberry mixture to a bowl. Lightly whisk in the oil and adjust the seasoning with salt and pepper. Serve the vinaigrette at room temperature for the best flavor.

2 Preheat the oven to 400°F.

3 Trim any excess fat from the duck breasts; using a very sharp knife, score the skin and fat layer in a crosshatch pattern without cutting into the meat below (this allows the fat to cook off and the skin to crisp up). Lightly season the duck with pepper. (Kosher duck can be very salty and doesn't need additional salt.)

4 Place the duck breasts skin side down in an unheated, large ovenproof sauté pan. Place the pan over medium-high heat.

5 Cook the duck until the skin is browned and most of the fat has rendered off, about 15 minutes. Keep draining the fat from the pan into a small bowl. When the breasts have browned, transfer the pan to the oven and roast the breasts until medium rare, 6 to 8 minutes, or a few minutes longer for medium. Remove the duck breasts and let cool. (See page 211 for more information on duck.)

6 To serve the salad, toss the greens in a large bowl with a spoonful of olive oil and season with salt and pepper. Slice the duck breasts thinly on the bias. Mound a generous amount of greens on each plate or on a platter, and lay the duck slices on top. Generously drizzle the vinaigrette over the duck and greens. Pass extra vinaigrette in a separate bowl. Reserved duck fat can be stored, if desired, and used for sautéing.

54

Leek and Onion Tart

D ▪ *Serves 6*

I am a major fan of tarts. I just love the idea of all the flavor and creamy texture tied up securely in a buttery, flaky crust. Tarts travel well and can be prepared far in advance of serving. A tart is the perfect centerpiece for a Shabbat luncheon. It goes from refrigerator to oven to table, or skip the oven and eat it cold. Serve it with a salad on the side, or start with a soup—and enjoy.

MAKE AHEAD/STORAGE The baked tart can be stored, wrapped tightly, in the refrigerator up to 3 days or frozen for 1 month.

2 tablespoon unsalted butter

3 medium leeks, white and light green parts only (save the dark green tops for stock), thinly sliced

1 medium shallot, chopped

2 cipollini onions, sliced into rings

1 garlic clove, chopped

Kosher salt and freshly ground black pepper

3 large eggs, beaten

1½ cups heavy cream

¼ teaspoon freshly grated nutmeg

¼ cup freshly grated Parmesan cheese

9- or 10-inch prebaked Tart Shell (recipe follows)

¼ cup chopped fresh chives

1 Preheat the oven to 350°F.

2 Heat a large sauté pan over medium heat. Add the butter, leeks, shallot, onions, garlic, and salt and pepper to taste, and cook until the onions are very soft and fragrant, about 15 minutes. Let the leek mixture cool to room temperature.

3 Whisk the eggs, cream, nutmeg, cheese, and salt and pepper to taste until combined.

3 Spread the cooled onions in the bottom of the tart shell and pour the custard over. Sprinkle with the chives. Bake the tart until the custard is set, about 30 minutes. Serve the tart hot or cold.

Tart Shell

D ■ *Makes one 9- or 10-inch tart shell*

Here's a classic recipe for all-butter pastry dough to make a tart shell. I never use vegetable shortening or margarine in my pastry. Those products don't taste good, and they aren't good for you either. Butter is always best. You can use this dough for making any kind of tart. For a fruit tart, you might want to add a couple of tablespoons of sugar along with the flour.

MAKE AHEAD/STORAGE The dough can be stored, wrapped tightly, in the refrigerator for 2 days or frozen for 2 months. The baked shell can be refrigerated, wrapped tightly in plastic wrap, for 1 day or frozen for 1 month.

> 1¾ cups all-purpose flour, plus extra for rolling
>
> Pinch of kosher salt
>
> 9 tablespoons cold unsalted butter, cut into ½-inch pieces
>
> 1 large egg, lightly beaten
>
> ¼ cup ice water, if needed

1 Place the flour, salt, and butter in a food processor, and pulse until the mixture is mealy and the butter forms small chunks the size of peas. Add the egg and continue to pulse until the dough comes together and begins to form a ball on the blade. If dough seems very dry, add ice water, a small spoonful at a time, continuing to pulse the dough just until it comes together.

2 Lightly flour a board or work surface and turn out the dough. Gently knead the dough several times, just until it comes together evenly (try not to overwork dough or it may toughen). Form the dough into a ball, then flatten it into a disk. Wrap the dough tightly in plastic wrap and chill at least 30 minutes, to make it easier to roll out.

3 Roll out the dough on clean, floured surface with a floured rolling pin, until it is 1 inch larger in diameter than the size of your tart pan. If the dough sticks, add a little more flour and roll again. Carefully roll the dough around your rolling pin and unroll it into the tart pan, pressing it down lightly. Cut off any excess dough and reserve for another use. Use a fork to prick holes in the bottom of the tart shell to prevent large air pockets. Refrigerate the tart shell before baking for at least 30 minutes.

4 While the shell is chilling, preheat the oven to 350°F.

5 Fit a piece of foil in the bottom and up the sides of the tart shell. Fill the bottom of the shell with dried beans or rice. Bake the tart shell for 10 to 15 minutes, until it is lightly golden. Remove the foil and beans and continue baking until the shell is golden brown and dry, about 10 minutes longer.

MAIN DISHES

Asparagus and Goat Cheese Lasagna

D ▪ *Serves 6 to 8*

I like lasagna but occasionally need a change from the usual tomato-based concoction. This version is bursting with the flavors of caramelized asparagus, lemon, and goat cheese. Serve it with a salad and crusty bread for a lovely spring meal. This is a great do-ahead dish, perfect for entertaining; all you have to do is pop it into the oven to bake.

MAKE AHEAD/STORAGE The lasagna can be assembled up to 2 days ahead and stored in the refrigerator, covered. Bring to room temperature before baking.

1 pound lasagna pasta

Extra-virgin olive oil

2 pounds fresh asparagus, trimmed and cut into 1½-inch pieces

Kosher salt and freshly ground black pepper

2 tablespoons unsalted butter

2 tablespoons all-purpose flour

2 cups whole milk

4 ounces goat cheese

2 tablespoons grated lemon zest (about 2 lemons)

Freshly grated Parmesan cheese

1 Bring a large pot of salted water to a boil and cook the lasagna pasta according to package directions until it is al dente. Drain the pasta and gently toss with a spoonful of olive oil to prevent it from sticking.

2 Preheat the broiler to high. Toss the asparagus pieces with salt and pepper and olive oil and transfer to a baking sheet. Broil the asparagus until golden brown and caramelized on all sides, about 12 minutes, turning the pieces frequently. Set the asparagus aside to cool.

3 Melt the butter in a medium saucepan over medium heat. Whisk the flour into the butter and cook the roux, stirring, about 2 minutes, to cook out the raw flour taste. Add the milk all at once and whisk constantly. Bring the sauce to a boil; the mixture will thicken when the milk reaches a boil. Remove the pan from the heat, and stir in the goat cheese, lemon zest, and salt and pepper to taste. Set the goat cheese sauce aside to cool slightly.

4 Spread enough of the goat cheese sauce in the bottom of a casserole dish or 9 × 13–inch lasagna pan to cover lightly, and top with a layer of pasta. Scatter one-third of the asparagus over the pasta and pour one-third of the cheese sauce over the asparagus. Repeat the layering process to make 3 layers, finishing with the cheese sauce. Sprinkle the top with enough Parmesan cheese to cover it lightly. The lasagna can be assembled up to this point and refrigerated.

5 To bake the lasagna, preheat the oven to 350°F. Cover the casserole loosely with aluminum foil and bake for 45 minutes. Remove the foil and bake an additional 15 minutes or until the top is golden brown and bubbly. Remove the casserole from the oven, and let rest for 15 minutes to allow it to set up before slicing.

Morel Mushrooms Stuffed with Ground Veal

M ▪ *Serves 4 as a first course or light main course*

Serving morel mushrooms is a surefire way to celebrate the return of spring. Morels have a light earthiness that makes them perfect for pairing with spring's more delicate meats and vegetables. They also have a very convenient hollow center that makes them perfect for stuffing. Fresh morels have a very short season, so when they appear in the markets, don't delay scooping them up and enjoying them. They won't be around for long!

MAKE AHEAD/STORAGE The mushrooms can be stuffed the night before and stored in the refrigerator, covered.

Extra-virgin olive oil

2 medium shallots, finely minced

2 garlic cloves, very finely minced

¼ pound ground veal

Kosher salt and freshly ground black pepper

¼ cup dry white wine, such as Sauvignon Blanc

¼ cup Chicken Stock (page 15)

3 tablespoons fresh, untoasted bread crumbs

1 teaspoon finely chopped fresh thyme

2 teaspoons finely chopped fresh flat-leaf parsley

1 tablespoon fresh lemon juice

12 large fresh morel mushrooms

Balsamic Reduction (page 19), warmed

1 Heat a medium sauté pan over medium heat, and lightly coat the bottom of the pan with olive oil. Sweat the shallots and garlic, without browning them, until translucent and very soft, about 10 minutes. Add the veal and salt and pepper to taste and continue cooking the mixture, stirring to break up the meat, until the veal is cooked through. Add the white wine, Chicken Stock, and bread crumbs, and stir to combine. Cook the mixture until the liquid has evaporated and the mixture is only slightly moist. Add the herbs and lemon juice and adjust the seasoning with salt and pepper. Transfer the mixture to a bowl and set aside to cool.

2 Using a soft brush, lightly brush the mushrooms to clean them. Trim off the tip of the tops (not the stems) of the mushrooms to make holes for the stuffing. Using a small spoon, fill the mushrooms until they are fairly full and firmly stuffed.

3 Lightly coat the bottom of a large sauté pan with olive oil, and heat the pan over medium-high heat. Gently transfer the mushrooms to the pan, and cook until the filling is warmed through and the mushrooms lightly caramelized, about 10 minutes. Use a large spatula or tongs to turn the mushrooms so they do not break. Place the mushrooms on individual plates or a platter and drizzle with the warm Balsamic Reduction before serving.

VARIATION

Stuffed Portobellos (M) Use 12 small portobello or large cremini mushrooms in place of the morels. Remove stems and scrape out the gills. Mound the stuffing in the centers. Bake the mushrooms at 400°F for 15 minutes, or until the filling is lightly browned.

Herbed Roasted Chicken with Quinoa-Mushroom Pilaf

M ▪ *Serves 4 to 6*

Just about everyone loves roasted chicken, because sometimes you just need a really good piece of chicken. I love the homey aromas that waft through my house from the herbs, citrus, and roasting juices. I think of roasted chicken as the "little black dress" of dinners—it's perfect for Shabbat dinner, a family celebration, or even a weekday meal. The quinoa pilaf is perfect for absorbing all the herbed juices, but there are many other sides that would also be delicious accompaniments. Try the Roasted Purple Potatoes (page 120) or the Roasted Sweet Potatoes (page 184) for a change.

2 whole chickens, about 4 pounds each

½ cup chopped fresh flat-leaf parsley

3 tablespoons chopped fresh thyme

1 tablespoon chopped fresh rosemary

1 tablespoon chopped fresh chives

Juice and grated zest of 1 lemon

Juice and grated zest of 1 orange

¼ cup extra-virgin olive oil

½ teaspoon kosher salt and ½ teaspoon freshly ground black pepper

½ cup dry white wine, such as Sauvignon Blanc

2 medium shallots, chopped

Water or Chicken Stock (page 15), if necessary

Quinoa-Mushroom Pilaf (recipe follows)

1 Preheat the oven to 400°F.

2 Rinse the chickens thoroughly, pat them dry, and place breast side up on a roasting rack set in a roasting pan. Whisk together the herbs, citrus juices and zests, olive oil, and salt and pepper in a small bowl. (Kosher chickens are salty to begin with, so use salt sparingly.) Use your hands to rub the chickens thoroughly inside the cavity and out with the herb mixture. Tuck the wings under the body of the chicken and tie the legs together if you wish (this helps keep the shape a little nicer).

3 Roast the chickens for 20 minutes. Turn down the oven temperature to 200°F and slowly roast, brushing on more of the herb mixture 2 or 3 times, until a thermometer inserted into the thigh registers 160°F, about 1½ hours. Remove the pan from the oven and transfer the chickens to a cutting board or platter. Allow the chickens to rest, loosely covered with foil, before carving. Discard any herb mixture that you haven't used.

4 Pour the juices from the roasting pan into a small bowl or measuring cup, and set aside to allow the fat to rise to the top. Skim off the fat; you should have about 1 cup juices (add some water or chicken stock if needed). Set the roasting pan over medium-high heat and add the wine and shallots. Reduce the wine, stirring and scraping the bottom of the pan to incorporate any browned bits. Pour in the reserved juices and boil the sauce, stirring, until reduced by one-third. Transfer the sauce to a warmed gravy boat or small pitcher for serving.

5 To carve the chickens, cut down the center along the breast bone on both sides and remove the breast bone. Pull the chicken apart slightly to expose the back bone. Cut along both sides of the back bone and remove it. Cut each half in half again and place the quarters on a serving platter. Serve with the sauce and Quinoa-Mushroom Pilaf.

Quinoa-Mushroom Pilaf

M ▪ *Serves 4 to 6*

Quinoa, with its delicate texture and taste, makes a nice change from rice. Botanically, quinoa is a grass, not a grain, so it's a good option for Passover or anytime you want to try a side that's a little different.

MAKE AHEAD/STORAGE Quinoa pilaf can be made up to 2 days ahead and stored in the refrigerator, covered. Reheat over gentle heat and toss with additional olive oil.

2 cups quinoa

Extra-virgin olive oil

1 medium shallot, finely diced

2 cups sliced fresh mushrooms (use shiitake, cremini, button, or a combination)

2 tablespoons fresh lemon juice

½ cup pine nuts, toasted

Kosher salt and freshly ground black pepper

1 Thoroughly rinse the quinoa in a large bowl filled with cold water, rubbing the grains together to remove their slightly "soapy" film. Drain the quinoa in a fine-mesh sieve. Transfer the quinoa to a medium saucepan and add 4 cups of water. Bring to a boil and cook the quinoa over medium heat until it is tender, about 20 minutes. Drain off any excess water, and lightly drizzle the quinoa with olive oil.

2 Heat a medium sauté pan over medium heat, and lightly coat the bottom of the pan with olive oil. Sauté the shallot and mushrooms until lightly browned and most of the liquid from the mushrooms has evaporated, about 15 minutes. Add the mushrooms to the quinoa with the lemon juice and pine nuts and season with salt and pepper.

Persian Meatballs (Kufteh)
in Tomato-Saffron Broth

M ▪ *Serves 4*

Serve these meatballs as part of a Purim feast. Traditionally, the meatballs would not be browned before being poached. As a chef, though, I think the caramelized crust on the meatballs is essential and gives them a great texture and more pronounced flavor. You can opt to do it either way. Although only a small amount of the cinnamon and spice mixture, Advieh (page 64), is used, it makes a delicious difference in the taste.

63

MAKE AHEAD/STORAGE The meatballs can be prepared up to cooking and stored in the refrigerator, covered, up to 2 days, or frozen for 1 month.

For the Meatballs

½ cup dried yellow split peas

½ cup raw basmati rice (or 2 cups leftover cooked rice, cooled)

1 pound ground chicken, turkey, or beef

½ cup finely chopped fresh dill

½ cup chopped fresh flat-leaf parsley

2 teaspoons Advieh (recipe follows)

1 cup chopped scallions (white and light green parts)

2 garlic cloves, chopped

2 large onions, chopped

2 large eggs

Kosher salt and freshly ground black pepper

Olive oil

For the Broth

One 14- to 15-ounce can whole peeled plum tomatoes with their juices

2 cups Chicken Stock (page 15)

1 teaspoon saffron threads

Juice and grated zest of 1 lime

Juice and grated zest of 1 lemon

Kosher salt and freshly ground black pepper

Saffron Rice with Almonds, Raisins, and Caramelized Onions (page 225)

1 **Make the Meatballs** Place the yellow split peas in a medium saucepan and cover with water. Place the raw rice in a separate medium saucepan and cover with water. Bring peas and rice to a simmer and cook until al dente, about 30 minutes for the peas, and about 20 minutes for the rice. Drain any excess water and toss lightly with salt and pepper. Let the peas and rice cool.

2 Combine the cooked rice, peas, ground meat, dill, parsley, Advieh, scallions, garlic, onions, and eggs in a large bowl; using your hands, mix together until well combined. (Do not overmix, as the mixture will be too tight and tough.) Season the mixture to taste with salt and pepper (I like to take a small amount and fry it to taste if the seasoning is correct.)

3 Lightly pat together meatballs with your hands, making about 12 or 16 meatballs. (I find that wetting my hands with cold water and using a light rolling motion keeps the meatballs from getting too packed and tight.) Heat a large sauté pan over medium heat, and lightly coat the bottom of the pan with olive oil. Brown the meatballs in batches if necessary to prevent without crowding, turning them. Remove the meatballs from the pan and drain on paper towels.

4 **Make the Broth** Break up the tomatoes with your hands, then bring the tomatoes with their juices, the stock, saffron, and citrus juices and zests to a simmer in a large saucepan. Season with salt and pepper. Place the meatballs in the pan and gently poach them until cooked through, about 20 minutes. (Do not stir the pan, as the meatballs will break apart.)

5 To serve, spoon the saffron rice into large, shallow bowls and top with 3 or 4 meatballs. Spoon some broth over saffron rice and meatballs.

Advieh

P ■ *Makes 2 tablespoons*

Advieh is as essential to the Persian kitchen as garam masala is to Indian cuisine and *ras el hanout* is to Moroccan. I like to make small batches of this mix to keep in my spice cabinet. I find myself sprinkling it on grilled and braised meats, adding a pinch to sautéed vegetables and salad dressings, and even stirring it into basmati rice for a Persian rice pudding.

MAKE AHEAD/STORAGE Advieh can be stored for up to 1 month in a cool dark place.

1 tablespoon ground cinnamon

1 teaspoon ground cardamom

1 teaspoon ground cloves

1 teaspoon ground ginger

Mix the spices together and store in a sealable jar or container.

Roasted Red Snapper
with Preserved Lemon Broth
and Artichokes

P ■ *Serves 4*

Snapper has a clean freshness that pairs beautifully with citrus flavors. A whole snapper is easy to cook and present dramatically. I like to let everyone serve themselves some of the tender fish off the platter. You could use fillets instead; just reduce the cooking time to 10 minutes. If you don't have preserved lemons, don't let that stop you from making this dish. Simply use strips of fresh lemon zest; even seeded kumquat slices would make a nice alternative. This is wonderful over Ivory Lentils (page 171) or Barley Pilaf (page 240).

Olive oil

2 Preserved Lemons (page 21)

½ cup Fumet (page 18)

½ cup dry white wine, such as Sauvignon Blanc

¼ cup fresh lemon juice

4 fresh or canned artichokes

1 whole red snapper, about 4 pounds, cleaned and scaled

1 medium fennel bulb, stalks trimmed and fronds reserved, quartered and cored

2 medium shallots, thinly sliced

¼ cup chopped fresh flat-leaf parsley

Kosher salt and freshly ground black pepper

1 Preheat the oven to 350°F. Line a baking sheet with parchment paper and lightly oil paper.

2 Open the Preserved Lemons and remove and discard the pulp. Rinse the rinds and cut them into julienne. Place a small saucepan over medium heat. Add the Fumet, wine, and Preserved Lemons. Simmer the mixture to reduce by one-half.

3 Place a large saucepan over medium-high heat. Fill the pan three-quarters with water. Add the lemon juice. Snap off the outer leaves at the base of an artichoke. Use a paring knife to trim off the green outer layer of the stem; try to leave the stem attached to the artichoke. Continue to peel off the outer layer of leaves from the artichoke using a paring knife or a vegetable peeler. Continue trimming until the inner leaves are yellow. Scoop out the fuzzy choke in the center using a melon baller or small spoon. Drop the cleaned artichoke into the pan of lemon water. Clean the remaining artichokes in the same manner.

4 Cook the artichokes until tender but not mushy (about 10 minutes). Remove from the water and place upside down to drain the water. When the artichokes are cool, slice them thin and add them to the pan with the preserved lemons.

5 Rinse the snapper and pat dry. Slice the fennel into julienne, using an Asian slicer if desired. Stuff the cavity of the fish with the fennel, shallots, and parsley. Salt and pepper the fish on both sides. Place on the baking sheet, and roast the fish until the skin is lightly browned and the fish feels slightly firm to the touch, about 30 minutes.

6 To serve the snapper, place on a platter and pour the sauce over the fish. Chop the reserved fronds and sprinkle over the top of the fish before serving.

Olive Oil–Poached Halibut with Herbed Semolina Gnocchi

D and P ■ *Serves 4*

I remember the first time I watched a chef-friend poach fish in olive oil. Just when you think you've seen it all and you know what you're doing, along comes a revelation like this one. It was one of those moments when the light bulb goes off—what genius! The fish cooks through a gentle heat transfer and absorbs the delicate olive oil flavor. The end result is fish that's moist and truly luscious. It may seem like a waste to use up practically a whole bottle of olive oil but have faith—this is a winning recipe. Enjoy the fish hot, cold, or at room temperature; it will be delicious any way you serve it.

MAKE AHEAD/STORAGE The oil can be used two times for poaching fish. Strain it through a fine-mesh sieve and store in the refrigerator, covered, up to 2 weeks, discard the oil after poaching fish twice.

4 skinless, boneless 6-ounce halibut fillets

About 4 cups extra-virgin olive oil (or 2 cups olive oil and 2 cups extra-virgin olive oil)

Kosher salt and freshly ground black pepper

Herbed Semolina Gnocchi (recipe follows)

Mint pesto (see page 40; optional)

1 Preheat the oven to 275°F.

2 Place the fillets in an ovenproof dish in which they fit snugly but do not overlap. Add enough olive oil to cover the fish about three quarters of the way up the sides of the fillets. Bake the fish in the oven until firm when lightly pressed on the sides and completely opaque, about 15 minutes.

3 Lift the fillets from the dish with a spatula, letting any excess oil drip off. Serve the fillets, sprinkled with salt and pepper to taste, with the gnocchi. Dollop with a spoonful of mint pesto, if using.

Herbed Semolina Gnocchi

D and P ■ *Serves 4*

Generally, gnocchi recipes are made with potatoes or other starchy vegetables. I'm really enthusiastic about this Roman version, which yields a noodlelike texture and rich creamy flavor. It's a wonderfully rich side dish for the Olive Oil–Poached Halibut (recipe above), or serve it on its own as a light supper with a tossed salad.

MAKE AHEAD/STORAGE The gnocchi can be assembled up to 2 days ahead and stored in the refrigerator, covered.

Olive oil

3 cups whole milk

1½ cups semolina*

4 tablespoons unsalted butter

1 cup freshly grated best-quality Parmesan cheese

¼ cup finely chopped fresh flat-leaf parsley

1 tablespoon finely chopped fresh mint

Kosher salt and freshly ground black pepper

*Semolina is available in most grocery stores or gourmet markets

1 Lightly grease a large cutting board with olive oil.

2 Bring the milk to a simmer in a medium saucepan over medium heat and add the semolina, whisking constantly. Add the butter and continue to stir the mixture with a wooden spoon. Cook the mixture, stirring constantly, until the semolina becomes very thick and bubbly, about 10 minutes (be careful, as the semolina may begin to sputter out of the pan). Set aside 3 tablespoons of the cheese, and stir the remaining cheese and the herbs into the semolina. Season with salt and pepper. Remove the pan from the heat.

3 Pour the semolina onto the prepared cutting board and smooth the top with a spatula. Let the semolina mixture rest until cooled and completely set, about 30 minutes.

4 Cut the semolina mixture into 2 x 2–inch gnocchi. Place the gnocchi in a lightly greased ovenproof casserole (the gnocchi can be stacked in 2 layers). The gnocchi can be assembled up to this point and chilled, covered. Allow the gnocchi to warm to room temperature before reheating.

5 Preheat the oven to 350°F. Sprinkle the top with the 3 tablespoons of reserved cheese. Bake until the cheese has melted and the gnocchi are hot and lightly browned, about 12 minutes.

Pan-Roasted Wild King Salmon with Mustard-Chive Sabayon

P ▪ *Serves 4*

Typically people think of sabayon for dessert, but it's just a sauce made from eggs and wine that's whisked and warmed over a water bath. For a savory dish, instead of sugar I add flavors, like mustard and chives, that complement the fish. I created this sabayon for some beautiful salmon that our fishmonger got at the very beginning of the season for wild kings, after a long winter of doing without. I whisked up the sauce right before dinner and spooned it over the fish. The customers caught on to my enthusiasm and gobbled it up.

MAKE AHEAD/STORAGE The sauce can be prepared several hours ahead and kept in a container placed in a water bath over very low heat. The sauce can also be stored in the refrigerator, covered, up to 2 days; heat it up very slowly in a water bath.

For the Sabayon

1 cup dry white wine, such as Sauvignon Blanc

3 large egg yolks

1 tablespoon Dijon mustard

3 tablespoons finely chopped fresh chives

Kosher salt and freshly ground black pepper

4 skinless 6-ounce fillets wild Alaskan king salmon

Kosher salt and freshly ground black pepper

2 tablespoons finely chopped fresh chives

Olive oil

Chive Mashed Potatoes (recipe follows; optional)

1 Make the Sabayon: Heat a medium saucepan filled about three-quarters full with water over medium heat and fit a large bowl over the pan (the bowl should fit securely in the pan, but the bottom should not touch the water). Add the wine, yolks, and mustard to the bowl and whisk constantly about 15 minutes, until the eggs are creamy and fluffy and a thermometer reads 140°F. Check the heat from time to time to make sure that the water is not simmering or boiling, or the eggs can scramble. Stir in the chives and adjust the seasoning with salt and pepper. Cover the bowl and keep warm over very low heat.

2 Season the salmon with salt and pepper and rub the chives onto the top side (nonskin) of the fillets.

Spring

3 Heat a large sauté pan over medium-high heat, and lightly coat the bottom of the pan with olive oil. When the oil begins to shimmer, place the fillets in the pan, skinned side up. Brown the salmon until dark golden and crispy, about 5 minutes. (Try not to touch or move the fillets until they are browned, as they can stick to the pan.) Carefully turn over the fillets with a spatula and remove the pan from the heat. Cover the pan with foil; the fish will continue to cook to a perfect medium rare. If you prefer your fish well done, transfer the fillets to an ovenproof baking dish, and roast the fish in a preheated 400°F oven for 5 to 8 minutes, until it feels firm to the touch.

4 To serve, place the fish on four plates and spoon the sauce over the fish. If using the potatoes, divide them among the plates, place the fish on top, add the sauce, then serve.

Chive Mashed Potatoes

D and P ▪ *Serves 4*

Classic comfort food at its best.

MAKE AHEAD/STORAGE If not being served immediately, the mashed potatoes can be kept warm, covered, on the back of the stove or in a warm water bath over very low heat, for up to 3 hours.

3 large russet potatoes, (about 3 pounds), peeled and cut into large dice

¼ cup whole milk, warmed

3 tablespoons unsalted butter

¼ cup chopped fresh chives

Kosher salt and freshly ground black pepper

Bring a large saucepan of lightly salted water to a boil over medium-high heat and cook the potatoes until tender, about 20 minutes. Drain the potatoes thoroughly. Rice the potatoes through a ricer or use a potato masher and mash until no longer lumpy. (Do not use a food processor, as the potatoes, have a tendency to get gummy). Stir the milk, butter, and chives into the potatoes and season to taste with salt and pepper.

70

Salmon

It may sound a little silly to say that I am passionate about salmon. Nevertheless . . . I am!
I could eat salmon almost every day. Since my kids also love salmon, sometimes I actually
do eat it every day. I have even been known to gather my staff around to admire an
especially beautiful fillet. I am not sure they always share my enthusiasm, and I'm positive
they don't think that it looks like jewelry. However, I do. The most exciting time of year for
me is when the Alaskan salmon season officially opens in April. The fish come in smelling
faintly of the sea. Their soft flesh ranges in color from an off-white for the Ivory Kings to a
brick red for the Copper River and Sockeyes. Among the best are the Chinook or wild kings
(my personal favorite), Copper River, Coho, and Sockeyes.

Most of the salmon that we buy for the restaurant or eat at home comes from Alaska.
Recently, there has been a lot of controversy over farmed salmon. I find that farmed fish do
not have the same texture and flavor nuances as wild fish. I don't serve any farmed fish at
my restaurant; when the wild salmon season is over, I don't even bother with the farmed
stuff. It just comes off the menu, both at the restaurant and at home.

It pays to make friends with a reliable fishmonger who will sell you the highest quality
fresh salmon on the market. Ask to smell your fish: It should have a clean and fresh smell.
It should not look dry, and the top may look slightly moist or oily. To store the salmon
at home, handle it as little as possible. Wrap it up tightly in plastic wrap or put it in a
resealable plastic bag. Place the wrapped fish on an ice pack in the coldest part of your
refrigerator, and use it within a day or two of purchase.

Salmon is so versatile that it lends itself to many preparations. I use salmon to make
appetizers, to garnish soup, and of course as a main course. My favorite way to cook
salmon is to start with a fillet that's at least one inch thick, with the skin removed. I season
the top (the nonskin side) with salt and pepper and sometimes pat on some finely chopped
herbs or a sprinkling of dried mushroom "dust." I heat my pan to a nice medium-high heat,
lightly coat the bottom of the pan with oil, and place the fillet top-side down in the pan.
Now comes the hard part: You cannot touch the fish until a crispy crust has formed. If you
try to move the fish, it may stick to the pan, which will mar the crust. The way to tell if it
is ready is to peek just under the edges after about 3 to 4 minutes, to see if it is lightly
browned and crispy-looking. Then gently turn the fish over and turn off the heat. Cover the
pan with some foil, and the fish will finish cooking all by itself in about 5 minutes. If you
don't want to eat it immediately, I recommend removing the salmon from the pan right after
searing, placing it in an ovenproof dish, and chilling it. Then you can finish cooking it in a
400°F oven a couple of hours later.

(continued)

Spring

When you have a really wonderful piece of fish, you can try making it into seviche (see page 94), which you can use to garnish a cold soup or even just enjoy on its own. When I'm planning a big party at home, one of the dishes I love to make is Gravlax (page 50). My version is a little different; it's a bit drier than typical gravlax, more like a salmon pastrami in fact. As with any beautiful piece of salmon, it's always a hit.

Some of my favorite salmon recipes:

Gravlax (cured salmon, page 50)

Mushroom-Crusted Wild Salmon (page 176)

Pan-Roasted Wild King Salmon with Mustard-Chive Sabayon (page 69)

Salmon Seviche (page 94)

Roasted Lamb Chops with Fava Beans and Minted Risotto

M ▪ *Serves 4*

As early as mid-March I start getting spring fever. I get anxious for warmer days and the smell of spring in the air. I long for the lighter, fresher flavors of the season. Using fresh mint and fava beans are a surefire way to put some classic spring flavors on the table. Fava beans is a bit of trouble to work with, but they are delicious and their season is short. Scoop them up while you can.

MAKE AHEAD/STORAGE The fava beans may be prepared up to 1 day ahead and stored in the refrigerator, covered.

2 racks of lamb, (each about 1½ pounds); ask your butcher to french them for an elegant presentation

About ½ cup extra-virgin olive oil

Juice of 1 lemon

1 pound fresh fava beans in the shell

Kosher salt and freshly ground black pepper

Fresh mint leaves, for garnish

For the Risotto

4 to 5 cups of Chicken Stock (page 15)

3 tablespoons olive oil

1 large shallot, finely chopped

1¾ cups Arborio rice

Kosher salt and freshly ground black pepper

½ cup dry white wine, such as Sauvignon Blanc

½ cup chopped fresh mint leaves

2 tablespoons chopped fresh flat-leaf parsley

1 Marinate the lamb in the olive oil and lemon juice in a covered shallow container or resealable plastic bag for at least 4 hours or overnight.

2 Shell the fava beans. Bring a medium saucepan of salted water to a boil, and prepare a bowl of ice water with a strainer that fits inside the bowl. Cook the fava beans until tender, about 5 minutes, and drain them into the strainer. Immediately shock the favas by submerging the strainer in the ice water (see page 41 for more information on blanching and shocking vegetables). When favas have cooled completely, remove the strainer from the ice water and peel the transparent skin off the beans.

3 Preheat the oven to 400°F. Season the lamb with salt and pepper.

4 Heat a large sauté pan over medium-high heat, and lightly coat the bottom of the pan with olive oil. Brown the lamb on all sides. Transfer the lamb to a baking sheet and roast until a thermometer registers 120°F for medium rare, about 15 minutes. Let the lamb rest, lightly covered with aluminum foil, for 10 to 15 minutes.

5 Make the Risotto while the lamb is browning, roasting, and resting. Bring the stock to a simmer in a saucepan over medium-high heat.

6 Heat a large sauté pan or medium saucepan over medium heat and add the olive oil. Sweat the shallot, without browning it, until translucent, about 5 minutes. Add the rice and salt and pepper to taste, and stir until each grain of rice is lightly coated and slightly transparent at the edges but still opaque in the center. Add the wine and continue to cook until the wine is absorbed. Slowly add the chicken stock to the pan, about one cup at a time, stirring and waiting until each addition is absorbed before adding the next, until the rice is al dente, about 25 minutes. Adjust the seasoning with salt and pepper and fold in the chopped mint and parsley.

7 To serve, cut the lamb into portions. Place a generous serving of risotto on each plate and sprinkle with fava beans. Place the lamb on the risotto and garnish with additional mint, if desired.

Ginger-Marinated Venison Loin with Purple Sticky Rice and Spring Pea Salad

M ▪ *Serves 4 to 6*

This dish has many great colors, textures, and flavors. Pairing the venison with the sticky rice and the tossed salad may be new for many but it works. I find that since venison is so lean, it's best when cooked rare (to 110°F on a meat thermometer); if you prefer your meat more cooked, you can try it at medium rare (120°F on a meat thermometer). But if you like well-done meat, venison loin isn't for you—it becomes tough and tasteless. Although this dish is delicious when hot, my preference is to serve it as a cold dinner or luncheon.

MAKE AHEAD/STORAGE The meat can be cooked and stored, covered, in the refrigerator up to 1 day. If prepared ahead, serve meat cold.

1 venison loin (3 to 5 pounds), silverskin removed by your butcher*

1 garlic clove, crushed

1 inch piece fresh ginger, thinly sliced

¼ cup extra-virgin olive oil

2 tablespoons fresh lemon juice

1 tablespoon unseasoned rice vinegar

½ teaspoon kosher salt and ½ teaspoon freshly ground black pepper

Olive oil, for browning the venison

Purple Sticky Rice (recipe follows)

Spring Pea Salad (recipe follows)

*If venison is not available at your butcher, see Sources (page 257).

1 Place the venison in a large covered container or resealable plastic bag with the garlic, ginger, extra-virgin olive oil, lemon juice, vinegar, and salt and pepper. Marinate the venison, in the refrigerator, for at least 4 hours or overnight.

2 Allow venison to come to room temperature. Preheat the oven to 400°F.

3 Heat a large sauté pan over medium-high heat and lightly coat the bottom of the pan with olive oil. Brown the venison on all sides. Transfer the venison to a roasting pan and roast until a thermometer reads 110°F for rare (about 20 minutes) or 120°F for medium rare (about 25 minutes). Transfer the meat to a cutting board and loosely cover with foil. Let the meat to rest 10 to 15 minutes before slicing.

Spring

4 To serve, mound the rice on a large platter and top with the vegetable salad. Thinly slice the venison and lay the slices on top of the salad. Drizzle all over with any remaining vinaigrette from the Spring Pea Salad.

Purple Sticky Rice

P ■ *Serves 4 to 6*

Purple sticky rice, similar to Native American wild rice, grows in marshy areas in Asia. It is also called Forbidden Rice, as one time only royalty was allowed to enjoy this nutty, chewy delicacy. Thankfully, we can find this rice at most health food stores, many grocery stores, and online. The rice can be tossed with a little of the vinaigrette right before serving. It is delicious cold or hot.

MAKE AHEAD/STORAGE The rice can be stored in the refrigerator, covered, for several days. To reheat, place the rice in a small pan with several tablespoons of water and heat it gently over low heat.

> 2 cups purple sticky rice
>
> 4 cups water
>
> About ½ teaspoon kosher salt
>
> Extra-virgin olive oil

1 Place the rice and water in a large saucepan and add salt to taste. Bring the rice to a boil, and cook, covered, over medium-low heat until it is tender and the water has been absorbed, about 30 minutes.

2 Remove the pan from the heat and spread out the rice on a baking sheet or in a large bowl to cool. Drizzle the rice with a spoonful of olive oil and lightly toss the rice to coat the grains with the oil. To serve rice chilled, fluff with a fork and drizzle with a little of the vinaigrette from the Spring Pea Salad (recipe follows).

Spring Pea Salad

P ■ *Serves 4 to 6*

Different varieties of fresh peas and beans mixed with a gingery vinaigrette make this salad sprightly enough for spring. Pea sprouts are at their tender best in the springtime, when you can find them at the farmers' market and occasionally at the grocery store. If you can't find pea sprouts, try tossing the pea mixture with some other delicate sprouts or tender lettuce like spring frisée.

MAKE AHEAD/STORAGE The favas, peas, and sugar snaps may be prepared 1 day ahead and chilled, covered.

> 1 pound fresh fava beans, in the shell
>
> 1 pound fresh English peas, in the shell
>
> 1 pound fresh sugar snap peas
>
> ¼ cup extra-virgin olive oil
>
> 2 tablespoons unseasoned rice vinegar

1 tablespoon fresh lemon juice

1 teaspoon freshly grated ginger

1 garlic clove, finely minced

Kosher salt and freshly ground black
    pepper

1 cup fresh pea sprouts

1 Shell the fava beans and the English peas and trim the sugar snap peas. Bring a medium saucepan of salted water to a boil, and prepare a bowl of ice water with a strainer that fits inside the bowl. Cook the fava beans until tender, about 5 minutes, and drain them into the strainer. Immediately shock the favas by submerging the strainer in the ice water (see page 41 for more information on blanching and shocking vegetables). When favas have cooled completely, remove the strainer from the ice water and peel the transparent skin off the beans. Separately blanch and shock the English peas (10 to 12 minutes) and the sugar snap peas (2 minutes) in the same manner, adding more ice to the ice water if necessary.

2 In a small bowl, whisk together the olive oil, vinegar, lemon juice, ginger, and garlic. Toss the cooked vegetables with the pea sprouts in a large bowl and drizzle with the vinaigrette. Toss lightly to coat.

Standing Rib Roast
with Porcini Mushroom Crust
and Mushroom-Onion Ragout

M ▪ *Serves 8 to 10*

This dish really says holiday or special occasion! It is elegant and delicious, and it feeds a crowd. Plus it's practical, as many of the steps can be done ahead of time or in stages. You can put the whole thing together as you sit down to your Seder or as your guests arrive. For the mushroom ragout, it's worthwhile seeking out a few different mushroom varieties for their diverse flavors and visual appeal. If you're comfortable carving the meat in front of your guests, bring the roast to the table—the standing rib is so impressive and festive.

MAKE AHEAD/STORAGE The meat can be coated with the mushroom mixture then stored, covered, in the refrigerator overnight. Bring the meat to room temperature before roasting. The ragout can be stored in the refrigerator, covered, up to 3 days. Reheat before serving.

For the Roast

- ½ cup dried porcini mushrooms (about 2 ounces)
- 1 whole beef rib or standing rib roast (about 15 to 17 pounds); ask your butcher to french the roast for an elegant presentation
- Kosher salt and freshly ground black pepper
- Olive oil

For the Ragout

- 1½ to 2 pounds fresh mushrooms, preferably an assortment, such as cremini, button, shiitake, oyster, and morel
- Olive oil
- 2 large Spanish onions, thinly sliced
- 3 medium shallots, thinly sliced
- 6 garlic cloves, thinly sliced
- 3 leeks, white and light green parts only (save the dark green tops for stock), thinly sliced
- 1 bottle (750 ml) dry red wine, such as Cabernet Sauvignon (try Baron Herzog)
- 2 cups Chicken Stock (page 15)
- Juice of 1 lemon
- ½ cup chopped fresh flat-leaf parsley
- 3 tablespoons chopped fresh thyme

1 Make the Roast Preheat the oven to 300°F. In a blender or food processor, grind the dried porcini mushrooms until they are reduced to a dustlike consistency. Season the roast with salt and pepper to taste, and pat the mushroom dust onto the meaty side of the rib.

2 Heat a large roasting pan over 2 burners on medium heat and lightly coat the bottom of the pan with olive oil. Place the roast, meat side down, in the pan, and brown the meat, about 15 minutes.

3 Turn the roast rib side down and transfer to the oven. Roast until a meat thermometer placed in the center of the meat registers 120°F for medium rare, about 1½ hours.

4 Transfer the meat to a cutting board, and let it rest, loosely covered with foil, for 15 minutes before carving.

5 Make the Ragout while the meat is roasting. Trim the stems and slice the mushrooms into fairly thick slices.

6 Heat a large sauté pan over medium heat, and lightly coat the bottom of the pan with olive oil. Sauté the mushrooms, in batches, until lightly brown and crispy, 5 to 7 minutes. Add the onions, shallots, leeks, and garlic to the pan and slowly cook until caramelized, about 15 minutes. Add the wine, stock, and salt and pepper to taste, and cook until the liquids reduce by half (you should have about 2½ cups of mushroom ragout at the end), about 45 minutes. Remove the pan from the heat and stir in the lemon juice, parsley, and thyme. Adjust the seasoning with salt and pepper.

7 To serve, carve the meat from the bone in thick slices, and transfer the slices to a platter or to plates. Serve the meat with the mushroom ragout. Keep any remaining roast warm on the platter for second servings.

Strawberry Fruit Soup with Fresh Mint

P ▪ *Serves 4*

I am a big fan of fruit soups any time of the year but especially in the spring and summer months. Fruit soups are refreshingly healthy and beautiful, and they can be dolled up by adding more fruit, chopped herbs, or a scoop of sorbet. We use them in the restaurant as desserts, midcourse palate refreshers, and even as appetizers. Let your imagination go when it comes to the accompaniments and garnishes.

MAKE AHEAD/STORAGE This soup can be stored in the refrigerator, covered, up to 3 days.

5 cups fresh strawberries, stemmed

1 cup sugar, plus more if needed

2 tablespoons fresh lemon juice, plus more if needed

4 cups water

¼ cup Champagne, fruity white wine, or nonalcoholic sparkling fruit juice

½ cup packed fresh mint leaves cut into chiffonade (thin strips)

Suggested Garnishes Strawberry Sorbet (page 82), additional fresh mint cut into chiffonade

1 Toss the strawberries with the sugar and lemon juice in a large bowl to coat. Let the berries macerate (allow their juices to flow out) at room temperature, about 20 minutes.

2 Transfer the berries to a blender or food processor and process until completely pureed. Pour the strawberry puree through a fine-mesh sieve into a large bowl and discard the solids. Add the water and champagne to the strawberry puree and stir until well combined. Adjust the sweetness or tartness to taste with additional sugar or lemon juice, and sprinkle with the mint. Chill the soup thoroughly before serving.

3 Serve the soup in shallow bowls with your choice of garnish.

Sorbets and Granitas

When I was a child I ate sweets the way only a kid can—stacks of candy bars, cookies by the jarful, tooth-achingly sweet drinks, sugary syrup sealed up in wax bottles, and anything else I could get my hands on. Who didn't? It is practically a right of passage for children. My parents always said that my tastes would change when I got older. Of course, I didn't believe them.

Like many things that parents say . . . they were right. I don't eat many sweets anymore. I do, however, crave fruit, always at its seasonal best. I like to eat it straight from my hand. And I love it frozen. Sorbets and granitas are refreshing and sophisticated. With their gorgeous colors and textures, they show off the best of fruit.

A sorbet is a lightly sweetened mixture of pureed fruit (or sometimes even vegetables) that develops a creamy texture by being spun in an ice-cream machine, not from the addition of any dairy products. A granita is even simpler—it's water and sugar with a flavoring such as fruit juice, coffee, wine, or chocolate. Instead of being processed in a machine, a granita is frozen in a shallow pan and stirred with a fork from time to time to break up the ice crystals. The result is a sweet ice with a coarse and sandy texture.

Since these desserts are dairy-free, they are perfect for meat meals. They can be served as plain or as fancy as you wish. A few scoops in a pretty glass make a perfect end to a simple summer meal. Or you can jazz them up with sliced fruit, a dollop of sabayon sauce, or rich biscotti.

Granitas need to be enjoyed soon after making them, since the fine-textured ice crystals quickly melt and refreeze into clumps. Fruit sorbets can be kept for longer, and in fact really need to harden before you can scoop them into pretty balls. You can keep a sorbet for a week without losing any of its fresh taste; however, after several days the sorbet may separate. The fruit solids in the sorbet are heavier than water, so following the laws of gravity, they will slowly begin to sink to the bottom of the container. (Ice cream does not separate as easily because the cream or milk emulsifies with the fruit better and holds it in a suspension.) But with sorbet you'll notice the change after about five days. The best way to prevent this is to flip your container of sorbet upside down after a few days to reverse the progress. If your sorbet does separate, don't throw it out—you can thaw and reprocess it in your ice cream machine. After being stored for a week, though, the bright, fresh flavors of sorbet start to fade, so it's best to enjoy it quickly.

The sorbets and granitas you'll find in this book:

Strawberry Sorbet

P ■ *Makes 1½ pints*

This sorbet is fragrant and delicious. The secret to any sorbet, and especially one made with berries, is to use the best ingredients possible. The berries should be in season and fresh. Don't use berries that are "on the way out," as we say in the restaurant business. Find a local farmers' market, and make friends with the farmer so he or she will save some of the best berries for you. The tastiest berries will still be warm from the field and bright red throughout with no hollow spaces in the core. Take advantage of the season and stock up. Freeze the berries (spread them on baking sheets, freeze, then pack in resealable plastic bags) to use in the future when you get a taste for this luscious spring favorite.

MAKE AHEAD/STORAGE This sorbet can be made up to 4 days ahead and kept frozen. If the sorbet begins to separate, simply melt it and reprocess it in your machine. (See page 81 for more information on sorbets and granitas.)

2 cups water (bottled water yields a tastier sorbet)

1½ cups sugar

5 cups best-quality fresh or frozen strawberries, thawed

1 tablespoon fresh lemon juice

1 Heat the water and sugar in a medium saucepan over low heat, stirring, until the sugar has dissolved. Remove the pan from the heat and let cool.

2 Stem the strawberries and puree them in a blender or food processor. Blend the strawberry puree, lemon juice, and sugar syrup in a blender or using an immersion blender, and chill the mixture at least 2 hours.

3 Process the sorbet mixture in your ice cream machine, following the manufacturer's instructions. Transfer the sorbet to a covered container and freeze until hard, at least 4 hours or overnight.

Strawberry-Rhubarb Crisp

D ▪ *Serves 6 to 8*

Fruit crisps are a delicious and homey way to end a meal. I love tart, rosy-red rhubarb and am always looking for ways to work it into my menus. I've even used it for chutneys and salads, but the classic combination of rhubarb and strawberries makes for an unbeatable dessert. Try the crisp with some strawberry sorbet spooned over it—it's delicious as it melts.

MAKE AHEAD/STORAGE The fruit mixture can be stored in the refrigerator, covered, up to 2 days, and the crisp topping can be stored in a covered container or a resealable plastic bag up to 5 days. The crisps can be cooked earlier on the day of serving and held at room temperature, loosely covered. Pop them in a low oven to rewarm or serve at room temperature.

For the Fruit Mixture

   4 large rhubarb ribs

   4 pints fresh strawberries

   ¼ cup dry or semidry white wine

   1 cup granulated sugar

   Juice and grated zest of 2 lemons

For the Topping

   1½ cups oats, preferably quick-cooking Irish oats

   1 cup granulated sugar

   ¼ cup dark brown sugar

   ½ cup all-purpose flour

   4 ounces (1 stick) unsalted butter, cut into 1-inch pieces

   2 teaspoons ground cinnamon

   Strawberry Sorbet (page 82, optional)

1 Make the Fruit Mixture If the rhubarb is stringy, snap off the ends and pull to remove the coarse strings. Cut the rhubarb into small dice. Stem the strawberries and cut into quarters. Set aside 1 cup strawberries and combine the remaining strawberries, the rhubarb, the wine, and 1 cup sugar in a medium saucepan. Cook the mixture over medium heat, stirring occasionally, about 20 minutes, until it is quite thick and the fruit is completely tender. Stir in the reserved strawberries (this makes the mixture a little chunky). Stir in the lemon juice and zest and allow the mixture to cool.

2 Make the Topping Place the oats, sugars, flour, butter, and cinnamon in a food processor or in the bowl of an electric mixer. Pulse the mixture on and off until it just comes together to form pea sized pieces (or beat with the paddle at low speed in the mixer).

3 Preheat the oven to 350°F.

4 Spoon the strawberry-rhubarb mixture into eight 4-ounce ramekins or a 2-quart casserole. Pile the crisp topping over the filling, making sure it comes to the edges, and pat it into place to form a thick layer.

5 Bake the crisp until the topping is browned and the filling is bubbly, about 20 minutes for ramekins or 30 minutes for a casserole. Serve with Strawberry Sorbet, if desired.

Chocolate Mousse Puffs

P ■ *Serves 6*

This dessert looks and tastes as if you spent all day working on it, but it's remarkably simple to assemble (and you can even do it ahead of time). For serving, you can dress it up with fruit, whipped cream, sorbet, or whatever you're in the mood for. This is a perfect Passover dessert, as it requires no flour or leavening products—plus, it uses no dairy, so it's flexible for any menu. Use the best-quality chocolate and vanilla possible.

MAKE AHEAD/STORAGE The puffs can be assembled and refrigerated, covered, for 1 day before baking.

- 2 tablespoon neutral-flavored oil, such as canola
- Sugar for coating ramekins
- 6 ounces best-quality semisweet or bittersweet chocolate, chopped
- 1/3 cup brewed coffee, espresso, or water
- 4 large eggs, separated
- 1 teaspoon vanilla extract or seeds scraped from 1/2 of a vanilla bean
- 1 cup plus 3 tablespoons sugar
- **Suggested Garnishes** fresh fruit, sorbet, or Raspberry Coulis (page 29)

1 Preheat the oven to 350°F.

2 Lightly brush the bottom and sides of six 4-ounce ramekins with oil to coat. Sprinkle the ramekins with sugar to coat and turn the cups upside down to remove excess sugar.

3 Melt the chocolate with the coffee in a medium saucepan over very low heat, stirring occasionally. Set the chocolate aside to cool slightly.

4 Whip the egg yolks with 1 cup of the sugar at high speed until very light and fluffy, about 5 minutes. Fold in the chocolate mixture and vanilla extract or seeds using a rubber spatula.

5 In a clean bowl with clean beaters, whip the egg whites at medium-high speed until they hold soft peaks. Slowly add the remaining 3 tablespoons sugar and continue to whip until they hold stiff peaks. Gently fold the whites into the chocolate mixture using a rubber spatula. Ladle the mixture into the prepared ramekins, filling them to the top.

6 Bake the puffs in the oven until puffed and fairly solid, 10 to 12 minutes (if the puffs have been chilled, they may take a little longer). Serve puffs immediately with your choice of garnish.

84

Floating Islands with Strawberry Fruit Soup

P ▪ *Serves 10 to 12*

I love this dessert for its sophisticated simplicity. It is light, elegant, and beautiful. You can adapt the fruit soup, depending upon the time of year and the ripeness of fruit in the market. It is as perfect for Passover as it is for Mother's Day or any occasion.

MAKE AHEAD/STORAGE Meringues can be made up to 4 hours ahead and kept at room temperature, uncovered. Turn them out of the pans (or pan) just before serving.

Nonstick vegetable oil spray

6 large egg whites, at room temperature

1 vanilla bean, halved lengthwise

1 cup sugar

Strawberry Fruit Soup with Fresh Mint (page 80) or another fruit soup

Suggested Garnishes slivered strawberries, fresh mint leaves cut into chiffonade

1 Preheat the oven to 350°F. Lightly spray a muffin pan or 9 × 5 × 3–inch loaf pan with nonstick vegetable oil spray. Fill a large pot or kettle with water and bring to a boil.

2 Place the egg whites in a bowl and, using the tip of a paring knife, scrape the vanilla seeds into the whites (keep vanilla pod halves for another use). Whip the whites at medium speed until they hold soft peaks.

Slowly add 1 cup sugar and continue to whip until the whites hold stiff and glossy peaks.

3 Scoop the meringue into the prepared pan, then place the pan in a larger pan, such as a roasting pan. Carefully pour the boiling water into the roasting pan until it reaches about halfway up sides of the meringue pan. Take care not to splash hot water into the meringue. Transfer the water bath into the oven and bake the meringue until it is lightly browned on top and a tester comes out clean, 15 to 20 minutes. Remove the meringue from the roasting pan and let cool to room temperature.

4 To serve, run a sharp knife around the edges of the meringues. Invert a platter over the meringues and turn the platter and the meringue pan upside down to release the meringues. (Slice the meringue if using a loaf pan.) Spoon fruit soup into shallow soup bowls and float the meringues on top. Garnish with slivered strawberries and mint.

SUMMER

Loveliest of trees, the cherry now
Is hung with bloom along the bough.

A. E. HOUSMAN

FOR ME, THE HIGH POINT OF SUMMER comes when the farmers' market stalls are overflowing with magnificent produce and the culinary possibilities seem endless. I love watching busy shoppers select their produce while I sit and sip my iced coffee. My eyes scan for the shopper whose system mirrors my own antics—the one carefully inspecting the baby beets or, perhaps, trying to decide between two baskets of raspberries, one deep red, the other golden (and eventually just gives up and buys both).

I love to merge the rich colors of my purchases into one beautiful mosaic on the cutting board. Quickly, I begin to conjure up unique combinations so my family and I can savor this glorious summer bounty. I try to lighten up my cooking techniques and flavors. I prefer to lightly sauté, grill, or even poach food in the summer. In keeping with the rising temperature, I even look for ways to eat my dinner cold. I crave the bright flavors of Chilled Cucumber Soup (page 91) with the playful Cucumber-Lemongrass Sorbet (page 92). The colorful mix of Roasted Duck Breast with Cherry—

Red Wine Reduction, Sour Cherry Chutney, and Roasted Purple Potatoes (pages 118 to 120) might seem almost garish any other time of the year. But its bright flavors and colors are as appropriate to the season as my favorite beaded sandals and melon-colored blouse.

As the summer progresses, new subjects catch my attention on my trips to the market. Suddenly the berries are passé, and shoppers turn their attention toward shell beans, the fresh version of dried beans. Shell beans are sweeter, nuttier, less starchy, and quicker to cook than their dried counterparts, staples in my pantry during the fall and winter months. Cranberry and Dragon-Tongue beans are some of the kinds I seek out. Their names are fun; their tastes are delicate and sweet. With just a quick blanch, shock, and perhaps a moment in the sauté pan, they can become a gorgeous and unusual dish. Or, for a more elaborate presentation, the Summer Vegetable Cassoulet (page 112) shows off the beans and a profusion of other seasonal vegetables. The fresh licorice flavor of sweet fennel and fresh herbs combined with the beans make the cassoulet perfect for Shabbat lunch or a light dinner.

One of my favorite stock-up fruits is cherries. Not only are they delicious and beautiful, but they keep fairly well. Whereas berries must be eaten within a day or two of purchasing, cherries will last about a week or more in the refrigerator. That gives me plenty of time to use them for my favorite Sour Cherry Chutney (page 119), a Cherry–Red Wine Reduction (see page 118) to drizzle over duck breasts, Bing Cherry Fruit Soup (page 135), and my most favorite sorbet of all, Sour Cherry Sorbet (page 136). I love to serve the cherry soup in a wine glass with a sidecar of sweet and tart sorbet. It makes an elegant and refreshing dessert, snack, or even a first course.

Every summer, I'm amazed by all the different types of corn on the market. I seem to remember that when I was a child we didn't have such varied colors, sizes, or names. Now, sweet and toasty flavored corn can be purple, white, bicolored, and more. I love to garnish plates with the kernels, grill corn with fresh herbs, and make it into my favorite Grilled Corn Chowder (page 93). The soup makes a gorgeous chilled first course or a light lunch or dinner. It can be made a day before serving, so it's a delicious and impressive Shabbat soup.

If I had to pick my absolute "can't live without" summer food, it would have to be heirloom tomatoes. Heirloom varietals are open-pollinated (without human intervention), but more important, they are varieties chosen for their intense flavors and vibrant colors. In contrast, the mega-produced varietals have very little taste, nutrition, or appeal. The most magnificent heirloom tomatoes have unique names like Brandywine, Purple Cherokee, Zebra Stripe, and Hillbilly. Their colors are bright and flashy, and their flavors are almost mouth-wateringly intense. I toss them into Heirloom Tomato Salad (page 100), slow cook them into Tomato Confit (page 22), and whirl them in the blender to make Gazpacho (pages 95 to 98). My passion for summer tomatoes leads me to fantasize about them the rest of the year, thinking up the best ways to use them when they finally appear in the market. Can you blame me? If I could stretch just one part of summer, tomato season would be the one

SOUPS, STARTERS, AND SALADS

Chilled Cucumber Soup

Grilled Corn Chowder
with Salmon Seviche

A Quartet of Gazpachos
Tomato Gazpacho
White Gazpacho (Ajo Blanco)
Green Gazpacho
Shallots Bistro–Style Gazpacho

Heirloom Tomato Salad

Duo of Watermelon Granitas
Red Seedless Watermelon Granita
Golden or Yellow Seedless
Watermelon Granita

Grilled Stone Fruit Salad

Roasted Fig Salad with
Honey-Lavender Vinaigrette

Roasted Baby Carrots with
Ginger-Lemon Vinaigrette

Pickled Vegetable Antipasto

Feta Cheese Salad with Lettuce Wraps

Shredded Lamb Salad with Mint
and Fig-Balsamic Reduction

Red Pepper Tabbouleh in
Grilled Vegetable Wraps

MAIN DISHES

Summer Vegetable Cassoulet

Sumac-Dusted Beef Skewers
with Spicy Mango Chutney

Shallots Fried Chicken

Roasted Duck Breasts with Cherry–
Red Wine Reduction

My BLT (Bison, Lettuce, and Tomato)

Grilled Flatbreads

Grilled Rib-Eye Sandwiches with
Grilled Vegetables

Grilled Marinated Short Ribs with
Spicy Fruit Barbecue Sauce

Grilled Venison Loin Stuffed with
Slow-Roasted Tomatoes and Leeks

DESSERTS

Blackberry-Lemon Frozen Custard

Peaches in Moscato with Amaretti

Bing Cherry Fruit Soup

Sour Cherry Sorbet

Mixed Cherry Clafoutis

Granita al Caffè

Chilled Cucumber Soup

P ■ *Serves 6*

Cool, cool, cool! I enjoy making this light and refreshing soup when the summer heat has set in. It's perfect to start a Shabbat dinner, since it's served ice cold, no heating required. For a special occasion, add a scoop of the cucumber sorbet for an extra burst of icy flavor.

MAKE AHEAD/STORAGE This soup can be stored in the refrigerator, covered, up to 5 days.

- 2 large English (seedless) cucumbers, peeled, soft centers scraped out, and cut into chunks
- 2 cups peeled, seeded, and cubed honeydew melon
- 1 cup seedless green grapes
- Juice and grated zest of 2 limes
- ¼ cup finely chopped fresh cilantro
- ½ cup finely chopped fresh flat-leaf parsley
- 2 to 3 cups water
- Kosher salt and freshly ground black pepper to taste
- Cucumber Lemongrass Sorbet (recipe follows; optional)

1 Process the cucumber, melon, and grapes in a food processor until smooth. Stir in the lime juice, zest, cilantro, and parsley. Stir in 2 cups water and salt and pepper to taste. Add more water if needed to thin the soup to the consistency you like. Chill completely, at least 1 hour, before serving.

2 Scoop 6 balls of sorbet, if using, onto a small baking sheet and freeze, uncovered, until firm, at least 1 hour. Ladle the soup into shallow bowls and top each with a sorbet ball.

Cucumber-Lemongrass Sorbet

P ■ *Makes about 1½ pints*

Once you can get used to the idea that sorbet is not just for dessert, you can really have some fun. My staff and friends know that I don't have a high tolerance for summer's heat and am always looking for cool and refreshing ways to escape.

MAKE AHEAD/STORAGE This sorbet can be made up to 1 week ahead and kept frozen. If the sorbet begins to separate, simply melt it and reprocess it in your machine. (See page 81 for more information on sorbets and granitas.)

1 stalk lemongrass

2 cups water (bottled water yields a tastier sorbet)

½ cup sugar

3 large English (seedless) cucumbers, peeled, soft centers scraped out, and cut into chunks

2 ripe avocados, pitted and peeled

Juice and grated zest of 2 limes

Kosher salt and freshly ground black pepper

1 Peel off the outer layers of the lemon grass to expose the tender shoot. Cut off the hard root end and the dried top of the stalk, leaving about 4 inches of the shoot. Cut the shoot into ½-inch pieces.

2 Place the lemongrass, water, and sugar in a small saucepan, and cook over medium heat until the sugar has dissolved and the mixture begins to simmer. Remove from the heat and set aside to let the lemongrass infuse the mixture. When syrup has cooled, strain out and discard the lemongrass.

3 Process the cucumber and avocado in a food processor or blender until smooth. Add the syrup, zest, and juice, and process until combined. Season with salt and pepper. Chill the mixture completely. Process the sorbet mixture in your ice cream machine, following the manufacturer's instructions. Transfer the sorbet to a covered container and freeze until hard before serving.

Grilled Corn Chowder
with Salmon Seviche

P ■ *Serves 6*

Try this recipe when you have fresh-picked, sweet, flavorful corn from the farmers' market or farmstand. Look for the sweetest varieties, and try to avoid corn that has been stored for several days since it can be starchy. You'll be amazed at the difference that fresh corn makes. Chipotle peppers are dried, smoked jalapeño peppers with a deep, earthy smoke flavor that deepens the grilled corn flavor. Watch out, they can be quite spicy! If you use one for this soup, and I recommend that you do, put it in to cook whole. That way it's easier to fish out when the soup has finished cooking.

MAKE AHEAD/STORAGE This soup can be stored in the refrigerator, covered, up to 2 days. The seviche can be stored in the refrigerator, covered, up to 1 hour, but no longer.

- 10 ears very fresh corn
- 4 cups Vegetable Stock (page 17) or water
- 1 dried chipotle pepper (optional)
- Kosher salt and freshly ground black pepper

For the Seviche

- 1 pound skinless, boneless wild Alaskan salmon fillet (do not use farmed salmon)
- Juice of 2 lemons
- Juice of 2 limes
- Juice of 1 orange
- 2 medium shallots, thinly sliced

- 1 Roasted Red Pepper (page 25; use red peppers), cut into thin strips
- ½ cup chopped fresh cilantro
- 1 jalapeño pepper, diced into very small confetti (optional)
- Kosher salt and freshly ground black pepper
- Extra-virgin olive oil

1 Preheat the grill to medium heat (or use a grill pan for indoor cooking). While the grill is heating, soak the corn in cold water, about 20 minutes, to keep the husk and corn silk from burning.

2 Grill the corn until the kernels pop easily when pressed with a knife, 15 to 20 minutes. Remove the corn from the grill and cool. When the corn is cool enough to handle, strip off the husks and silk. To remove the corn kernels, stand an ear up on a cutting board. Run a knife down the ear, stripping off the kernels. Continue until all the kernels have been stripped.

Summer

3 Puree half the kernels with the vegetable stock or water in a food processor or blender, and set aside another ½ cup of kernels for garnish. Stir together the puree with the remaining kernels in a large saucepan and add the chipotle, if using, and salt and pepper to taste. Simmer the soup for 20 minutes. Discard the chipotle and chill the soup until cold, at least 4 hours.

4 **Make the Seviche** Cut the salmon into long, thin strips. Gently toss the salmon with the citrus juices in a large bowl and let the salmon cure for 3 to 5 minutes, until the fish is opaque. Add the shallot, red pepper, cilantro, jalapeño (if using), and salt and pepper to taste, toss lightly, and drizzle with a spoonful of olive oil.

5 To serve, divide the Salmon Seviche among 6 bowls, spooning the mixture into a tight bundle in the center. Adjust seasoning to taste with salt and pepper and ladle the soup around the seviche. Garnish with the reserved corn kernels.

A Quartet of Gazpachos

I know that gazpacho is a fairly misunderstood soup. The original Andalusian version had almonds, bread, grapes, olive oil, vinegar, and salt; sometimes anchovies were added. The bread was allowed to soak up water, then the mixture was pounded with a mortar and pestle. It was peasant food. The gazpacho that we know best came after Columbus brought peppers and tomatoes back to Spain.

The trick to great gazpacho is not to let any one ingredient be more pronounced than any other. The soup should be in harmony, very subtle and delicate in flavor. Any one of these gazpachos makes a lovely starter, but I particularly like the idea of presenting your family or guests with four mini servings of gazpacho and letting them decide which they like best. Have fun with it and make a gazpacho party. Let the sangria flow as well!

Tomato Gazpacho

P ■ *Makes about 6 cups (serves 4)*

This version of the soup that we commonly eat here in America is refreshing and delicious. In Spain, gazpacho is drunk from a cup. Only here do we eat it with a spoon. Either way, it's wonderful.

MAKE AHEAD/STORAGE This soup can be stored in the refrigerator, covered, up to 2 days.

4 large, plump, juicy garlic cloves

Kosher salt

1 red bell pepper, seeded and deveined

1 small English (seedless) cucumber, peeled, soft center scraped out

2 to 3 pounds very ripe tomatoes, cut into chunks

1 cup soft bread torn into pieces (leftover challah trimmed of crust will work nicely)

¼ cup unseasoned rice vinegar

Splash of sherry (optional)

⅓ cup extra-virgin olive oil (use your best-tasting oil)

2 cups unsalted tomato juice

1 teaspoon pimenton*

Freshly ground black pepper

Suggested Garnishes herbed croutons, chopped cucumber, chopped fresh parsley, chopped hard-cooked egg, chopped hot chiles, diced roasted peppers, extra-virgin olive oil

*Pimenton, Spanish smoked paprika, can't really be compared to the paprika found in most grocery stores. It has a wonderful sweet smokiness essential to paella, chorizo, and other Spanish delicacies. It can be found online or at specialty markets. The Spice House (see Sources, page 257) has a kosher-certified product that is excellent and easily shipped to your home.

Summer

1 Place the garlic and 2 teaspoons salt in a mortar and pound it to a paste; or use a cutting board and the side of your knife to smash and scrape it. Transfer the garlic paste to a food processor or blender. Add the bell pepper, cucumber, tomatoes, bread, vinegar, sherry (if using), olive oil, and tomato juice, and process until very smooth and the mixture is peach colored. Season with salt and pepper to taste. Chill soup, covered, until it is very cold, at least 4 hours.

2 To serve, ladle the gazpacho into bowls or cups and garnish it, if you like, with as many toppings as you want. Use your imagination!

White Gazpacho (Ajo Blanco)

P ■ *Makes about 6 cups (serves 4)*

I love this beautiful, pale green, delicate version of the classic gazpacho from Andalusia. Try serving it in a glass bowl or even a wine glass.

MAKE AHEAD/STORAGE This soup can be stored in the refrigerator, covered, up to 2 days.

4 large plump, juicy garlic cloves

Kosher salt

2 cups cubed bread (crusts removed first)

4 cups ice-cold water

6 ounces blanched almonds (about 1 cup)

2 cups seedless green grapes

¼ cup unseasoned rice vinegar

Splash of sherry

⅓ cup extra-virgin olive oil (use your best-tasting oil)

Freshly ground black pepper

Suggested Garnishes chopped toasted almonds, halved green grapes, chopped fresh flat-leaf parsley

1 Place the garlic and 2 teaspoons salt in a mortar and pound it to a paste; or use a cutting board and the side of your knife to smash and scrape it. Transfer the garlic paste to a food processor or blender.

2 Soak the bread in the water until soft. (Delicate bread will take just a minute, while firm bread may take up to 15 minutes to soften.) Squeeze the remaining water out of the bread and reserve the water. Add the soaked bread, grapes, vinegar, sherry, and olive oil to the garlic and process until very smooth. Add reserved water to thin soup to the consistency you like, and season with salt and pepper. Chill the gazpacho, covered, until it is very cold, at least 4 hours.

3 To serve, ladle the gazpacho into bowls or cups and garnish it with your choice of toppings.

Green Gazpacho

P ■ *Makes about 6 cups (serves 4)*

This gazpacho, a "shepherd's gathering soup," highlights the herbs and greens found in the mountains and alongside the streams in the Axarquia region of Malaga, in southern Spain.

MAKE AHEAD/STORAGE This soup can be stored in the refrigerator, covered, up to 2 days.

4 large, plump, juicy garlic cloves

Kosher salt

1 small fennel bulb, trimmed and chopped, fronds reserved for garnish

2 cups packed watercress leaves or other robust greens, such as arugula or baby spinach

¼ cup packed fresh flat-leaf parsley leaves

¼ cup packed fresh mint leaves

¼ cup unseasoned rice vinegar

Splash of sherry (optional)

⅓ cup extra-virgin olive oil (use your best-tasting oil)

4 cups ice-cold Vegetable Stock (page 17) or water

Freshly ground black pepper

Suggested Garnishes Garlicky Aioli (page 26), chopped fresh mint, diced cucumber, reserved fennel fronds

1 Place the garlic and 2 teaspoons salt in a mortar and pound it to a paste; or use a cutting board and the side of your knife to smash and scrape it. Transfer the garlic paste to a food processor or blender. Add the fennel, watercress, parsley, mint, vinegar, sherry (if using), olive oil, and 3 cups of the stock, and process until the gazpacho is completely smooth. Add more stock if needed to thin soup to the consistency you like, and season with salt and pepper. Chill the gazpacho, covered, until it is very cold, at least 4 hours.

2 To serve, ladle the gazpacho into bowls or cups and garnish it with your choice of toppings.

Shallots Bistro—Style Gazpacho

P ■ *Makes about 6 cups (serves 4)*

This version is purely and playfully American, featuring summer watermelon and tomatoes. Yellow tomatoes, considered low-acid tomatoes, are becoming fairly easy to find. I love their sweetness and gorgeous color. Use a favorite tomato or experiment with some heirlooms in the market. At the restaurant, we roast and peel the tomatoes, but at home I don't bother. For a special occasion, try this with a scoop of the Cucumber-Lemongrass Sorbet (page 92).

MAKE AHEAD/STORAGE This soup can be stored in the refrigerator, covered, up to 2 days.

4 large, plump, juicy garlic cloves

Kosher salt

3 pounds yellow tomatoes or favorite heirloom tomatoes, cut into chunks

1 cup cubed yellow seedless watermelon

⅓ cup extra-virgin olive oil (use your best-tasting oil)

¼ cup unseasoned rice vinegar

Splash of sherry

4 cups ice-cold water

Freshly ground black pepper

Suggested Garnishes Cucumber-Lemongrass Sorbet (page 92), watermelon cubes, diced tomatoes, Tomato Confit (page 22), Harissa Aioli (page 26), chopped fresh flat-leaf parsley

1 Place the garlic and 2 teaspoons salt in a mortar and pound it to a paste; or use a cutting board and the side of your knife to smash and scrape it. Transfer the garlic paste to a food processor or blender. Add the tomatoes, watermelon, olive oil, vinegar, sherry, and water, and process until smooth. Chill the gazpacho, covered, until it is very cold.

2 To serve, ladle the gazpacho into bowls or cups and garnish it with your choice of toppings.

Olive Oil

As any child who has spun a dreidel knows, olive oil has always played an important role in the history of the Jewish people. While olive oil is not considered sacred today, it certainly remains one of the most essential ingredients—especially to kosher cooks. In my restaurant, where we obviously don't use any butter, olive oil is the key to our cooking. Our kitchen is stocked with at least four different types, from fragrant, fruity, unfiltered organic extra-virgin oil for drizzling on delicate salads to the light olive oils that we use for sautéing. Every Mediterranean country produces its own olive oils, and each of these has a different texture, color, and flavor. The hardest thing is limiting my choices. Currently I favor an unfiltered, organic Spanish oil, but I always come across new ones to try—perhaps a smoother one, or one with a more peppery aroma, or one with hints of lemon or herbs. I want them all.

At home, I'm very restrained and have only two bottles of olive oil. But sometimes I can't help myself—I just have to check out another new oil from Portugal, or Greece, or Southern Italy, or Spain, Israel, or even California.

Fortunately for me and for all kosher cooks, all extra-virgin olive oil is kosher. Extra-virgin olive oil comes from the first cold press of the olives, a relatively long and costly process. The second pressing of olives involves heating already pressed olives and pressing them again to extract even more oil. Therefore, all olive oils that are not labeled as extra virgin must be *hechshered* (certified as kosher by one of the rabbinical governing authorities).

Extra-virgin olive oil has a rich, fruity flavor that enhances sauces, vinaigrettes, and the natural flavors of vegetables, fish, and meats. I recommend that you splurge on an amazing extra-virgin olive oil, and drizzle it over your vegetables and fish and into your favorite vinaigrettes. A great place to show off a delicious, high-quality olive oil is in the gazpacho recipes (pages 95 to 98), where the fruity oil will enhance all the other ingredients. Taste and compare before you buy—generally you will find that oils with deeper color have more flavor, but they may be more peppery; paler ones may be milder, with a light fruitiness. Try them and see which ones you like best.

It's also worthwhile to have some other olive oil options. Extra-virgin olive oil has a relatively low smoke point: Its fragrance diminishes in a single whiff as the temperature of a sauté pan reaches about 325 to 350°F, which is still too low for most sautéing or frying. Then, as the temperature continues to increase, the oil can even burn. So for sautéing I recommend either a "light" olive oil or a blend, such as one that is part olive oil and part vegetable oil. You will still have some of the health benefits of the olive oil without the expense of extra-virgin olive oil. And you will avoid the heaviness of some vegetable oils. A mix of oils also works best for Garlicky Aioli (page 26) and its variations, since the signature fragrance and flavor of extra-virgin-oil can overwhelm the flavor of this sauce.

Heirloom Tomato Salad

P ▪ *Serves 6*

I wait all year long for heirloom tomatoes. They are tomatoes the way nature intended, and grocery-store tomatoes can't compare. Do yourself a favor, seek out the heirlooms and give them a try. They are gorgeous—colorful and mouthwateringly delicious. They can be found in farmers' markets, specialty stores, and some grocery chains. I offer them almost completely unadorned in this salad. They're so good, they don't need me! Sometimes, though, I like to dress them up with a granita for a particularly pretty starter.

5 pounds heirloom tomatoes, mixed color for best looking salad

1 cup large chunks yellow seedless watermelon

1 cup large chunks red seedless watermelon

Extra-virgin olive oil (use your best-tasting oil)

Balsamic Reduction (page 19)

Coarse sea salt and freshly cracked black pepper

Duo of Watermelon Granitas (page 102; optional)

Core the tomatoes and cut into large chunks. Lightly toss the tomatoes and melons in a large bowl. Drizzle with olive oil and balsamic reduction. Sprinkle with sea salt and crack pepper over the salad just before serving.

For an alternate presentation, layer the salad in dessert glasses with the Watermelon Granitas.

Heirloom Produce

An heirloom is a variety of fruit or vegetable that is open-pollinated (it stays true to type from seed through succeeding generations). Some authorities also insist that a true heirloom must be at least fifty years old, and many have histories that date back more than 100 years.

But the true distinction of heirloom produce and what makes it really worth seeking out is that it tastes the way it is supposed to taste. Before mega agriculture took over with its engineered hybrids, produce was grown locally and shipped not much farther than a day's drive from the farm. Since they didn't have to travel across the country, fruits and vegetables were picked ripe instead of being harvested while still hard. The ripe produce was put out for sale immediately, not stored in chilled warehouses. That's not to say that everything was better in the old days, but produce did have more flavor. Today, these antique vegetables may not have supermarket mass appeal with their surface imperfections and odd sizing. They are, however, for lack of a better term "real."

You can find heirloom varieties of apples, potatoes, tomatoes, beans, carrots, and an ever-expanding list of other produce. Their flavor is unmatched. I really enjoy working with them and am passionate about finding ways to use them at the restaurant and at home. The heirloom apple varieties change from early fall through first frost. As soon as I am convinced that I have found the perfect apple, another comes along to challenge it. I find it exciting to experiment and try a little bit of everything.

One of the reasons that more heirlooms are now available is that more chefs and home cooks are using them and encouraging farmers to grow them. The farmers' market or a local farm stand are still the best places to find these beauties. If you start going regularly farmers will alert you to something "new" (or old, as the case may be). They will also let you know when something you love is about to be harvested. As more people insist on buying these varieties, they will become more available at your local grocery store and gourmet markets.

Duo of Watermelon Granitas

Prowl the farmers market and you will find different colors and varieties of watermelon—I love their color and fragrance. Feel free to add some complementary fresh herbs to the mint, if desired. Try adding a tablespoon of chopped chervil or lemon verbena, for example, to vary the flavor a bit.

Red Seedless Watermelon Granita

P ■ *Makes about 1½ pints*

MAKE AHEAD/STORAGE This granita can be made up to 4 days ahead and kept frozen. (See page 81 for more information on sorbets and granitas.)

4 cups large chunks red seedless watermelon

1 cup sugar

½ teaspoon fresh lemon juice

¼ cup chopped fresh mint

Process the melon with sugar and lemon juice in a blender or food processor until completely smooth and combined. Pour the mixture into a shallow metal pan and stir in mint. Freeze, scraping the granita every hour or so with a fork to break up the ice crystals. When finished, the crystals should be fine and sandy.

Golden or Yellow Seedless Watermelon Granita

P ■ *Makes about 1½ pints*

MAKE AHEAD/STORAGE This granita can be made up to 4 days ahead and kept frozen. (See page 81 for more information on sorbets and granitas.)

4 cups large chunks golden or yellow seedless watermelon

1 cup sugar

½ teaspoon fresh lemon juice

¼ cup chopped fresh mint

Process the melon with sugar and lemon juice in a blender or food processor until completely smooth and combined. Pour the mixture into a shallow metal pan and stir in mint. Freeze, scraping the granita every hour or so with a fork to break up the ice crystals. When finished, the crystals should be fine and sandy.

102

Grilled Stone Fruit Salad

P ■ *Serves 6*

Cooking fruit on the grill, or even in a grill pan, really brings out its sweetness and juices. If you're lucky enough to find flavorful local peaches, plums, and apricots, you'll want to enjoy them in as many ways as you can—and this is a great way to get them into another course of a summer meal.

MAKE AHEAD/STORAGE The fruit can be grilled 1 hour before serving and kept warm, covered with foil. Or the fruit can be grilled 1 day ahead and stored in the refrigerator, covered. Let it come to room temperature before serving.

3 ripe peaches, cut in half and pitted

3 ripe plums, cut in half and pitted

3 ripe apricots, cut in half and pitted

Olive oil

6 cups mesclun or favorite salad greens

Juice and grated zest of 1 lemon

Extra virgin olive oil

Kosher salt and freshly ground black pepper

1 Preheat the grill or grill pan to medium heat.

2 Lightly brush the cut side of fruit with olive oil and place on the grill, cut side down. Grill fruit, covered, about 10 minutes, until juicy and caramelized on the cut side. Remove the fruit from the grill and let cool slightly. Peel off the skin (it should come off easily). Cut each fruit in half again.

3 Place the greens in a large bowl or on a platter. Scatter the fruit on top of the greens, and sprinkle with the lemon zest and juice. Drizzle with a few spoonfuls of extra-virgin olive oil, season with salt and pepper and toss lightly just before serving.

Roasted Fig Salad
with Honey-Lavender Vinaigrette

P ■ *Serves 4*

The trick to this recipe is to use a high-quality honey—I like clover or European summer-flower honey. The lavender just barely perfumes the honey and brings out the deep flavors of the figs. I love lavender and have made believers out of many people. If you have never tried lavender before, it's an herb just like thyme or rosemary, so you can use the leaves or the flowers, or both. I always have a pot of lavender growing (it's an easy herb to grow), so when a recipe requires some, I just snip the amount I need.

MAKE AHEAD/STORAGE The vinaigrette can be stored in the refrigerator, covered, up to 5 days.

1 pint green or black fresh figs, stemmed and cut in half

2 tablespoons high-quality honey

1 tablespoon water

For the Vinaigrette

¼ cup high-quality honey

1 tablespoon chopped fresh lavender (or 2 teaspoons dried)

2 tablespoons fresh lemon juice

Dash of unseasoned rice vinegar

2 tablespoons water

⅓ cup neutral-flavored oil, such as canola

Kosher salt and freshly ground black pepper

4 to 5 cups baby greens or favorite mix of lettuces

1 Preheat the oven to 300°F.

2 Place the fig halves, cut side up, on a cooling rack set over a shallow baking pan or on a cookie sheet lined with parchment paper. Whisk together 2 tablespoons honey and 1 tablespoon water to thin out the honey. Brush the figs with the honey mixture and roast until the figs have softened and are slightly caramelized, about 20 minutes.

3 **Make the Vinaigrette** Place ¼ cup honey and the lavender in a small saucepan. Bring the honey to a simmer and remove from the heat. Allow the lavender to steep for 30 minutes. Strain the honey through a fine-mesh strainer into a small bowl and discard the lavender. Add the lemon juice, vinegar, water, and oil, and whisk together. Season with salt and pepper.

4 Place the greens on a large platter or individual plates, arrange the figs on top, and drizzle the honey vinaigrette over the salad.

Roasted Baby Carrots
with Ginger-Lemon Vinaigrette

P ■ *Serves 6*

Baby carrots start to appear in the markets in the late spring and early summer. They are sweet, delicate, and nothing like their tough, woody counterparts at the end of the season. Look for different varieties and colors. I love making this dish with a mix of red, orange, yellow, and white carrots.

MAKE AHEAD/STORAGE This salad can be stored in the refrigerator, covered, up to 2 days. Let the carrots come to room temperature before serving.

6 bunches baby carrots, about 3 pounds

3 medium shallots, finely chopped

1 tablespoon chopped fresh thyme

3 tablespoons extra-virgin olive oil

Kosher salt and freshly ground black pepper

For the Vinaigrette

1 tablespoon freshly grated ginger

Juice and grated zest of 1 lemon

Dash of unseasoned rice vinegar

⅓ cup extra-virgin olive oil

Kosher salt and freshly ground black pepper

1 Preheat the oven to 300°F.

2 Scrub the carrots well (baby carrots don't really need to be peeled, as they have not yet developed a tough skin). I like to leave the tops attached, as it gives the carrots a nice appearance, but trim any long or wilted tops. Toss the carrots with the shallots, thyme, olive oil, and salt and pepper to taste. Roast the carrots on a baking sheet until they can be easily pierced with a paring knife, 20 to 30 minutes.

3 **Make the Vinaigrette** while the carrots are roasting. Whisk the ginger, lemon juice and zest, vinegar, and olive oil together and season with salt and pepper. Spoon the vinaigrette over the warm carrots.

Pickled Vegetable Antipasto

P ■ *Makes about 2 quarts*

Refrigerator pickles are easy to make and can perk up salads, chutneys, and cold meats. You can make an assortment or stick to just one vegetable if you like. Some nice combinations to try are: beets with onions, mango with carrots, yellow wax beans with cauliflower, and gherkins with hot peppers. For an antipasto plate, try to offer at least three different vegetables.

MAKE AHEAD/STORAGE These pickles can be stored in the refrigerator, covered, up to 2 weeks.

About 4 cups total from the following fruit and vegetables:

Cauliflower florets, blanched and shocked (see page 41)

Carrots, peeled, sliced thin, blanched and shocked

Pearl onions, blanched, shocked, and peeled

Baby beets, blanched and shocked (keep beets separate from other vegetables, other than onions)

Red onions, thinly sliced

Mango, peeled and thinly sliced

Yellow wax beans, stemmed

Baby corn, husked

Kirby cucumbers, gherkins, or cornichons

Hot peppers, such as serrano or jalapeño

Firm grape tomatoes

For the Pickling Liquid

4 cups cider vinegar

1 cinnamon stick

1 whole star anise

1 teaspoon coriander seeds

1 teaspoon whole black peppercorns

1 garlic clove

1 whole serrano chile (optional)

1 tablespoon honey

2 tablespoons kosher salt

Kosher salt and freshly ground black pepper for serving

1 Bring all the ingredients for the pickling liquid to a boil in a medium nonreactive saucepan. Tightly pack the vegetables into two 1-quart glass jars with plastic-coated lids. Pour the hot pickling liquid over the vegetables. Allow the mixture to cool uncovered. Cover the jars and let stand at room temperature for 2 hours.

2 To serve, remove pickles from brine and season with salt and pepper.

Feta Cheese Salad with Lettuce Wraps

D ▪ *Serves 4 to 6*

There are a few things that I know for sure in this world. One is that Israeli feta cheese, with its creaminess and slightly sharp flavors, is just about the best thing I can think of eating on a hot summer day. Whenever I can find this cheese I grab it. It has a slightly sharper, saltier flavor than other feta cheeses. I fondly remember eating it in Israel, generously sprinkled with extra-virgin olive oil, with crisp vegetables. The sparkling sunshine may also have added to its poetic flavor, but whatever the reason, I urge you to try this recipe. It is perfect for a summer luncheon or a kickoff to a Shavuot meal. I love to grab a leaf of lettuce and eat it with my fingers as a healthy hors d'oeuvre.

MAKE AHEAD/STORAGE The salad can be wrapped with plastic wrap and stored in the refrigerator for several hours before serving (store lettuce separately). Mound salad on lettuce leaves right before serving.

- 2 medium heads of firm-leafed lettuce, such as radicchio or romaine (I like to use baby romaine—it is easier to hold)
- ½ pound feta cheese, preferably Israeli, broken into medium chunks
- 1 cup pitted kalamata olives
- ½ cup brine-packed capers, drained and rinsed
- 2 cups teardrop, grape, or cherry tomatoes, cut in half
- 1 medium red onion, cut into small dice
- 1 large English (seedless) cucumber, peeled, soft center scraped out, and cut into small dice
- ½ cup chopped fresh flat-leaf parsley
- ¼ cup chopped fresh mint
- Juice of 1 lemon
- 3 tablespoons extra-virgin olive oil, plus more for garnish
- 3 tablespoons Za'atar (page 28), plus more for garnish
- Kosher salt and freshly ground black pepper

1 Wash and dry lettuces. Separate the leaves and place them on a large platter or individual plates. Combine the feta, olives, capers, tomatoes, onion, cucumber, parsley, mint, lemon juice, olive oil, and Za'atar in a large bowl. Toss gently, and season with salt and pepper.

2 Before serving, mound the salad mixture onto the lettuce leaves. Drizzle with some more olive oil and sprinkle with additional Za'atar.

Shredded Lamb Salad with Mint and Fig-Balsamic Reduction

M ▪ *Serves 8 a first course and 4 as a lighter main dish*

Slow and *easygoing* are the key words for this recipe. Cooking the lamb slowly allows the natural juices to fully permeate the meat so it becomes deeply flavored, with a melting texture that just can't be had when the meat is rushed. I strongly believe that slow cooking just one recipe now and then really makes you pay attention to the food that you feed your family and friends. Who knows, you just might find yourself relaxing and enjoying the time with your guests even more as well. For a Shabbat luncheon or dinner, you can serve the lamb cold, which is my favorite way to eat it, or you can reheat it. (Keep greens separate if you are going to serve this dish warm.)

MAKE AHEAD/STORAGE The lamb and all the vegetables can be stored separately, covered, in the refrigerator up to 2 days; the Fig-Balsamic Reduction can be stored in the refrigerator, covered, for several days.

- 1 lamb shoulder (5 to 7 pounds), boned by your butcher
- Kosher salt and freshly ground black pepper
- 4 large leeks, white parts only (save the light and dark green tops for stock), cut into thin strips
- 6 garlic cloves, preferably spring garlic, thinly sliced
- 6 medium shallots, thinly sliced
- 1 cup dry white wine, such as Sauvignon Blanc
- 1 to 2 cups Chicken Stock (page 15) or water

- 2 pounds baby carrots, preferably multicolored, trimmed and scrubbed
- 1 pound baby beets, preferably golden or candy striped, trimmed and scrubbed
- Olive oil
- 1 pound baby zucchini, trimmed
- 1 pound baby patty pan squashes, trimmed

For the Reduction

- 2 pints fresh green or black figs, stemmed and cut in half
- 1 cup balsamic vinegar
- ¼ cup dark brown sugar
- 6 cups mesclun or favorite salad greens
- ¼ cup fresh mint leaves cut into a chiffonade (thin strips)

1 Preheat the oven to 200°F.

2 Season the lamb with salt and pepper. Place the leeks, garlic, and shallots in the bottom of a large casserole or Dutch oven, and place the lamb on top. Add the wine and enough stock to come one inch up the sides of the lamb. Cover and roast the lamb until the meat is very tender and almost falling apart, about 3 hours. Set aside to cool in the liquid, uncovered. When the lamb is cool enough to handle, use your hands or two forks to pull the meat apart and lightly shred it, incorporating any juices and vegetables.

3 Blanch and shock the carrots and beets. Bring a large pot of salted water to a boil and prepare a large bowl of ice water with a strainer that fits inside the bowl. Add the carrots to the boiling water and cook 5 to 7 minutes, until the carrots are tender enough to be pierced with the point of a paring knife. Remove the carrots with a slotted spoon and chill them in the strainer set in the water. Cook the beets the same way, 10 to 15 minutes and chill in ice water. Pat dry and season with salt and pepper.

4 Lightly coat the bottom of a sauté pan with olive oil and heat over medium heat. Season the zucchini and patty pan squashes with salt and pepper, and sauté them until they are lightly colored and cooked through, about 10 minutes.

5 Make the Reduction Cook the figs, balsamic vinegar, and sugar in a medium nonreactive saucepan over medium-low heat, uncovered, stirring occasionally, until the figs are very soft and the balsamic vinegar has reduced to a syrup, about 1½ hours.

6 If made ahead, the lamb, vegetables, and Fig-Balsamic Reduction can be served cold, or remove them from refrigerator about 30 minutes before serving to allow them to come to room temperature. The lamb and vegetables can also be reheated, covered with foil, in a low (250°F) oven for about 30 minutes. Rewarm the fig reduction over medium-low heat or in the microwave.

7 To serve, place the mesclun (or salad greens) on a large platter or on individual plates. Scatter the vegetables over the greens. Place the lamb over the vegetables and spoon the Fig-Balsamic Reduction over the whole dish. Sprinkle liberally with the chopped mint.

Red Pepper Tabbouleh
in Grilled Vegetable Wraps

P ■ *Serves 4 to 5*

Here's a substantial lunch or light dinner idea that's perfect for the hottest summer days. It's easy to assemble since the parts can be made ahead. It's also delicious as a side to any grilled meat or fish. I particularly enjoy serving it with grilled tuna steaks.

MAKE AHEAD/STORAGE The tabbouleh and the grilled vegetables can be stored separately, covered, in the refrigerator up to 2 days.

For the Tabbouleh

1 large purple, white or striped eggplant

1 cup bulgur wheat

3 cups boiling water

Extra-virgin olive oil

1 medium red onion, finely chopped

1 garlic cloves, finely chopped

2 Roasted Bell Peppers (page 25; use red peppers), cut into thin strips

Kosher salt and freshly ground black pepper

Juice of 2 lemons

½ cup finely chopped fresh flat-leaf parsley

For the Wraps

3 medium zucchini, sliced lengthwise ½ inch thick

3 medium yellow squash, sliced lengthwise ½ inch thick

2 medium purple, white or striped eggplant, sliced lengthwise ½ inch thick

Kosher salt and freshly ground black pepper

Extra-virgin olive oil

2 Roasted Bell Peppers (page 25; use red peppers)

1 garlic clove

Mixed Olive Tapenade (page 230; optional)

1 Make the Tabbouleh Slice the eggplant into ½-inch-thick rounds. Sprinkle the eggplant heavily with kosher salt and place on a rack or in a strainer in the sink (this helps draw out the bitter juices). After 1 hour rinse the eggplant thoroughly and pat dry.

2 Meanwhile, place the bulgur in a large bowl and pour the boiling water over it. Cover and set aside for 1 hour.

3 Drain any excess water from the bulgur and fluff with a fork.

4 Heat a large sauté pan over medium-high heat, and lightly coat the bottom of the pan with olive oil. Sauté the onion until lightly browned, 3 to 5 minutes. Add the garlic, roasted peppers, and salt and pepper. Sauté until the onions are browned and caramelized, about 5 minutes. Toss the vegetables with the bulgur. Stir in the lemon juice and generously drizzle with olive oil. Toss the parsley with the tabbouleh, and adjust the seasoning with salt and pepper.

5 **Make the Wraps** Preheat the grill or a grill pan to medium-high.

6 Season the sliced zucchini, yellow squash, and eggplant with salt and pepper and lightly brush with olive oil. Grill the vegetables on one side until well marked and caramelized, 5 to 7 minutes. Turn the vegetables and grill until grill marks appear, 3 to 5 minutes. Remove the vegetables to a platter in a single layer so they don't steam and overcook, and set aside.

7 Process the roasted red peppers and garlic in a blender or food processor until pureed and thick, adding water 1 tablespoon at a time only if necessary. Season the puree with salt and pepper.

8 To assemble the wraps, place a zucchini slice on a cutting board, then slightly overlap another slice to form a double-wide strip of the vegetable. Smear the red pepper puree over the zucchini slices. Mound about 3 tablespoons of tabbouleh at the narrow end of the strip. Roll up the strip to enclose the tabbouleh, and carefully transfer the roll to a serving platter. Continue making rolls with the remaining grilled vegetables, pepper puree, and tabbouleh; you will have 8 to 10 rolls. If desired, dollop the rolls with Mixed Olive Tapenade before serving.

Summer Vegetable Cassoulet

P ■ *Serves 6 as a main dish or 8 to 10 as a side dish*

There are no rules for making this slow-cooked vegetable and bean dish, so I have just given you my favorite combination of ingredients. The best time to make it is when the farmers' market is overflowing with fresh vegetables—each item at its peak. By all means, come up with your own favorites; just try to include some fresh shell beans to keep the original "cassoulet" idea. I usually try to serve this dish on a large mound of fresh salad greens liberally sprinkled with olive oil and fresh herbs. I prefer it served at room temperature, which makes it a great Shabbat afternoon dish; it can also travel easily to a friend's home or to a weekend adventure in the country.

MAKE AHEAD/STORAGE The cassoulet can be made 2 days ahead and refrigerated, covered. Bring to room temperature before serving. If reheating is desired, gently warm, covered, in a 275°F oven until a knife inserted in the center is hot (about 40 minutes).

Extra-virgin olive oil

6 garlic cloves

Kosher salt

1 cup soft bread crumbs

2 tablespoons Dijon mustard

Freshly ground black pepper

2 medium fennel bulbs, trimmed and thinly sliced crosswise

2 medium leeks, white and light green parts only (save the dark green tops for stock), thinly sliced

1 cup cut fresh green beans (sliced on the bias into 1-inch pieces)

1 cup cut fresh yellow wax beans (sliced on the bias into 1-inch pieces)

1 cup fresh shell beans, such as cranberry beans (about 1 pound in the shell)*

1 medium zucchini, sliced 1 inch thick

1 medium summer squash, sliced 1 inch thick

2 medium carrots, peeled and sliced 1 inch thick

2 cups cherry or grape tomatoes,
cut in half

For the Salad

4 cups fresh arugula or favorite greens

¼ cup chopped fresh flat-leaf parsley

¼ cup fresh basil, torn into small pieces

1 tablespoon chopped fresh thyme

Extra-virgin olive oil

Kosher salt and freshly ground black
pepper

*Fresh shell beans can be found in late summer at farmers' markets and some grocery stores. They are not as starchy as their dried counterparts and have a subtle flavor. Some, such as cranberry beans, are available in both a dried and fresh form. I like the texture and flavor fresh beans add to this dish. You can substitute dried beans: Soak them overnight, then cook them with plenty of fresh water until they are tender

1 Preheat the oven to 300°F. Lightly rub a large casserole or Dutch oven with olive oil.

2 Place the garlic and 1 teaspoon salt in a mortar and pound it to a paste; or on a cutting board, smash and scrape the garlic and 1 teaspoon salt with the side of your knife. Combine the garlic, bread crumbs, mustard, and salt and pepper in a small bowl and sprinkle liberally with olive oil. Stir the mixture together until it forms a chunky, slightly wet topping. Pile the fennel, leeks, beans, zucchini, squash, and carrots into the casserole and toss with salt and pepper. Scatter the tomatoes on top of the vegetables then sprinkle with the bread-crumb topping.

3 Bake the cassoulet for 45 to 60 minutes until the bread crumbs are toasty brown, the tomatoes are slightly browned, and the vegetables are tender.

4 **Make the Salad** Toss the arugula, parsley, basil, and thyme in a large bowl with olive oil and salt and pepper to taste.

5 To serve, place the salad on a large platter or individual plates. Spoon warm or room temperature cassoulet onto the greens and sprinkle with additional olive oil, if desired.

Sumac-Dusted Beef Skewers with Spicy Mango Chutney

M ▪ *Serves 6 as an hors d'oeuvre or 4 as a main course*

Sumac, a spice commonly used in the Middle East, comes from the bark of the sumac tree. It has an astringent quality that makes it taste almost lemony, and it pairs well with meats and many vegetables. So feel free to make these skewers with chicken, lamb, or even sturdier fish, such as salmon or bass, if you're not in the mood for beef. It's worthwhile making the Spicy Mango Chutney when you have some beautiful ripe mangoes. A good alternative for dipping is a fruit salsa with peaches or pineapple.

MAKE AHEAD/STORAGE The skewers can be stored in the marinade, covered, in the refrigerator up to 1 day. The spice rub can be stored tightly covered at room temperature up to 1 month.

¼ cup extra-virgin olive oil

1 tablespoon fresh lemon juice

Grated zest of 1 orange

1 garlic clove, smashed

Kosher salt and freshly ground black pepper

½ pound skirt steak or other tender cut, cut against the grain into thin 2- to 3-inch-long strips

For the Rub

2 tablespoons sumac (see Sources, page 257)

1 tablespoon ground coriander

1 teaspoon freshly ground black pepper

½ teaspoon ground cumin

Pinch of salt

Spicy Mango Chutney (recipe follows) or Spicy Fruit Barbecue Sauce (page 127)

1 If using wooden skewers, be sure to soak them in water first for 10 minutes so they don't burn on the grill. In a small bowl, whisk together the olive oil, lemon juice, orange zest, garlic, and salt and pepper for the marinade. Thread the beef strips onto the skewers. Place the skewers in a shallow dish and pour the marinade over. Marinate the meat in the refrigerator, covered, at least 4 hours or overnight.

2 Preheat the grill to medium heat or a grill pan to medium-high.

3 **Make the Rub** Combine the sumac, coriander, pepper, cumin, and salt in a small bowl. Sprinkle over the beef skewers.

4 Grill the beef skewers until browned on one side, 3 to 5 minutes. Turn the skewers and grill until browned, 1 to 2 minutes more for medium-rare meat. Serve the beef skewers with chutney or barbecue sauce for dipping.

Spicy Mango Chutney

P ■ *Makes about 2 cups*

This tangy, sweet chutney—one of our kitchen favorites at the restaurant—can be paired with plenty of other dishes as well. It dresses up even a simple piece of grilled chicken or salmon.

MAKE AHEAD/STORAGE The chutney can be stored in the refrigerator, covered, up to 1 week or frozen for several months.

- 2 very ripe mangoes, pitted, peeled, and cut into large chunks
- 3 tablespoons extra-virgin olive oil
- 1 tablespoon fresh lemon juice
- 1 tablespoon unseasoned rice vinegar
- ½ to 1 teaspoon Harissa (page 28) or chopped fresh serrano chile
- ¼ cup finely diced red bell pepper
- 3 tablespoons chopped fresh flat-leaf parsley
- 1 tablespoon chopped fresh cilantro
- ¼ cup thinly sliced scallions (white and light green parts only)
- Kosher salt and freshly ground black pepper

Mash the mangoes with a potato masher or pulse in a food processor. (You want the mangoes to have a little texture and not be too runny.) Stir in olive oil, lemon juice, vinegar, Harissa, bell pepper, parsley, cilantro, and scallions, and season with salt and pepper. If you like a very spicy chutney, you can add more Harissa.

Shallots Fried Chicken

M ▪ *Serves 6*

One Memorial Day weekend at the restaurant, we were bracing for the hoards of celebrants who flock to the lakefront and parks in Chicago. I was craving fried chicken—the kind that I remembered from a life before kosher—and thought some of our guests might like some, too. My co-chef Dennis needed very little arm-twisting before he set himself in front of the fryer and produced a fried chicken that brought tears not only to my eyes but to those of many customers, too. Since then, we have instituted our popular picnic menu at the restaurant on Memorial Day, and on some other summer weekends and holidays as well. Our delicious, crunchy version has a secret ingredient—rice flour—that keeps it extra crisp. We made a huge batch that day—and the staff feasted on it for several days after. PS, It stayed crunchy. Note also that the Za'atar Spiced Potato Salad (recipe follows) isn't essential but will make this a meal worth celebrating.

MAKE AHEAD/STORAGE The fried chicken can be stored in the refrigerator, covered, for several days.

2 chickens, each about 4 pounds, cut into 6 pieces, on the bone (see page 220)

Kosher salt and freshly ground black pepper

2 cups all-purpose flour

1 cup rice flour

1 cup yellow cornmeal

2 tablespoons dried thyme

3 tablespoons sweet paprika

1 tablespoon mustard powder

1 tablespoon ground cumin

2 teaspoons cayenne pepper (optional)

3 large eggs

¼ cup cold water

Oil for frying, such as corn, peanut, or your favorite

Fresh lemon or lime juice (optional)

Za'atar Spiced Potato Salad (recipe follows; optional)

1 Rinse and pat dry the chicken pieces. Season the chicken with salt and pepper. Combine the flours, cornmeal, thyme, paprika, mustard, cumin, and cayenne (if using) in a large shallow dish. Whisk the eggs and water together in another shallow dish.

2 Lightly dredge the chicken pieces in the flour mixture. Next, dip the chicken pieces in the egg mixture to coat. Finally, place the chicken back in the flour mixture and allow it to sit in the flour for several minutes.

3 Heat at least 2 inches of oil to 350°F in a large, deep skillet, wide, shallow saucepan, or Dutch oven. (Use a deep-frying thermometer and watch the temperature carefully: Overly hot oil will brown the chicken too quickly and cold oil will make the chicken soggy and greasy.) Shake off any excess flour, and fry the chicken in batches (to prevent crowding), turning the pieces a few times, until it is browned on all sides and registers an internal temperature of 160°F, about 12 minutes for the breasts and about 15 minutes for the dark meat.

4 Let the chicken drain on layers of paper towels. Squeeze a little lemon or lime juice over the chicken for extra flavor, if using.

Za'atar Spiced Potato Salad

P ▪ *Serves 6 to 8*

I know that every culture has its own version of the summertime classic potato salad. This comfort food makes the hottest days tolerable and turns the most casual food into a festive picnic. I have made many versions of the classic dish but come back to this jazzed up salad repeatedly. I like the mixture of textures and the unexpected lemony zing of the sumac in the za'atar.

MAKE AHEAD/STORAGE Potato salad can be stored in the refrigerator, covered, up to 5 days.

5 pounds small red new potatoes

1 large red onion, diced

2 cups red grapes, cut in half and seeded if necessary

¼ cup chopped fresh flat-leaf parsley

3 celery stalks, thinly sliced

½ cup Garlicky Aioli (page 26) or store-bought mayonnaise

3 tablespoons Za'atar (page 28)

¼ cup sliced toasted almonds (optional)

1 In a large pot of boiling, salted water, cook the potatoes 20 to 30 minutes until they are tender and easily pierced with a knife. Drain the potatoes and cool thoroughly. Cut potatoes in half or quarter if large.

2 Combine the cooled potatoes with the onion, grapes, parsley, celery, aioli, Za'atar, and almonds (if using) in a large bowl, and toss thoroughly. The potato salad is even better after it sits overnight.

Roasted Duck Breasts
with Cherry–Red Wine Reduction

M ■ *Serves 4*

This summer dish is a riot of color and flavor, and it's delicious served room temperature or even chilled on a summer night. Tart-sweet cherries and rich, meaty duck are a fantastic combination. When the sour cherries are in season, it's a wonderful opportunity to make the Sour Cherry Chutney (recipe follows) to serve with this. Then, you'll have three kinds of cherries (dried, sour, and sweet Bing) to dress up your duck. The Roasted Purple Potatoes (page 120), nicely round out the meal.

MAKE AHEAD/STORAGE The sauce can be stored in the refrigerator, covered, up to 5 days, or frozen for 1 month.

For the Reduction

1 tablespoon olive oil

1 medium shallot, thinly sliced

1 garlic clove, thinly sliced

3 tablespoons balsamic vinegar

2 tablespoons tomato paste

1 Roasted Bell Pepper (page 25; use red peppers), cut into thin strips

1 bottle (750 ml) dry red wine, such as Cabernet Sauvignon (try Baron Herzog)

2 cups Dark Chicken Stock (page 16)

¼ cup dried cherries, chopped

4 boneless duck breasts, skin on

Freshly ground black pepper

Sour Cherry Chutney (recipe follows)

Roasted Purple Potatoes (page 120; optional)

1 Make the Reduction Heat the olive oil in a large saucepan over medium heat and add the shallot and garlic; slowly cook until they are translucent and softened, about 7 minutes. Turn up the heat to medium-high, add the balsamic vinegar, and cook until the vinegar is reduced to a glaze, about 1 minute. Add the tomato paste and cook, stirring, until darkened and fragrant, about 5 minutes. Add the red bell pepper and the wine, reduce the heat to medium-low, and simmer until the mixture is reduced by about two-thirds.

2 Strain the sauce through a fine-mesh sieve into a medium saucepan and add the chicken stock and cherries. Bring the sauce to a boil, reduce the heat to medium-low and simmer until the sauce is reduced by about half and has a *nappé* consistency (the sauce should coat the back of a spoon thickly enough that you can draw a line through it with your finger). Keep warm on very low heat while preparing duck.

3 Preheat the oven to 400°F.

4 Trim any excess fat from the duck breasts, and, using a very sharp knife, score the skin and fat layer in a crosshatch pattern without cutting into the meat below (this allows the fat to cook off and the skin to crisp). Lightly season the duck with freshly ground black pepper. (Kosher duck can be very salty and doesn't need additional salt).

5 Place the duck breasts skin side down in an unheated, large ovenproof sauté pan. Place the pan over medium-high heat. Cook the duck until the skin is browned and most of the fat has rendered off, about 15 minutes. Keep draining the fat from the pan into a small bowl. When the breasts have browned, transfer the pan to the oven and roast the breasts until medium rare, 6 to 8 minutes, or a few minutes longer for medium. (See page 211 for more information on duck.)

6 To serve, slice the duck breasts on an angle and fan out the meat on each of 4 plates. If using the potatoes mound them on the side and place a heaping spoonful of chutney at the top of each fan. Drizzle with cherry–red wine reduction.

Sour Cherry Chutney

P ■ *Makes 1½ cups*

When sour cherries appear in the farmers' market, I race over to buy them. The season is so brief, but the cherries are luscious, especially the ones we get here in the Chicago area. They come from Michigan, where they are grown mostly for commercial freezing and canning, but a few dedicated farmers still sell the fresh ones. If you can't find them, you can use all sweet (Bing) cherries, or a mix of Bing and Rainier (sweet yellow cherries), although of course the chutney won't be as tart.

MAKE AHEAD/STORAGE This chutney can be stored in the refrigerator, covered, up to 5 days.

½ cup coarsely chopped pitted Bing cherries

½ cup coarsely chopped pitted sour cherries

2 tablespoons finely chopped shallots or red onion

3 tablespoons extra-virgin olive oil

1 tablespoon red wine vinegar

¼ teaspoon chili flakes

¼ cup finely chopped fresh flat-leaf parsley

2 tablespoons pomegranate molasses (see Sources, page 257, and page 161 for more information)

Grated zest of 1 orange, chopped

Kosher salt and freshly ground black pepper

Combine all the ingredients in a medium bowl and stir until combined. Season with salt and pepper. Allow the chutney to sit at room temperature about 1 hour before serving for the flavors to meld.

Roasted Purple Potatoes

P ▪ *Serves 4*

Cut the roasted potatoes before serving them so you can see their beautiful interior color. If you're making the Roasted Duck Breasts (page 118), the duck can be roasting while the potatoes finish cooking.

2 pounds purple Peruvian potatoes

¼ cup olive oil

1 medium shallot, finely chopped

1 garlic clove, finely chopped

¼ cup chopped fresh flat-leaf parsley

2 tablespoons chopped fresh thyme

Kosher salt and freshly ground black pepper

Preheat the oven to 400°F. Toss the potatoes with the olive oil, shallot, garlic, parsley, thyme, and salt and pepper in a large bowl and transfer them to a shallow roasting pan. Roast for 40 to 50 minutes, depending upon size of potatoes, until tender. Allow the potatoes to cool slightly before cutting them into halves or quarters.

My BLT (Bison, Lettuce, and Tomato)

M ▪ *Serves 4*

Bison is a relatively new specialty meat to the kosher world. I love the idea that kosher consumers have more options now, and as a chef I enjoy working with bison. The flavor is similar to beef with a slight sharpness—it has "big flavor," which makes it fun to pair with foods. Bison is typically grass-fed (which is more natural than corn- or grain-fed), so the meat, which is low in fat and very high in iron, doesn't have all the hormones and antibiotics that can sometimes be found in commercial meats. Bison is available at many kosher markets or can easily be found online (see Sources, page 257).

MAKE AHEAD/STORAGE The bison can be stored in the marinade, covered, in the refrigerator up to 1 day.

Juice of 1 lemon

4 Grilled Flatbreads (recipe follows) or pitas

1 cup very dark beer, such as Aventinus or Guinness

¼ cup extra-virgin olive oil

2 to 2¼ pounds of bison skirt steak, trimmed and tenderized by your butcher

2 heads of firm lettuce, such as radicchio or romaine, cut in half lengthwise

2 medium red onions, sliced into 1-inch-thick rounds

2 medium ripe tomatoes, cut in half crosswise

½ cup Serrano Chile Aioli (page 26)

1 Prepare flatbreads, if making.

2 Place the lemon juice, beer, and olive oil in a resealable plastic bag or shallow container with a tight-fitting lid and add the bison, turning to coat the meat. Marinate the bison in the refrigerator for at least 4 hours or overnight.

3 Preheat the grill or a grill pan to medium-high.

4 Remove meat from marinade and pat dry; discard marinade. Grill the steaks on one side 7 to 10 minutes, until browned and slightly charred. Turn the steaks and continue cooking until the steaks are medium rare, about 5 minutes. Remove the steaks from the grill and loosely cover with foil to keep warm. Brush the lettuces, onion slices, and tomatoes with olive oil and place on the grill. Grill the lettuce until it has caramelized and is slightly wilted, about 5 minutes. Continue grilling the other ingredients until the onions and tomatoes are hot and caramelized, about 10 minutes.

5 Briefly rewarm the flatbreads on the grill. Top each bread with some meat, grilled vegetables, and a dollop of aioli.

Summer

Grilled Flatbreads

P ■ *Makes about 12 flatbreads*

There is something very satisfying about preparing an entire meal—even the bread—on the grill in the summertime. Making flatbreads can be a fun project to do with your family, and it gives kids a good introduction to baking. Instead of rolling out the breads, you can bring the bread dough out to your grill and have your friends and children flatten the rounds with their hands. This is really rustic and fun, and great for serving with your favorite grilled foods. The dark beer in the dough gives this bread an earthy fragrance and flavor. Feel free to toss in fresh herbs such as rosemary, thyme, or oregano, or citrus zest, if you like.

MAKE AHEAD/STORAGE The dough can be stored in the refrigerator, covered, up to 3 days. The rolled-out rounds can be stored in the refrigerator for 1 day.

1 cup bulgur wheat

2 cups boiling water

½ cup whole-wheat flour

1 to 2 cups all-purpose flour

2 teaspoons kosher salt

¼ to ½ teaspoon freshly ground black pepper

2 cups very dark beer, such as Aventinus or Guinness

¼ cup chopped pitted kalamata olives (optional)

Olive oil

1 Place the bulgur in a large bowl. Pour the boiling water over it and cover with plastic wrap. Set aside for 1 hour.

2 Pour the bulgur into a sieve to drain any excess water, and return the bulgur to the bowl. Add the whole-wheat flour, 1 cup of the all-purpose flour, the salt, pepper, and 1 cup of the beer. Use your hands to mix the ingredients until well combined.

3 Add the remaining beer and knead the mixture until it comes together. Turn out the dough onto a generously floured work surface and knead until the dough is smooth and no longer sticks to your hands or the work surface, adding more flour as needed. If the dough seems very dry, add a bit more liquid (humidity plays a factor with dough, and sometimes you may need to use a bit more or less liquid or flour). Knead in the olives, if using. Form the dough into a ball. Wrap the dough in plastic wrap and allow it to rest at room temperature for 1 hour.

4 Lightly flour a work surface and rolling pin. Cut off a piece of dough the size of a golf ball. Roll out the dough ¼ inch thick. Continue with the remainder of the dough, stacking the rounds as you make them.

5 Preheat the grill to medium-high.

6 Lightly brush the breads with olive oil and grill about 5 minutes per side, until the breads are well marked and the surface feels dry and rough textured.

VARIATION

Indoor Flatbreads (P) These flatbreads can be made indoors all year long using a well-heated grill pan or flat-top griddle.

123

Grilled Rib-Eye Sandwiches with Grilled Vegetables

M ■ *Serves 4*

For a fun, casual summer dinner, there's nothing like throwing some juicy steaks and fresh summer vegetables on the grill. Then I like to grill some flatbreads or pitas, slice up the steaks, pile the meat and the vegetables on the breads, and smother the whole sandwich with aioli. This is perfect for Father's Day, July Fourth, or whenever you want to celebrate summer.

Four 8-ounce rib-eye fillets

Kosher salt and freshly ground black pepper

Grilled Summer Vegetables (recipe follows)

4 Grilled Flatbreads (page 122) or pitas

Harissa Aioli (page 26)

1 Preheat the grill or a grill pan to medium-high.

2 Generously season the steaks with salt and pepper. Grill the steaks on one side for 5 minutes, then rotate the steaks a quarter-turn (this gives the steaks a professional-looking diamond-shaped grill marking) and continue cooking for another 3 to 5 minutes. Turn the steaks over and continue cooking about 7 minutes for medium rare (the steaks yield slightly when the sides are pressed). Remove from the grill and loosely cover with foil.

3 To serve, slice the steaks against the grain into thin strips and pile on a platter with the grilled vegetables. Briefly warm the flatbreads on the grill and serve with Harissa Aioli.

Grilled Summer Vegetables

P ■ *Serves 4*

The only rule to grilling vegetables is that there are no rules—just keep your grill at medium to medium-high heat and go! You can even grill vegetables a day or two ahead of serving. My family loves the variety, so summertime dinners in my house frequently start with a large platter of grilled vegetables drizzled with extra-virgin olive oil and sprinkled with sea salt.

About 4 cups total from the following vegetables:

Carrots, thinly sliced lengthwise (use a mandoline or Asian slicer)

Eggplant, sliced into 1-inch-thick rounds

Red and yellow bell peppers, sliced into rings or wedges

Onions, sliced into rings or wedges

Zucchini, sliced into wedges or thinly sliced lengthwise

Yellow squash, sliced into wedges or thinly sliced lengthwise

Portobello mushrooms (scrape out the gills)

Tomatoes, cut into wedges or halves

Lettuces such as romaine, radicchio, or Bibb, cut in half lengthwise or quartered if large

Avocados, pitted, peeled, thickly sliced

Olive oil

Kosher salt and freshly ground black pepper

Suggested Garnishes extra-virgin olive oil and Balsamic Vinegar Reduction (see page 19), Charmoula (page 227), chopped fresh herbs, Za'atar (page 28), coarse sea salt, and freshly ground black pepper

Toss or brush the vegetables with olive oil and liberally sprinkle with salt and pepper. Grill the vegetables over medium-high heat from 5 to 10 minutes on each side, according to their size and thickness, until hot and caramelized. (Avocados need only a minute or two per side, just to warm them slightly.) Transfer the vegetables to a platter and sprinkle with your choice of garnishes.

125

Grilled Marinated Short Ribs with Spicy Fruit Barbecue Sauce

M ■ *Serves 6 to 8*

I love the play of sweet fruit and spicy flavors. It wakes up your palate and keeps your taste buds tingling bite after bite. Sometimes sweet barbecue sauce can be too cloying—but not this sauce. Pick the ripest fruit you can find and use as much Harissa (page 28) as you dare. These short ribs are deliciously sticky and messy; the only way to eat them is with your fingers. Serve the ribs hot off the grill or tent them with foil and eat them at room temperature; they'll also travel well to a picnic. Be sure to bring extra sauce on the side—and plenty of napkins!

MAKE AHEAD/STORAGE The short ribs can be stored in the marinade, covered, in the refrigerator up to 1 day.

10 pounds short ribs, cut into individual ribs, each about 3 inches long

One 12-ounce bottle ale or favorite beer

Juice and grated zest of 2 lemons

⅓ cup olive oil

2 garlic cloves, crushed

¼ cup chopped fresh flat-leaf parsley

¼ cup chopped fresh cilantro

Kosher salt and freshly ground black pepper

Spicy Fruit Barbecue Sauce (recipe follows)

Za'atar Spiced Potato Salad (page 117; optional)

1 Rinse the short ribs to remove any bone fragments and debris. Pat the ribs dry. Combine the ribs with the ale, lemon juice and zest, olive oil, garlic, parsley, and cilantro in a large container with tight-fitting lid or several resealable plastic bags. Marinate the short ribs at least 4 hours, or overnight.

2 Preheat the grill to medium-low, or the oven to 275°F.

3 Remove the ribs from marinade and pat dry. Season the ribs with salt and pepper and grill the ribs, covered, turning the ribs several times until browned on all sides, 1½ to 2 hours, or until the meat is very tender. If oven cooking, bake the ribs on racks, uncovered, in 2 to 3 large roasting pans.

4 During the last 30 minutes, brush the ribs frequently with the barbecue sauce. Serve the ribs with plenty of extra sauce, with potato salad on the side, if you like.

Spicy Fruit
Barbecue Sauce

P ▪ *Makes about 3 cups*

If you don't have mangoes, use pineapple, or simply increase the amount of peaches and plums instead.

MAKE AHEAD/STORAGE The sauce can be stored in the refrigerator, covered, up to 5 days, or frozen for 2 months.

Olive oil

2 large Spanish onions, thinly sliced

8 garlic cloves, chopped

½ teaspoon kosher salt and ½ teaspoon freshly ground black pepper

2 large ripe mangoes, pitted, peeled, and cut into large chunks

3 large ripe plums, pitted and cut into large chunks

2 large ripe peaches, peeled, pitted, and cut into large chunks

One 6-ounce can tomato paste

½ cup unseasoned rice vinegar

¼ to ½ cup Harissa (page 28)

1 tablespoon ground coriander

1 teaspoon ground cumin

½ teaspoon ground ginger

One 28- or 29-ounce can whole peeled tomatoes with their juices

½ cup chopped fresh cilantro

½ cup chopped fresh flat-leaf parsley

½ cup neutral-flavored oil, such as canola, or regular olive oil (not extra virgin)

1 Heat a large nonreactive saucepan over medium-low heat and lightly coat the bottom of the pan with olive oil. Add the onions, garlic, and salt and pepper, and slowly cook until golden brown, 15 to 20 minutes. Stir in the mangoes, plums, peaches, tomato paste, vinegar, Harissa, coriander, cumin, and ginger. Break up the tomatoes slightly with your hands and add them with their juices. Cook over medium heat, stirring occasionally, until the mixture is very fragrant and the fruit is soft, about 30 minutes. Cool the mixture completely.

2 Puree the mixture in a blender or food processor in batches. Add the cilantro, parsley, and oil. Return the sauce to the pan and simmer about 15 minutes, until the flavors have melded.

Grilled Venison Loin Stuffed with Slow-Roasted Tomatoes and Leeks

M ▪ *Serves 8*

Venison has more flavor than beef, but it's not gamey or assertive. It's equally buttery in texture, but it is actually leaner and healthier. This elegant presentation is a perfect do-ahead dish since it's equally delicious warm or cold.

MAKE AHEAD/STORAGE The meat can be grilled and stored whole, covered, in the refrigerator up to 1 day. Allow it to come to room temperature, and slice just before serving.

For The Stuffing

Olive oil

2 leeks, light green parts only (save the dark green tops for stock, and the white for other uses), chopped

1 medium shallot, chopped

2 garlic cloves, chopped

1 cup Slow-Roasted Tomatoes (page 23) or chopped Roasted Bell Peppers (page 25; use red peppers)

Kosher salt and freshly ground black pepper

3 tablespoons balsamic vinegar

¼ cup Chicken Stock (page 15)

3 tablespoons chopped fresh flat-leaf parsley

1 tablespoon chopped fresh rosemary

1 tablespoon chopped fresh basil

½ cup fresh, untoasted bread crumbs

¼ cup extra-virgin olive oil

1 venison loin (about 5 pounds), silverskin removed and loin butterflied by your butcher*

Kosher salt and freshly ground black pepper

Tomato Coulis (recipe follows; optional)

Arugula Pesto (page 130; optional)

*If venison is not available at your butcher, see Sources (page 259).

■ **Make the Stuffing** Heat a medium sauté pan over medium heat, and lightly coat the bottom of the pan with olive oil. Cook the leeks and shallot until very soft and translucent, about 20 minutes. Add the garlic, tomatoes or Roasted Bell Peppers, and salt and pepper to taste and continue cooking until the flavors meld, about 10 minutes. Increase the heat to medium-high and add the vinegar. Cook the vegetables, stirring, until the vinegar is reduced to a glaze. Remove the pan from the heat and stir in

128

the stock, parsley, rosemary, basil, and bread crumbs. The mixture should stick together and be very thick. Transfer the stuffing mixture to a mixing bowl and let cool completely. Stir in the extra-virgin olive oil.

2 Preheat the grill or a grill pan to medium heat.

3 Open up the butterflied venison. Spread the stuffing in a thick layer, leaving a 1-inch border on all sides, and roll up the meat from long end. Using kitchen string, tie the loin every 2 to 3 inches to hold the meat closed. Season the venison with salt and pepper. Lightly rub the outside of the venison with olive oil.

4 Grill the venison on the first side for 15 minutes or until well browned. Turn the meat and continue grilling 10 minutes more for medium rare (the meat roulade should feel slightly firm when pressed gently). Remove from the heat and cover loosely with foil. Allow the meat to rest for 15 minutes before slicing.

5 To serve, slice the venison into 1½ inch sections. Place on a serving platter or individual plates and serve with Tomato Coulis and Arugula Pesto, if using, on the side.

Tomato Coulis

P ▪ *Makes about ¾ cup*

Even though the tomatoes are cooked, it's worthwhile using the best tomatoes you can find, as their flavor is intensified in this thick coulis. I have even used purple heirloom tomatoes, which made a vibrant, deep red coulis.

MAKE AHEAD/STORAGE The coulis can be stored in the refrigerator, covered, up to 3 days.

3 large ripe tomatoes (about 3 pounds)

2 medium shallots, chopped

¼ cup extra-virgin olive oil

¼ cup dry white wine, such as Sauvignon Blanc

Kosher salt and freshly ground black pepper

¼ cup packed fresh flat-leaf parsley

1 Bring a large saucepan of water to a boil. Prepare a large bowl of ice water with a strainer that fits inside the bowl. Core the tomatoes and cut an X shape at the other end before cooking. Cook the tomatoes for 15 seconds in the boiling water and drain them in the strainer. Immediately submerge strainer in the ice water (see page 41 for more information on blanching and shocking vegetables). When the tomatoes have cooled, peel off their skins. Slice the tomatoes in half and scoop out and discard the seeds. Dice the tomatoes.

2 In a large sauté pan, cook the diced tomatoes, shallots, olive oil, wine, and salt and pepper to taste over low heat until the mixture is thick, about 30 minutes. Cool the mixture slightly, then add the parsley and puree in a blender or food processor.

Arugula Pesto

P ▪ *Makes about 1 cup*

I love how the spicy, bold flavor of arugula in the pesto complements the tomatoes and the venison; it's a nice change from the usual basil pesto—less herbal and more peppery.

MAKE AHEAD/STORAGE The pesto can be stored, covered, in a small container in the refrigerator up to 3 days. Press plastic wrap directly onto its surface (this keeps it from oxidizing and turning very dark).

2 cups packed arugula, washed, dried, and stemmed

3 garlic cloves

½ cup toasted pine nuts

¾ to 1 cup extra-virgin olive oil (use your best-tasting oil)

Kosher salt and freshly ground black pepper

Process the arugula, garlic, and pine nuts in a blender or food processor just until finely chopped. With the motor running, slowly add the olive oil until the mixture becomes a thick paste. Season with salt and pepper.

Blackberry-Lemon Frozen Custard

D and P ■ *Serves 6*

I had a large quantity of blackberries in the restaurant one day when one of our farmer suppliers had a bumper crop and passed his good fortune on to us. I needed to quickly think of ways to use this treasure. This tart and fresh-tasting dessert was a winner and developed a large following. It is also lovely to look at and can easily be paired with a fruit soup, such as the Blackberry Soup included here or even just Chocolate Sauce.

MAKE AHEAD/STORAGE The frozen custard can be stored in the freezer, tightly wrapped, up to 1 week.

1 pound fresh, ripe blackberries or frozen, thawed and drained

¼ cup grated lemon zest (from about 4 lemons)

1 cup Simple Syrup (page 31)

1 cup whole milk or organic rice milk

1¼ cups sugar

Seeds scraped from 1 split vanilla bean

6 large eggs, separated

2 teaspoons cornstarch

¼ cup water

Blackberry Soup (recipe follows) or Chocolate Sauce (page 28), (optional)

131

1 Combine the blackberries, lemon zest, and Simple Syrup in a bowl. Cover and chill overnight. Strain the blackberry mixture and discard the liquid.

2 Line twelve 4-ounce ramekins with plastic wrap. For a smooth finish, pour very hot water into each plastic-lined ramekin. (This "shrink wraps" the ramekins for a wrinkle-free look.) Pour out the water and set aside the ramekins.

3 Heat the milk with ½ cup of the sugar and the vanilla bean seeds in a heavy-bottomed saucepan over medium heat until it simmers. Meanwhile, whisk the yolks with the cornstarch in a medium bowl until combined. Temper the egg mixture to prevent it from scrambling: Slowly pour a thin stream of the hot liquid into the yolks, whisking constantly, until about half of liquid has been added. Whisk the warmed yolk mixture back into the remaining hot liquid and cook the custard

Summer

over medium-low heat, stirring constantly with a rubber spatula, until it is very thick, about 1 minute. Transfer the custard to a large bowl and press a sheet of plastic wrap directly onto the surface of the custard. Set the custard aside to cool. When the custard has cooled completely to room temperature, stir in the blackberry mixture.

4 In the bowl of a stand mixer fitted with the whip attachment, begin whipping the egg whites on low speed. Meanwhile, heat the water and remaining ¾ cup sugar in small saucepan, stirring until sugar dissolves. Cook the syrup, without stirring, until a candy thermometer registers 250°F, 5 to 7 minutes. While the syrup is boiling, increase speed to medium and whip whites until they form soft peaks. Turn the mixer to low and slowly pour the sugar syrup into the center of the egg whites, keeping the motor running. When all of the syrup has been added, turn the mixer to high and continue to whip the meringue until the bottom of the bowl feels cool to the touch, about 10 minutes.

5 Fold the meringue into the custard in three additions until well combined. Spoon the custard mixture into the prepared ramekins. Cover the tops with plastic wrap and freeze the custards until firm, at least 6 hours or overnight.

6 To serve, invert the custards into shallow bowls, remove the plastic wrap, and spoon Blackberry Soup around or drizzle with Chocolate Sauce.

Blackberry Soup

P ■ *Serves 6 (makes about 3 cups)*

At the end of the summer, when the blackberry brambles are bursting with berries, pears start to appear on the market. The flavor of the berries and the fragrant pears are a match made in heaven. This soup is beautiful and tasty spooned around the frozen Blackberry-Lemon Frozen Custard (page 131). Or simply serve it with Poached Pears (page 191) or poured over fresh mixed berries with a scoop of vanilla ice cream.

MAKE AHEAD/STORAGE The soup can be stored in the refrigerator, covered, up to 2 days.

> 3 pints fresh ripe blackberries or frozen (thawed)
>
> 1½ cups sugar
>
> 3 large firm-ripe pears (I like Bartlett), peeled, cored, and cut into chunks
>
> 1 cup sweet white wine, such as Riesling
>
> 3 to 4 cups water

1 In a medium saucepan stir together the blackberries, sugar, pears, and wine with 3 cups water, and bring to a boil. Simmer the mixture over medium heat for 20 minutes, until the pears are very soft. Cool completely.

2 Puree the soup in a blender or food processor in batches until the fruit is no longer chunky. Strain the soup through a sieve set over a bowl to remove the seeds. If the soup is very thick, add some cold water to thin. Chill the soup until cold, at least 4 hours.

Peaches in Moscato with Amaretti

P ■ *Serves 6*

I had a perfect peach a long time ago. The hostess took fresh peaches that had been ripened in the sun and placed them in a bowl of ice water. Every guest got a paring knife and we peeled our slightly chilled peaches and let the juices run down our chins. Maybe it was the company, or the sun, or a combination, but I don't believe I will ever have a peach like that again. This recipe brings me back to that moment. End-of-the-summer peaches are sweet and juicy. This recipe lets you hang on to them a little longer, even when the first chill of autumn is in the air.

MAKE AHEAD/STORAGE The peaches can be stored in the syrup in the refrigerator, covered, up to 2 months.

6 medium ripe peaches

2½ cups Moscato (a slightly sweet Italian sparkling wine; leftover wine is fine to use)

2¼ cups sugar

¼ cup fresh lemon juice

2 cups water

Grated zest of 1 lemon, cut into strips (do not include bitter white pith)

Amaretti (recipe follows)

Champagne Sabayon (page 30) or vanilla ice cream (optional)

1 Bring a medium saucepan of water to a boil. Prepare a bowl of ice water. Blanch the peaches for 2 minutes, then transfer them to the ice water to cool. Peel the peaches, then halve and pit them.

2 In a medium saucepan, bring the moscato, sugar, lemon juice, and water to a simmer. Remove from the heat and add the lemon zest. Cool to room temperature. Place the peach halves in large mason jars and cover with the syrup. Cover the jars and refrigerate the peaches. They will be ready to eat in a week, but will get better after several weeks.

3 To serve, layer the peaches in beautiful bowls and top with crushed cookies. Drizzle with additional syrup and top with a dollop of Champagne Sabayon or ice cream, if desired.

Amaretti

P ■ *Makes about 2 dozen cookies*

Amaretti means "little bitter things." In Italy, amaretti are made from both bitter and sweet almonds, but we can't grow or import bitter almonds to the United States. Add a little almond extract instead to boost the flavor. I use these cookies in the restaurant to garnish desserts, especially those made with peaches, to crumble into the bottom of pie crusts, and to make little sandwiches with chocolate (a match made in heaven!)

MAKE AHEAD/STORAGE These cookies can be stored at room temperature in a covered container up to 5 days.

8 ounces almond paste (about ½ cup)

¾ cup sugar

2 large egg whites

½ teaspoon almond extract

1 Preheat the oven to 325°F.

2 Line 2 baking sheets with 2 layers of parchment each (this helps keep the cookies from overbrowning).

3 Place the almond paste in the bowl of a stand mixer fitted with the paddle attachment, and turn to low to break up the paste. Add the sugar and mix until the almond paste is fairly sandy. Add the egg whites, one at a time, and the extract; beat at a low speed just until the mixture is smooth and creamy. (Do not overmix the batter or it will be too fluffy.)

4 Scoop batter by the tablespoonful onto the prepared cookie sheets. You may need to use another spoon to push the batter out of the spoon, as the dough is quite sticky. Dab the tops of the cookies with water (this helps the cookies develop the crackly look that is characteristic of amaretti).

5 Bake the cookies for 15 minutes, until they are puffed and lightly browned. Cool the cookies in pans on racks for 5 minutes. Slide the cookies, still on the parchment, off the pans and cool completely before removing them from parchment.

Bing Cherry Fruit Soup

P ▪ *Serves 6*

I can't seem to get enough cherries during the short time they're available. So I try to serve them in as many ways as I can. This refreshing fruit soup with its vibrant magenta color looks gorgeous in a shallow bowl or even in a martini glass, garnished with a "sidecar" of sour cherry sorbet. If you love cherries as much as I do, it may be worthwhile buying an inexpensive pitter—it works for olives in the off-season, too.

MAKE AHEAD/STORAGE The soup can be stored in the refrigerator, covered, up to 3 days.

4 cups cubed red seedless watermelon

2 cups pitted Bing cherries

2 tablespoons fresh lemon juice

½ cup sugar

Suggested Garnishes diced kiwi, blackberries, raspberries, pitted cherries, fresh currants, blueberries, halved grapes, Sour Cherry Sorbet (page 136)

1 Process watermelon cubes in food processor until smooth. Strain the puree through a fine-mesh sieve set over a large bowl and discard the solids. Process the cherries in food processor until smooth and strain the cherry juices into the watermelon juice.

2 Stir half of the lemon juice and half of the sugar into the juices and taste. Add more lemon juice or sugar as needed to balance the sweetness and acidity to your taste. Chill the soup until cold, at least 4 hours, and serve garnished with fresh fruit and sorbet, if desired.

135

Sour Cherry Sorbet

P ▪ *Makes 1¾ pints*

Sour cherries are the unsung heroes of summer fruit. They are not as widely used as Bing cherries but are every bit as versatile and delicious. These little garnet-colored beauties can flavor chutneys and wine sauces—even martinis and this tart sorbet. Sour cherries are available in July in the farmers' markets and specialty produce stores. At other times of the year, you can make this with thawed frozen sour cherries.

MAKE AHEAD/STORAGE This sorbet can be made up to 1 week ahead and kept frozen. If the sorbet begins to separate, simply melt it and reprocess it in your machine. (See page 81 for more information on sorbets and granitas.)

- 4 cups pitted sour cherries
- 2 cups water (bottled water yields a tastier sorbet)
- 1 cup sugar

1 Puree the cherries in a food processor, then strain through a fine-mesh sieve set over a bowl and discard solids. Alternatively, process cherries through a food mill. (You should have about 1½ cups juice. Save the solids, if desired, to fold into the sorbet after processing in ice cream maker.)

2 Heat the water and sugar in a saucepan over low heat, stirring constantly until the sugar is completely dissolved. Let syrup cool completely to room temperature, at least 30 minutes. Blend the sugar syrup with the cherry juice in a blender or using an immersion blender. Chill the cherry mixture completely. Process the sorbet mixture in your ice cream machine, following the manufacturer's instructions.

3 Transfer the sorbet to a covered container and stir in the reserved cherry solids, if desired. Freeze until hard, at least 4 hours or overnight.

Mixed Cherry Clafoutis

D and P ▪ *Serves 5*

Baked custard, cherries, and crispy phyllo! What's not to love about this recipe? This is a great summer dessert for an elegant Shabbat dinner or a casual luncheon. I don't find many recipes that translate well between dairy and pareve, but substituting oil and rice milk for butter and milk when I want to serve this after a meat meal works perfectly. The secrets to making this great dessert are to use really fresh cherries and high-quality vanilla and to watch out not to overbake it.

MAKE AHEAD/STORAGE The clafoutis can be baked and cooled, then stored in the refrigerator, covered, up to 1 day.

20 sheets of phyllo, thawed if frozen

¼ cup melted butter or neutral-flavored oil

3 cups whole milk or organic rice milk

½ cup semidry white wine, such as Reisling or leftover Champagne or sparkling wine

Seeds scraped from 1 split vanilla bean (or 2 teaspoons high-quality vanilla extract)

3 large whole eggs

1 large egg yolk

1½ cups sugar

½ cup all-purpose flour

2 cups pitted mixed cherries, such as sour, Bing, and Rainier

Sour Cherry Sorbet (page 136; optional)

1 Preheat the oven to 350°F. Lightly brush five 4-ounce ramekins with melted butter or oil.

2 Place a sheet of phyllo on a work surface, keeping the remaining sheets covered with a damp cloth so they don't dry out. Lightly brush the phyllo with melted butter. (Brush all the way to the edges or the phyllo will crack or tear.) Place another sheet on top the first sheet and continue lightly brushing and layering until you have a stack of four sheets. Cut the phyllo stack into 2½-inch-wide strips and center a strip in a ramekin, allowing the ends of the strip to hang over the edges. Overlap with another phyllo strip and continue overlapping the remaining strips to completely cover the bottom and sides of the ramekin. Set the ramekin with the phyllo cup aside. Stack more phyllo sheets and cover remaining ramekins with strips in the same manner. Transfer the ramekins to a baking sheet, and bake until the phyllo is lightly browned, about 10 minutes.

3 Whisk together the milk, wine, vanilla bean seeds or extract, eggs and yolk, flour, and sugar in a large bowl until completely combined. Divide the cherries among the phyllo cups and ladle the custard over the cherries, filling the ramekins about three quarters full (leave some room, as the custard will puff slightly as it cooks).

4 Bake the custards for 30 minutes, or until the top is puffed and lightly browned but the custard is not completely set in the center (the centers will continue to set as the ramekins cool). If the centers are still very moist, continue baking up to 10 minutes longer, checking frequently; do not overbake or they will be dry. Allow the clafoutis to cool slightly.

5 To unmold, gently pull on the phyllo from two sides; the clafouti should slide out. Serve the clafoutis hot from the oven or cold with a scoop of sorbet on the side, if desired.

Granita al Caffè

P ■ *Makes about 1½ pints*

Cool and refreshing! This Italian concoction really hits the spot after a heavy meal. It is also my favorite afternoon treat on a hot day.

MAKE AHEAD/STORAGE This granita can be made up to 4 days ahead and kept frozen. (See page 81 for more information on sorbets and granitas.)

3 cups freshly brewed coffee or espresso

⅓ to ½ cup sugar

Chocolate Sabayon (page 31; optional)

Cocoa Nib Biscotti (page 193; optional)

1 Pour the coffee into a large bowl. Whisk in ⅓ cup of the sugar and taste; adjust sweetness if necessary, a spoonful at a time, it should be slightly sweet. Pour the mixture into a shallow metal pan. Freeze, scraping the granita every hour or so with a fork to break up the ice crystals. When finished, the crystals should be fine and sandy.

2 Serve the granita in tall glass mugs. Dollop with Chocolate Sabayon and serve Cocoa Nib Biscotti on the side, if desired.

FALL

Listen! The wind is rising
And the air is wild with leaves . . .

HUMBERT WOLFE

AUTUMN IS THE SEASON I ANTICIPATE THE most. The temperature outside is glorious, the trees are magnificent, and the produce is at its peak. Maybe it's the New Year holidays that bring about a renewal of the spirit, or maybe it's just a feeling left over from childhood and the excitement of beginning the school year, but in the fall, everything seems refreshed and new again. All through the summer, I've watched as the produce tumbles into the farmers' market. But there's so much to look forward to when fall comes again.

First, there are the end-of-season tomatoes to savor. Sometimes, unlike the summer ones, they're not the most gorgeous specimens, so I spend lots of time making Tomato Confit (page 22) and Slow-Roasted Tomatoes (page 23) to use in my recipes. There's so much of this season that I would love to preserve, so I do the best I can.

When the last of the stone fruits leave the market, I have pear and apple season

to look forward to. I marvel at all the varieties of apples and am grateful that I live in a part of the country where there are so many to choose from. We always get heirloom apples from the old orchards around here. I have the luxury of using a favorite apple for every recipe and changing my choices as the early ripening varieties give way to the frost-sweetened ones. I could serve baked apples at every meal, either stuffed with walnuts and dates for a simply elegant dessert or with shallots and rosemary for a delightful side (pages 189 to 190). I regularly run my sorbet machine late into the night to fill orders for Apple, Honey, and Walnut Sorbet (page 192), which I can scoop next to almost any dessert. I often celebrate the New Year with a favorite Crunchy Apple and Fennel Salad (page 154) that contrasts crisp raw shredded apples with the concentrated sweetness of roasted apple in the vinaigrette.

Pears also come in many shapes and sizes, from tiny Seckels to fragrant Forelles. There's nothing simpler or more elegant than a pear poached in red wine (page 191), so I make them time and again to use for desserts, salads, and even on cheese plates. I enjoy training new staff on the virtues of quince, an ancient fruit that complements apples perfectly, whether in a simple sauté, a baked crisp for dessert, or in an unusual stuffing for veal breast (page 191).

How I love the squashes that begin to pile up just as the weather turns crisp! They are not only gorgeous, with their hard shells shaded to rich colors or even fanciful stripes, but they are earthy, nutty, and so satisfying as well. Roasted Butternut Squash Bisque (page 145), with its drop-dead yellow-orange color and its sweet roasted flavor, can become practically a new dish, every time I make it, by simply changing the garnish. I can top it with squash chips or roasted squash seeds, an apple crouton, or a slice of poached pear, or just drizzle on some fruity olive oil and I have a new soup each time. I hit the farmers' market early in the autumn to be sure to catch all of the squash varieties from Delicata, Carnival, and Red Kuri to acorn and butternut. Squash is delicious alone, but it's also easy to mix in chunks with other vegetables, as I do with the Vegetable Tagine (page 157) and with Roasted Root Vegetables (page 181).

I dramatically change my cooking techniques as we turn the corner toward winter. I crave more abundant dishes, with rich, complex flavors. Fall is the time for a comforting pot of soup simmering on the stove: Sometimes it's a hearty stew, chockful of warming lentils and beans, like my favorite Lentil–Chick Pea Soup (page 150). I also use end-of-summer cauliflower to create a luxurious, silky puree (page 147) that is even a bit decadent, drizzled with porcini oil. I love what slow cooking does for my Boeuf Bourguignon (page 177). And I cannot imagine a more nurturing dish for an autumnal Shabbat than the Braised Venison with Dried Cherry Sauce and Roasted Root Vegetables (page 180). At this time of the year, it's such a pleasure to cook; I would be very happy to lock myself into the kitchen to work with the beautiful autumn palette of colors and flavors.

SOUPS, SALADS, AND STARTERS

Roasted Butternut Squash Bisque

Caramelized Cauliflower Soup

Celery Root, Apple, and Leek Soup

Lentil–Chick Pea Soup

Wild Mushroom Soup

Roasted Beet Salad
with Goat Cheese Crouton

Crunchy Apple and Fennel Salad
with Roasted Apple Vinaigrette

Homemade Gnocchi

MAIN DISHES

Vegetable Tagine

Pomegranate-Glazed Chicken

Duck Breast Schnitzel with Maple Mashed
Sweet Potatoes and Braised Swiss Chard

Crispy Roasted Duck with
Balsamic Pan Sauce

Fennel-Crusted Cod with Fennel, Orange,
and Red Onion Relish

Muhummarah-Crusted Halibut
with Saffron Broth and Ivory Lentils

Bourride

Pan-Roasted Black Bass with
Lemon-Caper Sauce and Farro Pilaf

Mushroom-Crusted Wild Salmon

Boeuf Bourguignon

Braised Venison with Dried Cherry Sauce
and Roasted Root Vegetables

Venison Loin Poivrade with
Roasted Sweet Potatoes

Stuffed Veal Chops with Melted Leeks and
Shallots and Pan-Fried Smashed Potatoes

Quince-Stuffed Veal Breast with
Roasted Fennel and Apples

DESSERTS

A Duo of Baked Apples
Baked Apples with Dates and Apricots
Baked Apples with Shallots and Herbs

Poached Pears

Apple, Honey, and Walnut Sorbet

Cocoa Nib Biscotti

Fig Confit

Chocolate Opera Torte
with Chocolate Ganache

Chocolate Sorbet

Roasted Butternut Squash Bisque

M or P ■ *Serves 6*

Roasting the squash intensifies its flavors and concentrates the sugars. It gives the soup a far creamier texture and richer color than simply simmering the squash would. This soup seems decadent, but it is actually low in fat and high in beta-carotene.

MAKE AHEAD/STORAGE This soup can be stored in the refrigerator, covered, up to 5 days.

2 butternut squash, cut in half and seeded

Olive oil

2 medium Spanish onions, chopped

1 large Granny Smith apple, peeled, cored, and thinly sliced

2 medium carrots, peeled and chopped

¼ cup dry sherry

3 to 4 cups Chicken Stock (page 15) or Vegetable Stock (page 17)

Kosher salt and freshly ground black pepper

Suggested Garnishes Apple Croutons and Butternut Squash Chips (recipe follows), freshly grated nutmeg, a slice of poached pear, fruity olive oil

1 Preheat the oven to 350°F.

2 Rub the cut side of squash with olive oil and place cut side down on a parchment paper–lined baking sheet. Roast the squash 30 to 40 minutes, until it is easily pierced with a knife. Remove from the oven and let cool.

3 While squash is cooling, heat a medium saucepan over medium heat and lightly coat the bottom of the pan with olive oil. Slowly cook the onion about 20 minutes, until soft, browned, and caramelized. Add the apple and carrots and continue to cook for an additional 10 minutes. Add the sherry and cook 5 more minutes. Remove the pan from the heat.

4 Peel the cooled squash and cut it into large dice. Add the squash to the onion mixture, then puree vegetable mixture with 3 cups of stock in batches in a blender or food processor until smooth. Return the pureed soup to the saucepan. If the soup is too thick, adjust the consistency with more

Fall

stock, and season with salt and pepper. Simmer soup for 30 minutes to meld flavors.

5 Serve the soup with your choice of garnishes.

Apple Croutons and Butternut Squash Chips

P ■ *Makes about 1 cup each croutons and chips*

Together or separately, the apple croutons and the squash chips make attractive garnishes for the Roasted Butternut Squash Soup (page 143). The Apple Croutons can also be used to top the Celery Root, Apple, and Leek Soup (page 149). Keep any leftovers for snacking—the apple ones are addictive dipped into a bit of peanut butter. And the squash ones are delicious sprinkled with a little sea salt.

MAKE AHEAD/STORAGE Apple Croutons and Squash Chips can be stored at room temperature, tightly covered, up to 3 weeks.

1 Granny Smith apple

¼ of a butternut squash

1 cup Simple Syrup (page 31)

Nonstick vegetable oil spray

1 Preheat the oven to 200°F.

2 Core the apple using an apple corer or sharp paring knife (do not peel). Thinly slice the apple into rounds using a mandoline or Asian slicer.

3 Peel and seed the squash. Thinly slice the squash using a mandoline, Asian slicer, or vegetable peeler. Transfer the apple and squash slices to separate bowls.

4 Heat Simple Syrup in a saucepan until it is simmering. Pour the syrup over the slices, and let them soak for 15 minutes.

5 Line 1 or 2 baking sheets with parchment paper and lightly grease the paper.

6 Transfer the slices to the baking sheets in a single layer and bake until dry, crisp, and lightly browned, about 1½ hours.

7 Let the apple croutons and the squash chips cool completely on the baking sheets, and transfer them to separate dry containers with tight-fitting lids.

Caramelized Cauliflower Soup

D, M, or P ■ *Serves 6*

My friend Stuart thinks that cauliflower is the most misunderstood vegetable. Many people think they hate cauliflower simply because they've only had it boiled. That's absolutely the worst way to prepare it. Try this rich and flavorful soup to see what browning and caramelizing does to cauliflower. The depth of flavor of the vegetables is complex and delicious, perfect for a cold autumn or winter night. I often make this for my family with a sprinkle of Parmesan cheese at the end (which, if you don't use the cream, makes it a dairy dish). If you haven't yet appreciated cauliflower, this soup can change your mind.

MAKE AHEAD/STORAGE This soup can be stored in the refrigerator, covered, up to 1 day.

- 1 head of garlic
- Kosher salt and freshly ground black pepper
- Olive oil
- 2 heads of cauliflower, cored and cut into florets
- 2 celery stalks
- 1 medium fennel bulb, trimmed and chopped
- 2 medium leeks, white parts only (save the light and dark green tops for stock), chopped
- 1 medium-large Yukon gold potato, peeled and diced
- 3 to 3½ cups Vegetable Stock (page 17) or Chicken Stock (page 15)
- ½ cup dry white wine, such as Sauvignon Blanc
- ½ cup heavy cream, plus additional if necessary (optional)
- Porcini Oil (recipe follows)

1 Preheat the oven to 400°F.

2 Cut ½ inch off the nonroot end of the head of garlic to expose the cloves. Place the garlic in a small baking dish or ovenproof ramekin and lightly sprinkle with salt and pepper. Lightly drizzle with olive oil and add enough water to come about 1 inch up the side of garlic. Cover the dish with foil and roast until the garlic is lightly browned and soft enough to squeeze out of the skins, about 1 hour. Set aside to let the garlic cool.

3 Heat a stockpot or large saucepan over medium heat and lightly oil pot. Cook the cauliflower, celery, fennel, leeks, and potato with salt and pepper to taste until they are lightly browned and soft, about 30 minutes, stirring occasionally. If desired, scoop out about ½ cup cauliflower florets with a slotted spoon and reserve them for garnishing. Add 3 cups stock and the white wine to the remaining vegetables, and simmer for 15 minutes.

4 Squeeze the garlic cloves from their skins and add the cloves to the soup. Let the soup mixture cool slightly. Puree the soup, in batches, in a blender or food processor, adding the cream, if using. Return the soup to the pan and season with salt and pepper. If the soup is too thick, adjust the consistency with more stock or cream.

5 Reheat the soup just to simmering and serve drizzled with Porcini Oil and garnished with the reserved florets.

Porcini Oil

P ■ *Makes ½ cup*

This oil is a little bit of luxury that you can use to drizzle on soup or even a baked potato. If you like, save the mushroom solids strained from the oil to toss with hot pasta and a bit more oil.

MAKE AHEAD/STORAGE Porcini oil can be stored in the refrigerator, covered, up to 1 month.

½ cup neutral-flavored oil, such as
    canola

¼ cup dried porcini mushrooms (about
    1 ounce)

1 Bring the oil with the porcinis just to a simmer in a small saucepan. Remove the pan from heat and set aside to allow the flavor of the porcinis to infuse into the oil. Let oil cool completely to room temperature, at least 30 minutes.

2 Transfer the oil and porcinis to a blender and process about 1 minute. Strain the oil through a fine-mesh sieve into a small bowl or into a small glass jar with a tight-fitting lid.

Celery Root, Apple, and Leek Soup

M and P ▪ *Serves 6*

The unexpected flavors of this soup really work well together. The sweetness of the apple complements the earthy and slightly bitter taste of the celery root to make an elegant and delicious soup that's anything but boring. If you usually think of apples only for dessert, try this combination; it's a fun twist on a familiar ingredient.

MAKE AHEAD/STORAGE This soup can be stored in the refrigerator, covered, up to 2 days, or frozen for 1 month.

Olive oil

1 large celery root (celeriac), about 2 pounds, peeled and diced

3 medium apples, preferably Gala, peeled, cored, and diced

3 medium leeks, light green parts only (save the dark green tops for stock, and the white part for other uses), thinly sliced

½ cup sweet white wine, such as Riesling

4 to 5 cups Chicken Stock (page 15)

Kosher salt and freshly ground black pepper

Suggested Garnishes diced apple, sautéed diced celery, celery seeds, Apple Croutons and Butternut Squash Chips (page 146)

1 Heat a large saucepan or stockpot over medium heat, and lightly coat the bottom of the pan with olive oil. Slowly cook the celery root and apples 20 to 30 minutes, until they are quite soft. Add the leeks and salt and pepper to taste, and continue to cook until the leeks are limp and translucent, about 15 minutes. Add the wine and continue cooking for several minutes until the alcohol has evaporated, then add 4 cups Chicken Stock.

2 Puree the soup in batches in a food processor or blender, and return it to the pan. If the soup is too thick, adjust the consistency with a bit more stock, and season with salt and pepper. Simmer the soup for 30 minutes for the flavors to meld. Serve the soup with your choice of garnishes.

Fall

Lentil–Chick Pea Soup

M or P ■ *Serves 6 or more*

When the weather starts to cool, I begin to crave hearty soups that are substantial and comforting. This aromatic soup, with its varied textures, is always satisfying. If you've never cooked red lentils before, they're unlike any other kind—they break down to a creamy orange puree that thickens the soup. The chick peas and vegetables, on the other hand, remain nicely textured and chewy.

MAKE AHEAD/STORAGE This soup can be stored in the refrigerator, covered, up to 3 days.

1 cup dried chick peas or one 28-ounce can chick peas

Olive oil

3 medium carrots, peeled and diced small

3 celery stalks, diced small

1 large Spanish onion, diced small

1 medium fennel bulb, trimmed and diced small

3 garlic cloves, finely chopped

3 cups red lentils

6 to 8 cups Chicken Stock (page 15), Vegetable Stock (page 17), or water

2 teaspoons ground coriander

1 teaspoon ground cumin

3 tablespoons fresh lemon juice

Kosher salt and freshly ground black pepper

Charmoula (page 227; optional)

1 If using dried chick peas, place them in a medium saucepan and cover the chick peas with water by 2 inches. Bring the chick peas to a simmer and cook until the chick peas are tender, from 1 to 2 hours, depending on their age. Drain the chick peas and set aside. If using canned chick peas, simply drain them in a sieve, rinse with cold water, and drain again.

2 Heat a large saucepan or stockpot over medium-high heat and lightly coat the bottom of the pan with olive oil. Sauté the carrots, celery, onion, fennel, and garlic, seasoned with salt and pepper, in batches if needed, until golden brown, about 25 minutes per batch. Set aside about ¾ cup of the sautéed vegetables. Add the lentils, chick peas, and 6 cups stock to the pan and bring to a simmer. Cook until the lentils are beginning to fall apart, about 20 minutes. Stir in the coriander, cumin, lemon juice, and reserved vegetables. Reduce heat and continue cooking the soup 15 minutes longer for the flavors to meld. If soup is too thick, add some stock, a half cup at a time, to thin, and adjust the seasoning to taste with salt and pepper.

3 Serve the soup with a spoonful of Charmoula stirred in, if desired.

Wild Mushroom Soup

M or P ▪ *Serves 6*

The rich flavor of this soup doesn't come from a lot of expensive mushrooms but from the extraction of flavor from the stems of the mushrooms, a classic technique called *duxelles*. I mince the stems in my food processor and then slowly cook them with shallots and garlic. I also like to add a touch of cinnamon. It's an unexpected ingredient that carries the flavor of the mushrooms with each mouthful.

MAKE AHEAD/STORAGE This soup can be stored in the refrigerator, covered, up to 3 days, or frozen for 1 month.

1 pound button mushrooms

1 pound cremini mushrooms

½ pound shiitake mushrooms

Olive oil

2 medium shallots

1 garlic clove

1 teaspoon ground cinnamon

Kosher salt and freshly ground black pepper

1 cup dry white wine, such as Sauvignon Blanc

6 cups Chicken Stock (page 15) or Veal Stock (page 18)

¼ cup dried porcini mushrooms (about 1 ounce)

Juice of ½ lemon

Porcini Oil (page 148; optional)

1 Trim the bottoms and cut the stems from the button and cremini mushrooms, reserving the stems. Discard the shiitake mushroom stems. Process the button and cremini mushroom stems with the shallots and garlic in a food processor until finely minced. Cut mushroom caps into quarters.

2 Heat a large saucepan over medium-low heat and lightly coat the bottom of the pan with olive oil. Add the mushroom stem mixture, the cinnamon, and salt and pepper to taste. Slowly cook the mixture, stirring occasionally, until the liquid from the mushrooms has evaporated and the mixture is dry and fragrant, about 20 minutes.

3 Add the wine and turn up the heat to medium. Cook until the wine has been absorbed and the alcohol has cooked off. Add the stock and the porcini mushrooms, and bring soup to a simmer.

4 Meanwhile, heat a large sauté pan over medium heat and very lightly coat the bottom of the pan with olive oil. Sauté the mushrooms, seasoned with salt and pepper, in batches until lightly browned, 5 to 7 minutes.

5 Add the mushrooms to the soup and continue simmering about 20 minutes longer, to allow the flavors to meld. Add the lemon juice and adjust the seasoning with salt and pepper. Serve with a drizzle of Porcini Oil, if desired.

Fall

Roasted Beet Salad
with Goat Cheese Croutons

D ■ *Serves 4*

Some people might be disappointed to learn that chefs don't eat everything, but I didn't really enjoy beets very much until fairly recently. Now, I'm wild about beets! I love their color, their earthy-peppery flavor and their resilience. What made me change my mind? Pairing beets with goat cheese makes a perfect match; the two foods seem made for each other. The tanginess of the goat cheese really complements the earthy qualities of the beets. This salad turned me into a beet fan. Try it as an autumn starter to a dairy meal or as a light lunch with friends.

MAKE AHEAD/STORAGE The beets can be roasted and peeled ahead and stored in the refrigerator, covered, up to 4 days.

1 large red beet

1 large golden beet

4 ounces soft goat cheese, preferably in a log

⅓ cup dry bread crumbs, preferably panko*

2 tablespoons finely chopped fresh flat-leaf parsley

1 tablespoon finely chopped fresh thyme

Kosher salt and freshly ground black pepper

All-purpose flour

1 egg

Olive oil

1 blood orange or navel orange

4 cups baby greens or mesclun

Extra-virgin olive oil

1 medium red onion, very thinly sliced

Balsamic Vinegar Reduction (page 19)

*Panko is a Japanese bread crumb with a coarse flake. It is very light and becomes very crispy when fried. It makes a superb crust for many items. Panko is available with a *hechsher* online or at specialty markets. (See Sources, page 257.)

1 Preheat the oven to 300°F.

2 Wrap the beets in foil and roast until easily pierced with a knife, about 1½ hours. Open the foil pack and let the beets stand until cool enough to handle. Peel the beets.

3 Cut the goat cheese into 4 coins (about 1 ounce per coin). Place the cheese coins in the freezer about 30 minutes, until firm and easy to handle.

4 Mix the bread crumbs, parsley, and thyme on a small plate and season with salt and pepper. Place the flour on another small plate. Whisk the egg in a small bowl.

5 Heat a medium sauté pan over medium heat, and lightly coat the pan with olive oil. Dredge a cheese coin in the flour. Then dip it into the beaten egg to cover. Finally coat the cheese all over with the breadcrumb mixture. Repeat with remaining cheese coins. Sauté the cheeses, 2 at a time, until browned on each side, about 3 minutes per side. Remove the cheeses to a plate lined with paper towels. Continue cooking remaining cheese.

6 Cut off the top and bottom of the orange to expose the fruit. Put orange on work surface, a cut side down and cut off the peel and white pith, following the contours of the fruit. Continue until the orange is completely peeled. Cut between the sections, letting the sections and any juices drop into a small bowl and leaving the membrane behind. Squeeze the membrane to extract the juice. Cut the beets into wedges or thin strips. Toss the greens with a spoonful each of extra-virgin olive oil and juice from the orange, and season with salt and pepper. Mound the greens on four plates or a serving platter and place the beets, red onion, and orange sections on top. Place the cheese croutons on top of the salad and drizzle with the Balsamic Vinegar Reduction.

153

Crunchy Apple and Fennel Salad with Roasted Apple Vinaigrette

P ▪ *Serves 6 to 8*

I was considering a light starter for our special menu on Rosh Hashanah one year. It was still unseasonably hot out, and I was longing for something cool and refreshing. One of our suppliers came in with a gorgeous bunch of apples—and they inspired this salad. To me, apples and fennel are a perfect match. Ever since, I have served this salad throughout the holiday season, and I try to change the apple varieties as they become available. At the restaurant we serve it at the beginning of the meal; at home my boys and I like it best as a midcourse salad, between the entrée and dessert.

154

MAKE AHEAD/STORAGE The vinaigrette can be stored in the refrigerator, covered, up to 2 days.

For the Vinaigrette

- 2 apples, preferably Braeburn or Jonathan, cored
- 2 tablespoons honey, preferably clover
- 2 tablespoons apple cider
- 1 teaspoon fresh lemon juice
- ½ cup neutral-flavored oil, preferably canola
- Kosher salt and freshly ground black pepper

- 2 celery stalks
- 2 medium fennel bulbs, trimmed
- 1 medium celery root (celeriac), peeled
- 1 medium red onion
- 4 medium apples, cored (use 2 or more varieties for color and flavor)

- 2 cups red grapes, cut in half and seeded if necessary, or seedless
- 5 cups mesclun or favorite salad greens

1 Make the Vinaigrette Preheat the oven to 300°F. Roast the apples on a baking sheet until they are very soft, about 1 hour. Set the apples aside to cool. Remove the apple peel and scoop the cooked flesh into a food processor or blender. Add the honey, cider, and lemon juice and process until smooth. With the motor running, add the oil and process until the vinaigrette is smooth and thick. Season with salt and pepper.

2 Thinly slice the celery, fennel, celery root, onion, and apples using a mandoline or Asian slicer, or slice with a knife. Toss the vegetables, apples, and grapes together in a large bowl with a few spoonfuls of the vinaigrette. Serve the salad on a bed of greens, drizzled with additional vinaigrette.

Homemade Gnocchi

D or P ▪ *Serves 6 as a first course or 4 as a main dish*

We have been serving gnocchi at Shallots for years. I regularly change the way I serve them according to the season and my whim. Some of my favorite gnocchi topping combinations are: Tomato Confit (page 22) tossed with sautéed mushrooms; Basil Pistou (page 45) and freshly grated Parmesan cheese; sautéed butternut squash cubes with fresh sage; chopped roasted beets with freshly cracked peppercorns; chopped swiss chard sautéed with garlic and golden raisins; and the simplest, just browned butter and chopped fresh herbs. At the restaurant, we started out making them tiny and calling them *gnocchetti*. Make them large, make them small, just make plenty, as they will be gobbled up before you know it!

MAKE AHEAD/STORAGE The gnocchi can be prepared through Step 5 and stored in the freezer in a resealable plastic bag up to 1 month.

3 large Idaho or russet potatoes (about 3 pounds)

1 large egg

¼ teaspoon freshly grated nutmeg

½ teaspoon kosher salt and ¼ teaspoon freshly ground black pepper

¼ cup freshly grated Parmesan cheese (optional)

1 to 2 cups all-purpose flour

Suggested Garnishes see above

1 Preheat the oven to 350°F.

2 Prick potatoes with a fork and bake until very soft, 1 to 1½ hours. Peel the potatoes while they are still hot (the hotter and flakier the potato, the lighter the gnocchi) and pass the potato flesh through a potato ricer onto a baking sheet. Spread out the riced potato and allow it to cool completely.

3 Beat the egg with the nutmeg and salt and pepper to taste.

4 Lightly flour a work surface. Place the cooled potato, cheese (if using), and 1 cup flour on the work surface and form a well in the center, just as you would to make pasta. Pour the egg into the center of the well and start working the egg into the potato mixture with your fingertips to form a dough. Use more flour to keep the dough from sticking to your hands and to the surface, and add more flour to the dough a spoonful at a time, if needed, to make a dough that's smooth and easy to handle. Lightly knead the dough just until it comes together and no longer sticks to the surface, about 3 to 5 minutes, but try not to knead any longer or the gnocchi can become tough.

5 Cut the dough into 8 pieces. Roll the pieces on the work surface or between floured hands to form long ropes about 1 inch thick. Cut the dough into 1-inch pieces. Dip a fork into flour. Gently roll the gnocchi off the back of the fork to form grooves for the sauce to cling to. Continue until all the gnocchi have been cut and grooved. Lay the gnocchi in a single layer on a floured sheet pan as they are made. The gnocchi can be prepared up to this point and frozen on the sheet pan. Gather them together and place in a resealable plastic bag in the freezer.

6 Bring a large stockpot or saucepan of salted water to a rolling boil. Gently add the gnocchi to the boiling water, and cook until they float to the top, about 3 minutes. Remove the gnocchi with a slotted spoon to a platter lined with paper towels as they finish cooking.

7 Heat a large sauté pan over medium-high heat and lightly coat the bottom of the pan with olive oil. Add the boiled gnocchi and brown on one side, about 2 minutes. Turn the gnocchi and add your choice of garnishes. Toss the gnocchi to coat and warm the garnish, if needed. Serve the gnocchi immediately.

Vegetable Tagine

P ■ *Serves 8 generously*

This riotously colored stew, full of beautiful squash and dried fruits, is one of my favorite dishes. The barley and potatoes also make it my ultimate comfort food. For a special occasion, this stew looks gorgeous served from a large pumpkin that's been hollowed out. Alternatively, you can use scooped-out mini pumpkins for individual servings. Of course, if you have a tagine or Dutch oven, it can be served directly from the pan. If you decide to use the pumpkin as your serving vessel, simply scoop out the pulp and seeds. Rub the inside with a little olive oil and roast the pumpkin in a 400°F oven for about 20 minutes until lightly colored.

MAKE AHEAD/STORAGE This tagine is a great dish to make ahead, as it seems to get better overnight. The cooked tagine can be stored in the refrigerator, covered, up to 5 days. Reheat tagine, covered, at 350°F until hot, adding a cupful of stock if the mixture seems dry.

1 tablespoon coriander seed

One 2-inch cinnamon stick

1 teaspoon anise seed or fennel seed

2 whole cloves

½ teaspoon chili flakes

Olive oil

1 medium Spanish onion, diced

3 garlic cloves, minced

1 medium fennel bulb, trimmed and diced

2 medium carrots, peeled and diced

2 medium parsnips, peeled and diced

1 acorn squash, peeled, seeded, and diced

1 butternut squash peeled, seeded, and diced

1 large sweet potato, peeled and diced

1 large russet potato, peeled and diced

2 medium zucchini, diced

Kosher salt and freshly ground black pepper

½ cup tomato paste

½ cup dry white wine, such as Sauvignon Blanc

3 to 4 cups Chicken Stock (page 15) or Vegetable Stock (page 17)

½ cup pitted dates, thinly sliced

½ cup dried apricots, thinly sliced

1 cup pearled barley

½ cup chopped fresh flat-leaf parsley

1 Preheat the oven to 325°F.

2 Combine the coriander seeds, cinnamon, anise seeds, cloves, and chili flakes in a spice grinder, and process until finely ground. Set aside spice mix.

3 Heat a large sauté pan and lightly coat the bottom of the pan. Sauté the vegetables, seasoned lightly with salt and pepper, in batches until lightly browned, adding more olive oil between batches if needed. Transfer the vegetables to a tagine, a large, deep casserole dish, or an enameled cast-iron Dutch oven.

4 Lightly coat the pan with oil again and sear the tomato paste until visibly darkened, about 2 minutes. Add the ground spices to the tomato paste and stir to combine. Add the wine and 3 cups stock, stirring to dissolve the paste, then pour the liquid over vegetables. Stir in the dates, apricots, barley, and salt and pepper to taste over the tagine and roast about 1½ hours, until the barley is tender and most of the liquid has been absorbed.

Pomegranate-Glazed Chicken

M ■ *Serves 4 to 6*

Many chefs put chicken on their menus just because they have to—it's the safe option for diners who don't know what else to order. I happen to love chicken, and I'm not shy about preparing it in unusual ways. This take on "barbecue chicken" has a deeply flavored, complex basting sauce that's anything but boring. The secret ingredient is pomegranate molasses, one of my favorite pantry ingredients. It adds a tart, syrupy sweetness that makes this chicken dish really stand out. Add a sprinkling of fresh pomegranate seeds at the end—they make the dish look as wonderful as it tastes. Bulgur Pilaf with Golden Raisins and Pine Nuts (recipe follows) is a great accompaniment.

MAKE AHEAD/STORAGE The glaze can be stored in the refrigerator, covered, up to 2 days.

- 2 chickens, about 4 pounds each, cut by your butcher into 6 pieces each, on the bone (see page 220)
- Kosher salt and freshly ground black pepper
- Olive oil

For the Glaze

- Olive oil
- 2 garlic cloves, finely chopped
- 1 medium shallot, finely chopped
- ½ cup pomegranate molasses (see Sources, page 257, and page 161 for more information)
- 3 tablespoons dark brown sugar
- 1 tablespoon tomato paste
- ¼ cup Dark Chicken Stock (page 16)

Suggested Garnishes fresh pomegranate seeds, chopped fresh flat-leaf parsley

1 Preheat the oven to 350°F. Season the chicken pieces with salt and pepper.

2 Heat a large, deep sauté pan over medium-high heat, and lightly coat the bottom of the pan with olive oil. Brown the chicken pieces on all sides, in batches, without crowding. When the pieces are well browned (the drumsticks and thighs will take longer than the breast and wing pieces), transfer the white and dark meat pieces to two separate baking dishes.

3 **Make the Glaze** Heat a small saucepan over medium-high heat, and lightly coat the bottom of the pan with olive oil. Sauté the garlic and shallot until lightly browned. Add the pomegranate molasses, sugar, tomato paste, and stock. Lower the heat to medium and cook, stirring, until well combined and the glaze has thickened, about 10 minutes.

Fall

4 Brush the chicken pieces with pomegranate glaze, and roast until cooked through and a thermometer inserted into the thigh registers 160°F, 30 to 35 minutes for white meat and about 45 minutes for dark meat. Brush the chicken with the glaze halfway through cooking and again when it is removed from the oven.

5 Serve the chicken with the pilaf, sprinkled with your choice of garnishes.

Bulgur Pilaf with Golden Raisins and Pine Nuts

P ▪ *Serves 4 to 6*

Bulgur is most commonly used to make tabbouleh, but it's also delicious when simply tossed with a few tasty ingredients. There are raisins for sweetness, preserved lemon for sour and salty flavors, and pine nuts for crunch. It's a nice change from rice and the perfect accompaniment for the Pomegranate-Glazed Chicken (page 159). This pilaf is best made with medium-grind bulgur. It can also be made with fine-grind but not with coarsely ground bulgur, which really needs to be cooked.

MAKE AHEAD/STORAGE The pilaf can be stored in the refrigerator, covered, up to 5 days.

2 cups bulgur wheat

Boiling water

¼ cup pine nuts

½ cup golden raisins

Rind of 1 Preserved Lemon (page 21), chopped

Kosher salt and freshly ground black pepper

1 Place the bulgur in a large, heat-resistant bowl and pour in enough boiling water to cover. Cover the bowl with plastic wrap or a large plate and let stand until most of the liquid is absorbed and the bulgur is tender, about 30 minutes.

2 Meanwhile, toast the pine nuts in a medium saucepan over medium-high heat, stirring frequently, until they are golden brown and fragrant, about 10 minutes. (Keep an eye on the pan, as pine nuts can burn easily.)

3 Drain the bulgur in a fine-mesh sieve or a a strainer, pressing to remove any excess liquid and return to the bowl. Stir in the pine nuts, raisins, and Preserved Lemon rind, and season with salt and pepper.

Pomegranate Paste

Every chef—and many a home cook—has a secret weapon. You know what I mean: The ingredient that you pull out to make your food distinctly your own. My weapon of choice is pomegranate paste or pomegranate molasses (they're the same thing). Pomegranate molasses or pomegranate paste is a thick, syrupy reduction of pomegranate juice. It is slightly sweet and sour with a gorgeous deep magenta color. I stock an arsenal of this bottled magic, hiding it in my refrigerator, at my stovetop, in the restaurant storage room by the case, at the bar for tasty martinis, and even at friends' houses, from the time that they requested my "secret."

I discovered the power of pomegranate paste years ago quite by accident. I was making a marinade and felt that it lacked the "smack" I was looking for. I tried lemon juice; then I tried vinegar of every variety. I was about to give up and just go with it when I spied an uninspiring-looking bottle lurking on my countertop, where a supplier had dropped it off for us to try. I pulled off the plastic sleeve and seal, dabbed my finger on the underside of the cap and . . . it was love at first taste! Now my paste and I are inseparable. When I worked in New York, my paste came with me. When I moved the restaurant to a suburb outside of Chicago, my paste was there; and when I travel to teach cooking classes, my paste is my companion.

I use this gem when my vinaigrettes aren't zippy enough; I use it when my marinades are flat. I brush it on meat when I'm feeling too lazy to do anything else (yes, that happens, even to chefs!). Our bartender at Shallots Bistro even shakes it into a pomegranate martini. It is my "fixer-upper"; I hope it works for you as well.

Most brands are kosher. I have had many brands of pomegranate paste over the years. Some are great; others are medicinal and flat. My recommendation is to buy several and find your favorite. Pomegranate paste can be found in many Middle Eastern markets, gourmet stores, and online. (See Sources, page 257.)

Duck Breast Schnitzel with Maple Mashed Sweet Potatoes and Braised Swiss Chard

M ■ *Serves 4*

I adore duck and I'm always thinking up new ways to prepare it. Duck can be a little tricky to cook, since the breasts cook at a different rate than the legs. At the restaurant, we get whole ducks from our supplier, so one of the challenges is using up the different parts of the duck equally. We had a very popular salad on the menu that used the leg and thigh, so this recipe was originally created to use up a bunch of duck breasts. It caught on, and then I needed more recipes for the legs and thighs . . . the rest is history!

MAKE AHEAD/STORAGE The duck breasts can be pounded thin and stored in the refrigerator, wrapped tightly in plastic wrap, up to 2 days before cooking.

4 skinless, boneless duck breasts

½ cup all-purpose flour

1 egg

1 cup fresh, untoasted bread crumbs

¼ cup finely chopped fresh flat-leaf parsley

Freshly ground black pepper and kosher salt

Olive oil

Maple Mashed Sweet Potatoes (recipe follows)

Braised Swiss Chard (page 164)

1 Preheat the oven to 350°F.

2 Remove the tender (a small finger-sized piece of meat from the under side of the duck breast) and reserve for another use. Place a duck breast on a cutting board and cover with plastic wrap. Pound the breast using a mallet or the bottom of a heavy sauté pan. Pound from the center of the breast out to all sides. When the breast is about ¼ inch thick, set it aside and continue with the remaining pieces until all are flattened.

3 Place the flour in a large shallow dish and whisk the egg in another shallow dish. Mix the bread crumbs with the parsley in a third shallow dish. Season all three with pepper and sparingly with salt (kosher duck is already salty). Heat a large sauté pan over medium heat, and lightly coat the bottom of the pan with olive oil. Dredge a breast in the flour, shaking off excess, then in the egg, and finally in the bread crumbs.

4 Brown the coated duck breasts, in batches if necessary to prevent crowding, about 3 minutes, until the crumbs are golden. Turn the schnitzels and brown the other side about 3 minutes longer. Transfer the schnitzels as they are browned to a baking sheet or ovenproof platter in one layer. Bake the schnitzels 5 to 7 minutes, or until all the schnitzels are hot and crispy. (Do not overcook or the duck will be tough and chewy.)

5 To serve, spoon a generous amount of sweet potatoes onto each plate and top with a schnitzel. Spoon the chard around the schnitzel.

Maple Mashed Sweet Potatoes

M or P ■ *Serves 4*

This deep orange sweet potato puree gets additional sweetness from the maple syrup and a bit of crunch from the pecans. If you can find sweet potatoes with dark reddish skin (sometimes labeled ruby or garnet yams, although they're really sweet potatoes) give them a try; they're very flavorful and have an extra-creamy texture when mashed.

MAKE AHEAD/STORAGE The sweet potatoes can be kept warm, covered, for up to 2 hours, set over a warm water bath or on the back of the stove.

- 2 to 3 sweet potatoes (about 3 pounds), peeled and cut into large dice (you should have about 4 cups)
- ½ to 1 cup warm Chicken Stock (page 15) or water reserved from cooking sweet potatoes
- Kosher salt and freshly ground black pepper
- ¼ cup pure maple syrup
- ¼ cup chopped toasted pecans (optional)

Cover the sweet potatoes with lightly salted water in a large saucepan and bring to a boil. Cook the potatoes until tender, about 20 minutes. Drain the potatoes, reserving a cup of cooking liquid if desired, and mash them in a large bowl or put them through a ricer. Add ½ cup warm stock (if using) or water, salt, and pepper, and stir until smooth and creamy. If potatoes are too thick, stir in more liquid, a spoonful at a time, until they reach desired consistency. Stir in the maple syrup and pecans, if using, and adjust the seasoning with salt and pepper.

163

Braised Swiss Chard

P ▪ *Serves 4*

At the farmers' market you can find chard in different color combinations. There's white-stemmed Swiss chard with dark green leaves; ruby-stemmed red chard with green leaves veined with red; and sometimes you'll even find rainbow chard, with stems and veins of different colors ranging from white and yellow to pink and orange. Choose a bunch with glossy leaves that aren't wilted or frayed.

1 large bunch of Swiss chard

Olive oil

Kosher salt and freshly ground black pepper

1 Tear the leaves from the stems and discard the stems. Tear the leaves into medium pieces, and wash well under cold running water. (You should have about 3 packed cups.) Let the leaves drain slightly in a strainer, but do not dry.

2 Heat a large sauté pan over high heat, and lightly coat the bottom of the pan with olive oil. Add the chard and season with salt and pepper. Add several teaspoons of water to wilt the chard if the pan seems dry. Cook, stirring, until the chard is wilted and tender, 3 to 5 minutes.

Crispy Roasted Duck
with Balsamic Pan Sauce

M ▪ *Serves 4 to 6*

Whenever I do a cooking demonstration or teach a class, I discover that many of my students think duck is one of the most intimidating things to cook. People imagine kitchen fires, smoke billowing out their ovens, and grease everywhere! Fear not, home chefs, this method is foolproof and delicious. It makes a delicious and different Shabbat dinner. If you still find this dish a challenge, serve it with your favorite simple-made side dish, or for a perfect accompaniment try the Braised Chestnuts, Fennel, Leeks, and Golden Raisins (recipe follows).

MAKE AHEAD/STORAGE The ducks can be boiled and then stored in the refrigerator, covered, up to 2 days. The ducks can be roasted about an hour ahead and kept in a warm oven, loosely covered with foil.

2 whole ducks, 4 to 5 pounds each, fresh or thawed

6 medium carrots, peeled and coarsely chopped

4 medium onions, coarsely chopped

4 celery stalks, coarsely chopped

Several fresh thyme sprigs

Freshly ground black pepper and kosher salt

3 medium shallots, finely diced

½ cup balsamic vinegar

1½ cups Chicken Stock (page 15)

Braised Chestnuts with Fennel, Leeks, and Golden Raisins (recipe follows)

Fig Confit (page 194; optional), warmed

1 Bring 6 quarts water to a boil in a very large stockpot. Using a very sharp knife, prick the skin and fat layer of the duck breasts and legs without cutting into the meat below (this allows the fat to cook off). Add half of the carrots, onions, celery, and thyme (reserve the rest for roasting the duck) and carefully lower the ducks into the stockpot. Boil the ducks, covered, for 45 minutes.

2 Preheat the oven to 450°F.

3 Remove the pot from the heat and set aside until the ducks are cool enough to handle. Scatter the remaining vegetables and thyme sprigs in a large roasting pan. Carefully remove the ducks from the stockpot, allowing any water in the cavities to drain out, and place them, breast side up, on top of the vegetables. Season the ducks with pepper and a small amount of salt. (Kosher duck can be salty, so add salt sparingly.)

4 Roast the ducks for 30 to 40 minutes, until the skin is crispy and the ducks are browned all over. Transfer the ducks, breast sides up, to a large cutting board or platter and cover loosely with foil. Let the ducks rest 10 to 15 minutes before carving, while you make the sauce.

5 Drain off fat from the roasting pan and discard the vegetables. Place the pan across 2 burners on low heat. Add the shallots and gently scrape up any browned bits that remain in the pan. Add the balsamic vinegar and continue stirring and scraping until the vinegar has reduced to a glaze. Add the chicken stock, and whisk until the sauce comes together. Adjust the seasoning with salt and pepper, and keep sauce warm while carving the ducks.

6 Using either a sharp knife or poultry shears, cut along both sides of the breast bone and remove the bone in the center. Gently pull the duck apart to expose the back bone. Cut on either side of the back bone and remove it. The duck is now cut in half. Cut the duck into quarters, separating the leg and breast sections, and place the pieces on a serving platter. Carve second duck and pour the sauce over the duck pieces. Serve duck with braised chestnuts and fig confit, if desired.

Braised Chestnuts, Fennel, Leeks, and Golden Raisins

P ■ *Serves 4 to 6*

Chestnuts are one of those foods that baffle many cooks. They look so appealing, and yet they are a culinary puzzle. The method I use to cook and peel them is easy and foolproof. The combination of flavors in this festive dish is rich, nutty, and slightly sweet.

MAKE AHEAD/STORAGE The braised chestnuts can be stored in the refrigerator, covered, up to 3 days. Reheat, covered, over medium-low heat, stirring occasionally, until warmed through.

1 pound chestnuts in the shell

Olive oil

½ cup water

1 medium fennel bulb, trimmed and sliced ¼ inch thick

2 medium leeks, white and light green parts only (save the dark green tops for stock), thinly sliced lengthwise

1 cup Chicken Stock (page 15) or Vegetable Stock (page 17)

½ cup golden raisins

Kosher salt and freshly ground black pepper

3 tablespoons fresh thyme leaves

1 With a sharp paring knife, cut a small X shape into the rounded side of each chestnut shell. Toss the chestnuts in a large bowl with a drizzle of olive oil until lightly coated.

2 Heat a large sauté pan over medium heat and add the chestnuts. Cook, stirring the chestnuts occasionally to prevent them from burning, about 10 minutes. Add ½ cup water to the pan and cover. Lower the heat and allow the chestnuts to steam for 15 to 20 minutes, until they are quite tender and most of the water has evaporated from the pan. Remove the chestnuts and allow them to cool until they can be handled comfortably.

3 Peel the chestnuts; the shells and skins should be easy to pull off. Heat the same pan over medium-high heat and lightly coat the bottom of the pan with olive oil. Add the leeks and fennel, and sauté until the vegetables are golden brown, about 10 minutes. Add the stock, peeled chestnuts, the raisins, and salt and pepper to taste. Cover the pan and lower the heat to a simmer. Simmer the chestnuts until they are tender and the liquid has reduced to a glaze, about 20 minutes. Add the thyme and adjust seasoning to taste with salt and pepper.

Fennel-Crusted Cod with Fennel, Orange, and Red Onion Relish

P ▪ *Serves 4*

I love to coat fish fillets with a crust, but I'm always looking for something more interesting and flavorful than bread crumbs. I got the idea to make this spice crust one evening when preparing a Sicilian-inspired salad of fennel and oranges. I thought it would make a delicious topping for fish, so I crusted some cod fillets with fennel seeds to intensify the fresh fennel flavor in the relish. The combination of the toasted fennel and the cool relish works perfectly.

MAKE AHEAD/STORAGE The fillets can be browned ahead and stored in the refrigerator, covered, up to 4 hours.

2 tablespoons fennel seeds

4 skinless, boneless 6-ounce cod fillets

Kosher salt and freshly ground black pepper

Olive oil

For the Relish

2 large navel oranges

2 medium fennel bulbs, trimmed

1 medium red onion

3 tablespoons finely chopped fresh flat-leaf parsley

Extra-virgin olive oil

1 Preheat the oven to 450°F.

2 Heat a small sauté pan over medium heat, and add the fennel seeds. Toast the seeds, shaking the pan or stirring from time to time, until the seeds are fragrant and visibly darkened, about 3 minutes. Season the fish with salt and pepper, and lightly pat the fennel seeds onto top (nonskin) side of the fillets.

3 Heat a medium sauté pan over medium-high heat, and lightly coat the bottom of the pan with olive oil. Place the fillets in the pan coated side down, and sear until the cod is golden brown. Transfer the fillets to a baking dish, crust side up, and set aside while you prepare the relish.

4 Make the Relish Peel the orange (see Step 6, page 152) and cut between the sections, letting the sections and any juices drop into a small bowl and leaving the membrane behind. Squeeze the membrane to extract more juice (you should have about 3 tablespoons juice). Using a mandoline, Asian slicer, or a very sharp knife, thinly slice the fennel and onion. Toss together the fennel, onion, orange sections, and parsley in a medium bowl and drizzle with a spoonful of extra-virgin olive oil and the fresh-squeezed orange juice. Season relish with salt and pepper.

5 Roast the cod until it is cooked through but not dry, 7 to 10 minutes, depending upon thickness. Divide the relish among four plates, mounding it in the center of the plates, and top with a cod fillet. Drizzle the cod and plate with additional extra-virgin olive oil.

Muhummarah-Crusted Halibut with Saffron Broth and Ivory Lentils

P ■ *Serves 4*

Muhummarah is one of my favorite condiments and it makes a delicious crust for fish fillets. Mild, flaky halibut provides the perfect contrast to the decadent creaminess and exotic spices of muhummarah crust. The crust doesn't overpower the fish—it just gilds it. The saffron broth adds beautiful color and flavor to the dish; if you don't have fish fumet, you can use vegetable stock instead.

MAKE AHEAD/STORAGE All the parts can be done ahead of time; you just pop it in the oven when you're ready for dinner. The fish can be topped and stored in the refrigerator, covered, up to 2 hours. The saffron broth can be stored in the refrigerator, covered, up to 1 day; reheat to simmering.

Olive oil

4 skinless, boneless 6-ounce halibut fillets

½ cup Muhummarah (page 25)

Kosher salt and freshly ground black pepper

For the Broth

½ cup dry white wine, such as Sauvignon Blanc

2 cups Fumet (page 18) or Vegetable Stock (page 17)

1 teaspoon saffron threads

Kosher salt and freshly ground black pepper

Ivory Lentils (recipe follows)

1 Preheat the oven to 400°F and oil a large baking dish.

2 Season the halibut with salt and pepper and smear the tops (nonskin side) of the fillets thickly with Muhummarah. Place the fish in the baking dish.

3 **Make the Broth** Bring the wine to a simmer in a medium saucepan over medium heat. Add the stock and saffron, and season lightly with salt and pepper. Continue to simmer until the broth is reduced by half. Taste broth and adjust seasoning.

4 Roast the fish until the Muhummarah has formed a crust and the fillets are cooked through, 12 to 15 minutes. To serve, spoon the lentils into shallow bowls and top with fish. Spoon the saffron broth around the lentils.

Ivory Lentils

P ■ *Serves 4*

There's a whole world of lentils out there beyond the little brown lentil you can buy at the grocery store. Even the brown ones aren't so bad, but one of my favorites is a tender yellow-white lentil, called an ivory lentil. In India, where it's used frequently, it's known as *urad dal*. Try it if you can find it—the lentils cook to a tender texture but don't fall apart into mush like the brown or light green varieties. If you can't find it, small, dark-green French lentils are the best substitute in terms of taste, though not in color.

MAKE AHEAD/STORAGE These lentils can be stored in the refrigerator, covered, up to 3 days. Reheat gently over low heat before serving.

Olive oil

1 medium fennel bulb, diced small

1 medium shallot, thinly sliced

1 medium leek, white part only (save the light and dark green tops for stock), thinly sliced

2 cups ivory lentils or small green French lentils (see Sources, page 257)

Kosher salt and freshly ground black pepper

Heat a medium saucepan over medium-high heat, and lightly coat the bottom of the pan with olive oil. Gently sauté the fennel, shallot, and leek just until lightly browned. Add the lentils and enough water to cover the lentils by about 1 inch. Cover the pan and reduce the heat to medium. Simmer the lentils until they are tender but still al dente, about 25 minutes. Season with salt and pepper.

Bourride

P ▪ *Serves 4*

Bright yellow saffron, fragrant garlic, roasted tomato, and succulent fresh fish—here are the flavors of Provence rolled into one delicious dish. The garlicky aioli is traditionally stirred into the dish but I like to just dollop it on a crouton and let it work its way into the stew. For another delicious break with tradition, I like to serve this stew on a bed of homemade saffron pasta instead of the more traditional boiled potatoes.

MAKE AHEAD/STORAGE The fish can be browned (Step 1), the vegetables sautéed (Step 2), and the soup prepared (Step 3) and all stored separately in the refrigerator, covered, overnight.

4 skinless, boneless 4-ounce fillets of fresh, firm-fleshed fish, such as bass, grouper, or cod

Kosher salt and freshly ground black pepper

Olive oil

5 or 6 plump garlic cloves

Kosher salt

1 medium leek, white and light green parts only (save the dark green tops for stock), thinly sliced

2 medium shallots, thinly sliced

1 large fennel bulb, trimmed and thinly sliced

½ cup dry white wine, such as Sauvignon Blanc

2½ cups Fumet (page 18)

1 cup Tomato Confit (page 22) or canned whole peeled plum tomatoes, juices drained and tomatoes broken up with your hands into smaller pieces

1 tablespoon finely chopped lemon zest

1 tablespoon finely chopped orange zest

1 teaspoon saffron threads

¼ cup torn or chopped fresh basil leaves, plus extra for garnish

¼ cup chopped fresh flat-leaf parsley, plus extra for garnish

Freshly ground black pepper

1 small baguette, thinly sliced and toasted for croutons

Garlicky Aioli (page 26)

Saffron Pasta (page 21; optional), cooked, or boiled potatoes

1 Lightly season fish fillets with salt and pepper. Heat a large saucepan over medium-high heat, and lightly coat the bottom of the pan with olive oil. Lightly brown the fish on both sides, but do not cook through. Transfer the fish to a plate and set aside.

2 Place 4 of the garlic cloves and 2 teaspoons salt in a mortar and pound to a paste; or use a cutting board and the side of your knife to smash and scrape it. Sauté the garlic paste, leek, and shallots in same pan until lightly browned, about 5 minutes. Add the fennel and sauté until lightly browned, about 5 minutes more. Transfer the vegetables to the plate and set aside.

3 Add the wine to the pan and cook, stirring and scraping up any browned bits that remain in the pan, until the wine has reduced to a glaze. Stir in the fish stock, the Tomato Confit, with its juices, zests, saffron, and chopped basil and parsley, and season with salt and pepper. Reduce the heat to medium and bring the mixture just to a simmer. Gently simmer the soup for 10 minutes (do not boil).

4 Add the fish and vegetables to the simmering soup. Simmer until the fish cooks through completely, about 8 to 10 minutes. Meanwhile, rub the croutons with the remaining garlic and top with a dollop of the Garlicky Aioli.

5 To serve, place some pasta or potatoes in the bottom of 4 large, shallow bowls, and top with fish and some of the vegetables. Top the fish with the garlicky croutons and sprinkle with the additional herbs. Spoon the soup over and around the pasta, if using, and serve with extra croutons on the side.

173

Pan-Roasted Black Bass with Lemon-Caper Sauce and Farro Pilaf

P ▪ *Serves 4*

I whisk this lemon-caper sauce together whenever I need a quick topping to dress up a piece of fish or chicken. It's really more like a warm vinaigrette, since you make it separately from whatever you're cooking. That makes it convenient for grilled dishes as well. The tartness of the lemons and capers cuts right through any oiliness from the fish.

MAKE AHEAD/STORAGE Sauce can be made 1 day ahead and chilled, covered. Reheat sauce over low heat.

4 skinless, boneless 6-ounce black bass fillets or salmon fillets

Kosher salt and freshly ground black pepper

2 teaspoons finely chopped fresh thyme

2 teaspoons finely chopped fresh flat-leaf parsley

2 teaspoons finely chopped fresh chives

Olive oil

For the Sauce

½ cup drained capers

Juice and grated zest of 1 lemon

¼ cup dry white wine, such as Sauvignon Blanc

¼ cup extra-virgin olive oil (use your best-quality oil)

Kosher salt and freshly ground black pepper

Farro Pilaf (recipe follows)

1 Season the fillets with salt and pepper. Mix the herbs in a small bowl, and sprinkle on the top (nonskin) side of the fish. Heat a medium sauté pan on medium-high heat, and lightly coat the bottom of the pan with olive oil. When the pan is very hot, place the bass fillets in the pan, herbed side down. Brown the fillets until very crispy, about 5 minutes. Turn over the bass and remove the pan from the heat. Cover the pan loosely with foil and set aside to allow the bass to finish cooking. (There is enough residual heat in the pan to finish cooking the bass.) If you prefer your fish well done, transfer the fillets to a baking dish and bake in a preheated 400°F oven, 5 to 7 minutes, until firm.

2 Make the Sauce Place the capers, lemon juice and zest, wine, and extra-virgin olive oil in a small saucepan over medium-high heat, and simmer the sauce, stirring occasionally, until it has reduced by half. Season the sauce with pepper and a small amount of salt. (Capers are very salty, so add salt sparingly.)

3 To serve, place a generous mound of Farro Pilaf on each plate and top with bass fillets. Drizzle with lemon-caper sauce.

Farro Pilaf

P ▪ *Serves 4*

Farro, also called emmer wheat, has been cultivated since prehistoric times, but many chefs have only recently discovered this ancient grain and are now putting it on their menus. Farro resembles barley, but it has a nutty flavor and cooks to an al dente texture. The only country producing it today is Italy, where it is quite popular. It's also healthy and unprocessed, high in vitamin E, and fiber. Farro can be found in most health food stores and in some specialty markets (see Sources, page 257). I serve farro as a side dish, as a salad, and even as an appetizer.

MAKE AHEAD/STORAGE The farro pilaf can be stored in the refrigerator, covered, up to 3 days, or frozen for several weeks. Leftover farro can be served cold or warm. Reheat covered, over medium heat or in the microwave.

Olive oil

1½ cups farro

3 to 4 cups water

Kosher salt and freshly ground black pepper

¼ cup dried fruit, such as currants, cranberries, or dried cherries

¼ cup walnuts

1 Heat a medium saucepan over medium heat and lightly coat the bottom of the pan with olive oil. Toast the farro, stirring gently, until coated with olive oil and slightly toasted. Add 3 cups water and salt and pepper to taste to the pan and cook, covered for 10 minutes. Without opening the pan, reduce the heat to low and simmer for 30 minutes longer. Check the farro for doneness by tasting it: The farro should be al dente but slightly firm; it should not be crunchy. If it needs more time, add a little more water and continue cooking over low heat 5 to 15 minutes longer.

2 Transfer the farro to a bowl and let it cool slightly. Add the dried fruit and nuts, adjust seasoning with salt and pepper and toss well. Farro can be kept warm, covered with foil, for several hours.

175

Mushroom-Crusted Wild Salmon

P ▪ *Serves 4*

Salmon is a staple in my house, and I would be embarrassed to reveal how often we eat this dish. But as long as no one complains, I will continue to make this a weekly dinner. My son Ari is a big fan of this meal—he seems content and happy whenever this dish is on the menu for the night. He loves any combo of salmon and potatoes, so sometimes we have roasted fingerling potatoes with fresh herbs and garlic instead of the mashed potatoes. I always drizzle on a bit of Balsamic Reduction (page 19) at the end; the syrupy sweetness complements the earthy mushrooms.

Olive oil

1 ounce dried porcini mushrooms

½ ounce dried black trumpet mushrooms (or your other favorite dried mushroom)

2 tablespoons all-purpose flour

4 skinless, boneless 6-ounce wild salmon fillets

1½ cups sliced fresh mushrooms, such as button, cremini, or shiitake

Kosher salt and freshly ground black pepper

Chive Mashed Potatoes (page 70)

Balsamic Reduction (page 19), warmed

1 Preheat the oven to 400°F and lightly oil a baking dish.

2 In a blender or food processor grind the dried mushrooms until they are reduced to a dustlike consistency. Combine the mushroom powder and flour in a shallow dish.

3 Heat a large sauté pan over medium-high heat, and lightly coat the bottom of the pan with olive oil. Dredge the tops (nonskin side) of the salmon fillets in the powder. Place the salmon in the pan crusted side down, and brown the fillets until crispy and golden, 3 to 4 minutes. Transfer the fillets to the baking dish, crust side up.

4 Sauté the sliced mushrooms in cleaned saute pan over medium heat until they are browned with slightly crispy edges, 8 to 10 minutes. While mushrooms are cooking, roast the salmon until cooked through, 6 to 8 minutes for medium rare. (The salmon should feel slightly firm when pressed on the sides.)

5 Serve the salmon on a mound of Chive Mashed Potatoes, and spoon the sautéed mushrooms around the salmon. Drizzle the salmon with Balsamic Reduction.

176

Boeuf Bourguignon

M ▪ *Serves 4 to 6*

Here is my version of the classic beef-and-red-wine stew from the Burgundy region of France. I start craving hearty stews like this in the autumn when the nights are cool. So do our customers at the restaurant; and so do my friends, so I frequently make this for dinner parties. What a pleasure to come in from a brisk fall walk to the aroma of this rich stew simmering in the oven. I think this makes a perfect one-pot meal for Sukkot or for any kind of casual get-together. The dish is easily doubled or tripled for a crowd. To make this meal heartier and a bit more elegant, serve it with the Roasted Garlic–Potato Galette (recipe follows).

MAKE AHEAD/STORAGE Beef stew improves if prepared a day ahead. The stew can be stored in the refrigerator, covered, up to 3 days.

2½ pounds boneless beef chuck, cut into 2-inch pieces

1 bottle (750 ml) dry red wine, such as a hearty Pinot Noir

2 teaspoons dried rosemary

1 tablespoon dried thyme

½ cup all-purpose flour

Kosher salt and freshly ground black pepper

Olive oil

2 medium leeks, white and light green parts only (save the dark green tops for stock), thinly sliced

2 medium carrots, peeled and cut into 1-inch pieces

4 garlic cloves, chopped

1 celery stalk, cut into 1-inch pieces

2 tablespoons tomato paste

1 cup Chicken Stock (page 15)

1 cup pearl onions

½ pound mushrooms (use cremini, button, or shiitake), trimmed and cut in half (about 2 cups)

Roasted Garlic–Potato Galette (page 178), Chive Mashed Potatoes (page 70), or cooked pasta

1 Place the meat in a large resealable plastic bag or a container with a tight-fitting lid and pour in the wine. (Each piece of meat should be submerged in the wine.) Let the meat marinate in the refrigerator at least 4 hours or overnight.

2 Preheat the oven to 300°F.

3 Combine the rosemary, thyme, and flour in a large shallow plate. Pour the meat into a colander set over a large bowl and set aside the wine. Dry the meat on paper towels and generously season each piece with salt and pepper. Dredge the meat in the flour mixture and shake the pieces to remove any excess flour.

4 Heat a large sauté pan over medium heat, and lightly coat the pan with olive oil. Brown the meat on all sides, in batches if necessary to prevent crowding, about 12 minutes. Transfer the meat to a large Dutch oven or a casserole with a lid as it is browned, and set aside. Add the leeks, carrots, garlic, and celery to the pan and cook, stirring occasionally, until they are browned, about 10 minutes. Add about 1 cup reserved wine to the pan with the tomato paste and cook, stirring and scraping up any browned bits that remain in the pan, until the wine has reduced to a glaze. Stir in Chicken Stock and the remaining wine and season with salt and pepper. Pour the wine mixture over the meat. Bring the stew to a simmer over medium-high heat, then transfer to the oven. Cook the beef until it is tender (the meat releases easily when pierced with a fork), 2½ to 3 hours.

5 While the beef is braising, blanch, shock, and peel the onions: Bring a medium saucepan of lightly salted water to a boil and prepare a large bowl of ice water with a strainer that fits inside the bowl. Cook the onions until tender, about 12 minutes, and drain them into the strainer. Immediately shock the onions by submerging the strainer in the ice water (see page 41 for more information on blanching and shocking vegetables). When onions have cooled completely, remove the strainer from the ice water, peel the onions, and set them aside.

6 Heat a large sauté pan over medium-high heat and lightly oil the pan. Sauté the mushrooms and onions until lightly browned and caramelized, 5 to 7 minutes. Add the mushrooms and onions to the beef and continue to cook 15 minutes longer for the flavors to meld and for the onions to become very tender.

7 To serve, place a wedge of potato galette on a plate or in a large shallow bowl and top with the beef, mushrooms, onions, and some of the braising liquid.

Roasted Garlic–
Potato Galette

P ■ *Serves 4*

Some chefs have an omelet pan that they guard protectively. For others, it's a crepe pan or a sugar saucepot. I have several pans dedicated to specific uses, but I'm most careful with my galette pan. It has a nonstick surface, so no one is allowed near it with anything resembling metal. It's worth it for this pretty potato dish that combines a potato-chip crisp exterior with a creamy interior. Once you have your galette pan and an Asian slicer, this dish is a snap to prepare, and it makes any cook look like a pro.

1 head of garlic

Kosher salt and freshly ground black pepper

Extra-virgin olive oil

¼ cup dry white wine, such as Sauvignon Blanc

4 large russet potatoes (about 4 pounds), peeled

1 teaspoon chopped fresh thyme

1 teaspoon chopped fresh chives

1 teaspoon chopped fresh flat-leaf parsley

1 Cut ½ inch off the nonroot end of the head of garlic to expose the cloves. Place the garlic in a small baking dish or ovenproof ramekin, and lightly sprinkle with salt and pepper. Lightly drizzle with olive oil and add the wine. Cover the dish with foil and roast until the garlic is lightly browned and soft enough to squeeze out of the skins, about 1 hour. Set aside to let the garlic cool. Squeeze the garlic cloves from the head into a small bowl and mash with a fork.

2 Using a mandoline or Asian slicer, slice the potatoes into paper-thin rounds. Toss the potato slices in a large bowl with a generous amount of olive oil and salt and pepper to taste. Add the thyme, chives, parsley, and the roasted garlic, and toss the potato slices until well coated.

3 Heat a medium sauté pan (8 to 10 inches, preferably nonstick or well-seasoned cast-iron) over medium-low heat, and generously coat the bottom of the pan with olive oil. Layer the potatoes in the pan, overlapping the slices to completely cover the bottom of the pan. (The bottom layer becomes the side that will be seen, so arrange the slices evenly in an attractive pattern.) Add the remaining potatoes, spreading them evenly, and cook the potatoes, without stirring, until the bottom layer is browned and can be shaken loose, about 30 minutes. (Gently lift up edge of the potatoes with a spatula to peek after about 25 minutes.)

4 Invert a large plate over the pan and, using potholders and a bit of courage, invert the potatoes onto the plate. Slide the potatoes back into the pan, uncooked side down, and continue cooking until the underside is browned and can be shaken loose, about 30 minutes more. Alternatively, if your pan is ovenproof, flip the potatoes and place the pan in a preheated 350°F oven to finish cooking.

5 Slide the potato galette onto a serving platter and cut into wedges.

179

Braised Venison with Dried Cherry Sauce and Roasted Root Vegetables

M ▪ *Serves 6*

One of the best ways to cook venison is to braise it. Venison is so lean that it can sometimes be tough, but a slow and gentle braise, bathed in stock, red wine, and spices, makes it tender enough to shred. If you have leftovers, try rolling up the meat in a warmed flatbread and topping it with a spoonful of salsa or a dollop of Muhammarah (page 25).

MAKE AHEAD/STORAGE The meat and braising liquid can be prepared through Step 4 and stored separately in the refrigerator, covered, up to 3 days, or frozen for 1 month.

Olive oil

3 medium Spanish onions, sliced

6 garlic cloves, finely chopped

1 venison shoulder or leg, on the bone, 6 to 8 pounds*

4 to 6 cups Chicken Stock (page 15) or water

1 cup dry red wine, such as Cabernet Sauvignon (try Baron Herzog)

1 bay leaf

1 large rosemary sprig

1 teaspoon juniper berries

For the Sauce

2 cups Chicken Stock (page 15) or water

1 cup dry red wine, such as Cabernet Sauvignon (try Baron Herzog)

6 thyme sprigs

Several flat-leaf parsley stems, plus chopped fresh flat-leaf parsley for garnish

½ cup dried cherries, plus extra for garnish

Roasted Root Vegetables (recipe follows)

*If venison is not available at your butcher, see Sources (page 259).

1 Preheat the oven to 275°F.

2 Heat a large Dutch oven over medium heat and lightly oil the pan. Slowly cook the onions until very brown, soft, and caramelized, about 20 minutes. Add the garlic and continue cooking for 5 minutes. Add the venison shoulder and enough stock to come about 1 inch up side of venison. Add wine, bay leaf, rosemary, and juniper berries. Cover the pan and bring the liquid to a boil.

3 Transfer the pan to the oven, and braise the venison until it is very soft and falling off the bone, about 2 hours. Remove the venison from the pan and set aside. Strain the braising liquid through a sieve into a bowl and set aside, discard the solids. When the venison has cooled, pull the meat off the bones. Cut up the larger chunks of meat or use 2 forks to pull apart the meat and slightly shred it.

4 Make the Sauce Pour the braising juices into a medium saucepan and add the stock, wine, thyme, and parsley stems. Boil the sauce until reduced by half. Strain the sauce through a fine sieve and return it to the saucepan. Add the cherries and continue to simmer the sauce until the cherries are soft and fragrant, 10 to 15 minutes.

5 Reheat the venison in 275°F oven in a baking dish for about 15 minutes with some of the sauce drizzled over, until warm but not dried out.

6 To serve, place Roasted Root Vegetables in a large, shallow bowl and top with the shredded venison. Drizzle with some sauce and garnish with additional dried cherries and chopped parsley. Serve extra sauce on the side.

Roasted Root Vegetables

M ■ *Serves 6*

Root vegetables are terrific candidates for roasting. The heat concentrates their sweetness and intensifies their flavor. If you wish, you can add or substitute cut-up squash (butternut or acorn) and halved or quartered small potatoes for any of the vegetables in this mixture.

- 2 medium parsnips, peeled and sliced about ⅓ inch thick
- 2 medium carrots, peeled and sliced about ⅓ inch thick
- 1 medium rutabaga, peeled and cut into medium dice
- 2 medium sweet potatoes, peeled and cut into medium dice
- 1 medium celery root (celeriac), peeled and cut into medium dice
- Olive oil
- 2 teaspoons Herbes de Provence (page 27)
- Kosher salt and freshly ground black pepper

Preheat the oven to 350°F. In a large bowl toss the parsnips, carrots, rutabaga, sweet potatoes, and celery root with olive oil to coat lightly. Sprinkle with Herbes de Provence and season with salt and pepper and toss again. Transfer the vegetables to a large, ovenproof casserole and roast until tender and golden brown, about 1 hour.

Venison

When I was a child, I thought the only people who ate venison were either grand gourmets or hunters who lived in rural areas. Since then, venison and other game meats have become much more accessible to chefs and discerning diners. It's still not everyday food, but it's certainly showing up on restaurant menus all over and is easily available from a good butcher shop. Perhaps it's because venison has a very low fat content. It could also be the rich, complex flavor that makes venison perfect for so many preparations. When you go to a restaurant and you want to test the chef's mettle, I suggest ordering the venison. An order of steak frites is delicious and satisfying, but a plate of venison is an adventure. In this modern age of specialty farmers and the growing popularity of kosher products, we can now have a venison adventure at home.

Venison is a huge boon to kosher cooks. In the United States, beef tenderloin is not available in the kosher market because the sciatic nerve is so difficult to remove, probably due to the fat content of beef. (For a detailed explanation, see Lisë Stern's *How to Keep Kosher* [New York: Morrow, 2004].) Venison has a very low fat content that makes butchering and removal of the sciatic nerve possible. The loin is an especially prized piece of meat with a buttery texture and beautiful appearance. Other delicious cuts of venison include the legs, which have large pieces of meat that can be used in place of the loin.

Because of their low fat content (comparable to turkey), I cook the loin and leg pieces quickly over high heat. This meat is best served rare or medium rare. The flavor of the meat is woodsy, rich, and delicious when cooked in this manner, and the texture is tender and supple. I enjoy this meat so much that I even recommend trying it raw (Venison Carpaccio with Artichoke Slivers and Preserved Lemon, page 51). If you are not ready for that type of adventure yet, try a cut of venison that will hold up to long cooking. (The loin and legs will become tough and chewy if cooked for a long time.) You could substitute venison osso buco for the veal in the Braised Veal Shanks with Moroccan Spices and Mango "Gremolata" on page 241 or enjoy the Braised Venison with Dried Cherry Sauce and Roasted Root Vegetables (page 180). Perhaps, when you have been seduced by the flavor and texture of venison, you will also try these other recipes:

Ginger-Marinated Venison Loin with Purple Sticky Rice and Spring Pea Salad (page 75)

Grilled Venison Loin Stuffed with Slow-Roasted Tomatoes (page 128)

Venison Loin Poivrade with Roasted Sweet Potatoes (page 183)

Venison Loin Poivrade
with Roasted Sweet Potatoes

P ■ *Serves 6 to 8 generously*

Many people automatically assume that anything crusted in pepper (*au poivre*) will be too hot and spicy. I believe that's mostly due to a bad experience in the past. Peppercorns have volatile oils stored inside them that are responsible for the flavor we get when the pepper is freshly ground. The oils are also responsible for the heat associated with peppercorns. The proper way to extract these oils is through direct heat: When the peppercorn crust hits the very hot pan, there will be a lot of "big" pepper aroma all at once. That is the volatile oils cooking off. What's left behind is a perfumed, light peppery flavor, not mouth-burning heat. Now that you know how to do it correctly—go ahead, try it!

MAKE AHEAD/STORAGE The venison can be coated and seared (through Step 4), and stored in the refrigerator, covered, up to 4 hours. Remaining peppercorn mixture can be stored at room temperature, tightly covered, up to 1 month before losing its flavor.

¼ cup black peppercorns (preferably Tellicherry)

¼ cup white peppercorns

½ cup pink peppercorns

½ cup dried green peppercorns

1 venison loin (about 5 pounds), silverskin removed by your butcher*

Kosher salt

Olive oil

¾ cup brandy

¼ cup pure maple syrup

2 cups Chicken Stock (page 15)

Roasted Sweet Potatoes (recipe follows)

*If venison is not available at your butcher, see Sources (page 259).

1 Preheat the oven to 400°F.

2 Place the black and white peppercorns on a cutting board or sturdy countertop and lightly crush the peppercorns with the bottom of a heavy pan until they are broken open and fragrant (do not oversmash them; you want the mixture to be a little chunky). Add the pink and green peppercorns and lightly crush them. Transfer the peppercorn mixture to a small bowl and stir to mix.

3 Using your hands, generously coat the venison with the pepper mixture and season with salt.

Fall

4 Heat a large sauté pan over medium-high heat, and lightly coat the bottom of the pan with olive oil. When the pan is very hot, add the venison and brown on all sides. Transfer the venison to a baking sheet.

5 Roast the venison until a meat thermometer inserted in the center reads 120°F for medium rare, about 30 minutes. (The venison and the sweet potatoes can be roasted at the same time).

6 While the venison is roasting, prepare the pan sauce. Remove the sauté pan from the heat and carefully add the brandy. Reduce the heat to low and boil to allow the alcohol to cook off. Be careful, as the brandy added to the hot pan may flame. When the flames have subsided, add the maple syrup and stock and boil, stirring and scraping up any browned bits that remain in the pan, until the sauce has reduced to about 1 cup. Keep the sauce warm.

7 Transfer the venison to a cutting board and loosely cover with foil. Allow the venison to rest for 10 minutes before carving. Slice the venison and fan out the pieces on a platter or plates. Place the sweet potatoes on the platter and drizzle with the warm sauce.

Tuna Steak Poivrade (P)   A beautiful hunk of tuna will also work well and stand up to the big flavor. Ask your fishmonger for a 2½- to 3-pound piece of center-cut tuna. The technique is the same. Coat and sear the tuna, then roast for 10 minutes for rare tuna. Prepare pan sauce in same manner, substituting Vegetable Stock (page 17) for the Chicken Stock (page 15). Serves 4 to 6.

Roasted Sweet Potatoes

P ■ *Serves 6 to 8*

If serving the sweet potatoes with the Venison Poivrade (page 183), start roasting the potatoes about 15 minutes before the venison.

8 medium sweet potatoes (4 to 5 pounds), peeled

Extra-virgin olive oil

Kosher salt and freshly ground black pepper to taste

Preheat the oven to 400°F. Cut the sweet potatoes into eighths. Toss the potatoes with olive oil and salt and pepper and place them on a baking sheet lined with parchment paper. Roast the potatoes until browned and tender, turning occasionally, about 45 minutes.

Stuffed Veal Chops
with Melted Leeks and Shallots
and Pan-Fried Smashed Potatoes

M ■ *Serves 4*

This is a dish that really says "special occasion." You'll need to purchase thick veal rib chops, or buy a rack of veal and cut the chops yourself. (Make sure your butcher cuts whole chops for you and doesn't halve them through the bone, or they will be too thin to stuff.) This cut of meat can be a little pricey, but it is absolutely delicious, moist, and succulent and looks gorgeous and festive. I just want to caution you not to overcook the veal, which can dry it out. The leeks aren't really "melted," but they are cooked so long that they turn soft and almost lusciously gooey.

MAKE AHEAD/STORAGE The chops can be stuffed a day ahead and chilled, covered. The stuffed chops can be seared (through Step 3) and the pan sauce made and stored separately in the refrigerator, covered, up to 4 hours. Bring chops to room temperature before roasting, and reheat pan sauce over low heat.

> Extra-virgin olive oil
>
> 2 medium leeks, white parts only (save the light and dark green tops for stock), thinly sliced
>
> 4 medium shallots, thinly sliced
>
> ¾ cup dry white wine, such as Sauvignon Blanc
>
> 1¼ cups Chicken Stock (page 15) or Veal Stock (page 18)
>
> Kosher salt and freshly ground black pepper

> 4 veal rib chops, each with a 2-inch pocket cut into the side by your butcher
>
> Pan-Fried Smashed Potatoes (recipe follows)

1 Preheat the oven to 350°F.

2 Heat a large sauté pan over medium-low heat, and lightly coat the bottom of the pan with olive oil. Add the leeks, shallots, ¼ cup white wine, ¼ cup Chicken Stock, and salt and pepper. Cook until very soft and fragrant, about 45 minutes. Cool the stuffing mixture completely to room temperature.

3 Season the veal with salt and pepper. Stuff the pocket of each veal chop with the leek stuffing. Heat a large sauté pan over medium-high heat, and lightly coat the bottom of the pan with olive oil. Brown the veal chops on both sides until they are golden brown. Transfer the chops to an ovenproof casserole or roasting pan.

Fall

4 Roast the chops until the meat feels slightly firm when pressed on the sides, 15 to 20 minutes.

5 Make the Sauce while the chops are roasting. Heat the sauté pan over medium heat and add the remaining ½ cup white wine. Cook, stirring and scraping up any browned bits that remain in the pan, until the wine has reduced by half. Add 1 cup stock and simmer, stirring occasionally, until the sauce is reduced by half. Keep the sauce warm.

6 Serve the roasted veal chops with the potatoes, and drizzle with pan sauce.

Pan-Fried Smashed Potatoes

P ■ *Serves 4*

This is one of my favorite ways to make crispy fried potatoes. These are addictive simply sprinkled with sea salt and freshly ground black pepper. If serving with the Stuffed Veal Chops (page 185), panfry the potatoes while the veal is roasting.

MAKE AHEAD/STORAGE The potatoes can be roasted ahead and stored in the refrigerator, covered, up to 2 days.

1½ pounds new potatoes, scrubbed well

Olive oil

Coarse sea salt and freshly ground black pepper

1 Preheat the oven to 350°F.

2 Roast the potatoes on a baking sheet for 1 hour, or until they are easily pierced with a thin knife.

3 Cover your hand with a kitchen towel and gently smash each potato to flatten it.

4 Heat a large sauté pan over medium-high heat, and generously coat the bottom of the pan with olive oil. Panfry the potatoes until they are crispy and golden brown, about 5 minutes on each side. Transfer the potatoes to paper towels to drain and sprinkle with salt and pepper.

Quince-Stuffed Veal Breast with Roasted Fennel and Apples

M ▪ *Serves 6 to 8 generously*

Though quinces have been around for millennia, every time I prepare them at the restaurant, my customers think I'm doing something new and fancy. Similar in appearance to apples, quinces are dry and astringent when cut open and much too hard for eating out of hand. The trick with quinces is to cook them slowly, so their pectin releases to thicken the mixture. Here, the quince helps to hold together a sweet and savory stuffing mixture simply made from fruit and seasonings.

MAKE AHEAD/STORAGE This recipe is perfect for holidays, as it feeds a crowd, is very festive, and can be made ahead for serving. The veal can be roasted and the sauce made and stored separately in the refrigerator, covered, up to 2 days. Bring veal to room temperature, then reheat in a baking dish, covered, at 350°F until warmed through. Warm pan sauce over low heat.

Olive oil

2 apples, preferably Granny Smith, peeled, cored, and diced

3 quinces, peeled, cored, and diced

1½ cups chopped shallots (about 8 medium)

3 garlic cloves, chopped

½ cup chopped fresh flat-leaf parsley

2 tablespoons chopped fresh thyme

1 tablespoon chopped fresh rosemary

1 bottle (750 ml) dry red wine, such as Cabernet Sauvignon (try Baron Herzog)

2½ cups Chicken Stock (page 15)

Kosher salt and freshly ground black pepper

1 boneless veal breast, butterflied by your butcher (about 4 pounds when bones are removed)

Roasted Fennel and Apples (recipe follows)

1 Heat a medium saucepan over medium heat, and lightly coat the bottom of the pan with olive oil. Slowly cook the apples and quinces until the apples are slightly softened, about 15 minutes. Add 1 cup of the chopped shallots and the garlic, and continue cooking until the shallots have softened, about 15 minutes. Add the parsley, thyme, and rosemary, 1 cup of the wine, ½ cup of the stock, and salt and pepper, and continue to cook until the liquid has been reduced to a glaze and the mixture is very soft and falling apart, about 1 hour. Remove the pan from the heat, and let the mixture cool completely.

Fall

2 Preheat the oven to 325°F.

3 Lay the veal breast on a work surface with the short end facing you. Spread the stuffing evenly over the meat, leaving a 1-inch border on all sides, and roll up the meat. Using kitchen string, tie the breast every 2 to 3 inches to hold the meat closed. Season the veal with salt and pepper.

4 Heat a large sauté pan over medium-high heat, and lightly coat the bottom of the pan with olive oil. Brown the veal on all sides. Transfer the veal to a lightly oiled roasting pan or baking dish (set sauté pan aside for making sauce), and roast veal in the oven until a meat thermometer inserted in the center of the meat registers 140°F, about 1½ hours. Transfer the veal to a platter and let rest, loosely covered with foil.

5 While veal is roasting make pan sauce. Drain any fat from the sauté pan and heat over medium heat. Add the remaining ½ cup shallots and sauté until they are lightly colored, gently scraping up any browned bits that remain in the pan. Add the remaining wine and simmer until the wine has reduced to about 1 cup, about 30 minutes. Add the remaining 2 cups stock, and continue to simmer until the sauce has reduced again to about 1 cup, about 20 minutes more. Adjust the seasoning with salt and pepper, and keep sauce warm over low heat.

6 To serve, slice the veal into 1-inch slices and place on a bed of Roasted Fennel and Apples. Drizzle the veal with sauce and serve extra sauce on the side.

Roasted Fennel and Apples

P ■ *Serves 6*

Instead of the crunch and acidity that you expect from a raw fennel and apple combination, this roasted mixture is mellow and slightly caramelized. Put the baking dish in the oven to roast when the veal has cooked for about 30 minutes.

- 2 medium fennel bulbs, trimmed and thinly sliced
- 4 medium apples (use 2 or more varieties for color and flavor), peeled, cored, and thinly sliced
- 2 medium leeks, white and light green parts only (save the dark green tops for stock), cut into julienne

Extra-virgin olive oil

Kosher salt and freshly ground black pepper

Preheat the oven to 325°F. Toss the fennel, apples, and leeks in a large bowl with olive oil to coat lightly and season with salt and pepper. Transfer the mixture to a baking dish and roast, stirring occasionally, until the mixture is browned and the apples are fairly soft, about 1 hour.

A Duo of Baked Apples

Here are two variations on baked apples, one of my favorite dishes for fall. The sweet variation makes a wonderful dessert, the savory one is a perfect side. Serve the dessert with Apple, Honey, and Walnut Sorbet (page 192) to make it extra special.

Baked Apples with Dates and Apricots

P ■ *Serves 6*

I think that many people (myself included) can get hung up on making holiday desserts. The problem with so many cakes, pies, and other treats is that they feel too heavy after a big meal. That's not to mention the massive number of calories that are packed into some favorites! Here's a solution: Baked apples are picture perfect and really very good for you. Place them on a gorgeous platter, spoon some sorbet around them and feel good about serving your family something natural and healthy.

MAKE AHEAD/STORAGE Apples can be baked 4 hours ahead and kept loosely covered at room temperature.

½ cup chopped pitted dates

½ cup chopped dried apricots

1 tablespoon pomegranate molasses (see Sources, page 257, and page 161 for more information)

3 tablespoons best-quality honey

¾ cup sweet white wine, such as Riesling

1 teaspoon ground cinnamon

Pinch of ground cloves

⅛ teaspoon freshly grated nutmeg

6 large firm apples, cored, preferably Pink Lady or Rome Beauty

1 Preheat the oven to 300°F.

2 Pulse the dates and apricots in a food processor 10 to 12 times, until the fruits are chopped and clumping together. You don't want them to form a smooth paste. Transfer the fruit to a bowl and stir in the pomegranate molasses, ¼ cup of the wine, and cinnamon, cloves, and nutmeg.

3 Stuff the mixture into the cored apples. You should have enough stuffing to generously stuff the apples and have some of the stuffing "pop" out of the top of the apples (I love this part, as it gets crispy on top).

4 Place the apples in a baking dish, and pour the remaining ½ cup wine around the apples. Bake the apples until they are soft and fairly wrinkly, 30 to 45 minutes. Occasionally, spoon some of the wine and juices onto the apples so they do not dry out.

5 Serve the apples warm or at room temperature with some of the cooking juices spooned around the apples.

Baked Apples with Shallots and Herbs

M and P ■ *Serves 6*

Who says apples have to be only for dessert? This savory variation is perfect served alongside any poultry, especially duck.

MAKE AHEAD/STORAGE Apples can be baked 4 hours ahead and kept loosely covered at room temperature.

6 medium shallots, thinly sliced

1 garlic clove, chopped

¼ cup chopped fresh flat-leaf parsley

1 tablespoon chopped fresh thyme

2 teaspoons chopped fresh rosemary

½ cup dried cherries or cranberries

½ cup chopped dried figs

1 tablespoon pomegranate molasses (see Sources, page 257, and page 161 for more information)

3 tablespoons best-quality honey

¾ cup dry white wine, such as Sauvignon Blanc

6 large firm apples, cored, preferably Pink Lady or Rome Beauty

1 Heat a small sauté pan over medium heat, and lightly coat the bottom of the pan with olive oil. Sauté the shallots, stirring occasionally, until golden brown and caramelized, about 15 minutes. Stir in the garlic, parsley, thyme, and rosemary, and continue to cook until garlic is tender, about 5 minutes.

2 Preheat the oven to 300°F.

3 Pulse the cherries and figs in a food processor 10 to 12 times, until the fruits are chopped and clumping together. You don't want them to form a smooth paste. Transfer the fruit to a bowl and stir in the shallot mixture, pomegranate molasses, honey, and ¼ cup of the wine.

4 Stuff the mixture into the cored apples. You should have enough stuffing to generously stuff the apples and have some of the stuffing "pop" out of the top of the apples (I love this part, as it gets crispy on top).

5 Place the apples in a baking dish, and pour the remaining ½ cup wine around the apples. Bake the apples until they are soft and fairly wrinkly, 30 to 45 minutes. Occasionally, spoon some of the wine and juices onto the apples so they do not dry out.

6 Serve the apples warm with the cooking juices spooned around them.

Poached Pears

P ▪ *Serves 6*

I love the rich garnet color that the pears take on after they've been poached in this fragrant spiced wine syrup. I serve them as a simple dessert in the fall or winter, usually drizzled with Raspberry Coulis (page 29) or Chocolate Sauce (page 28), but plain is fine too. I also love them on a cheese plate with dried fruits and nuts, in place of a sweet dessert. Or forget about dessert altogether and slice them into a salad, or serve them with roasted meat.

MAKE AHEAD/STORAGE The pears can be stored in the poaching liquid, covered, in the refrigerator, up to 5 days. Remove pears and syrup from refrigerator an hour before serving.

1 bottle (750 ml) dry red wine, such as Merlot (try Baron Herzog)

2 cups water

3 cups sugar

2 bay leaves

1 branch fresh rosemary

1 sprig fresh thyme

5 whole black peppercorns

1 2-inch cinnamon stick

1 vanilla bean, split (or use a vanilla pod saved after seeds have been scraped out)

Grated zest of 1 lemon, slivered

6 medium firm-ripe pears (preferably Forelle, Bosc, or other firm-fleshed pear)

1 In a large nonreactive saucepan or stockpot, stir the wine with the water, sugar, bay leaves, rosemary, thyme, peppercorns, cinnamon, vanilla bean, and lemon zest, and bring to a boil over high heat.

2 Meanwhile, peel the pears and remove the cores with a melon baller. Reduce the wine mixture to a simmer and add the pears. Poach the pears until they are tender enough for a knife to pierce them without resistance, at least 20 minutes, longer if the pears are less ripe. Let the pears cool in the poaching liquid.

3 Remove the pears and set aside. Strain the poaching liquid through a sieve into a large saucepan and discard the solids. Bring the liquid to a boil, then reduce heat and simmer until the liquid is reduced to a thick syrup, about 45 minutes. Let syrup cool slightly, and serve the pears drizzled with the warm syrup.

Apple, Honey, and Walnut Sorbet

P ■ *Makes 1½ pints*

This sorbet is a great way to show off the fall flavors of apples and honey. I love to serve this with baked apples and a little glass of sweet Riesling. The flavor of the fruit really shines through. I enjoy the crunch of the nuts in the sorbet, but if you don't, just leave them out—the sorbet will be delicious anyway. Honey really varies in flavor and fragrance, so I urge you to taste a few kinds and find one you really enjoy. I usually use an organic summer flower honey. Farmers' markets are great sources for high-quality, flavorful honey.

MAKE AHEAD/STORAGE This sorbet can be made up to 4 days ahead and kept frozen. (See page 81 for more information on sorbets and granitas.)

2 cups water (bottled water yields a tastier sorbet), plus 2 tablespoons

¼ cup sugar

½ cup best-quality honey

5 cups peeled, cored, diced apples (4 to 5 large apples; use 2 or more varieties for best flavor)

1 teaspoon high-quality ground cinnamon

1 cup chopped walnuts (optional)

1 Place the sugar and 2 cups water in a medium saucepan and cook over low heat until the sugar has completely dissolved. Add the honey and remove from the heat. Allow the mixture to cool completely.

2 Cook the apples with remaining 2 tablespoons water in a medium saucepan over medium-low heat until they are very soft and break up when mashed with a fork, about 20 minutes. Remove pan from the heat and cool completely. Place the apples and honey syrup in a blender and process until the apples are broken up and the mixture is combined, or add the syrup to the apples and use an immersion blender to mix. Stir in the cinnamon. Chill completely.

3 Meanwhile, toast the walnuts, if using, in a dry sauté pan over low heat until they are fragrant and visibly darkened, about 7 minutes. Let cool completely.

4 Process the sorbet mixture in your ice cream machine, following the manufacturer's instructions. After the sorbet has been processed, fold in the toasted walnuts. Transfer the sorbet to a covered container and freeze until hard, at least 4 hours or overnight.

Cocoa Nib Biscotti

P ▪ *Makes 24 biscotti*

I prefer a cookie that stands up to dipping and saucing. Chocolate chip cookies can't compete with these crunchy biscotti, chockful of fragrant cocoa nibs. They are perfect for garnishing any granita or sorbet; they can be dipped in melted chocolate to jazz them up; or they're great all by themselves. I keep a batch in the freezer at home, and they're a staple at the restaurant.

MAKE AHEAD/STORAGE The biscotti can be stored at room temperature, covered, up to 3 days, or frozen for 1 month.

2½ cups all-purpose flour

¾ cup sugar, plus extra for sprinkling

1½ teaspoons baking powder

3 large eggs

Grated zest and juice of 1 lemon

1 teaspoon vanilla extract

6 ounces cocoa nibs* (about 1 cup)

Ground cinnamon

*Cocoa nibs are the hulled and roasted pieces of the cocoa bean before it is ground and the chocolate liquor is extracted. They are very fragrant and contain 54 percent cocoa butter solids. They are not at all sweet and are not really for eating out of hand (unless you are a die-hard chocolate fan like me). Cocoa nibs can be found *hechshered* in many gourmet shops and online. (See Sources, page 257.)

1 Preheat the oven to 375°F. Line a baking sheet with a double layer of parchment paper.

2 Place flour, sugar, and baking powder in the bowl of a stand mixer fitted with a paddle. Add the eggs, lemon zest and juice, and vanilla, and mix until the dough just comes together, about 2 minutes. (Do not overbeat.) Add the coca nibs and beat for another few seconds. Turn the dough out onto the baking sheet and form it into a 2×12 inch log.

3 Bake the dough until the top is lightly golden, about 12 minutes. Let the log cool slightly. Cut into ½-inch-thick slices. Return the cookies to the baking sheet a cut side up, and sprinkle tops with cinnamon and sugar. Bake the cookies again until they crisp up and the sugar melts slightly, about 5 minutes.

193

Fig Confit

P ■ *Makes about 3 cups*

Figs are one of my favorite fruits. I love their sexy little shape and their multitextural insides. The crunchy seeds and juicy flesh make them irresistible. They are really versatile and can be used in many recipes both sweet and savory. For an elegant, pareve dessert that is really rich yet light after an autumnal meal, layer the confit in a glass with Champagne Sabayon (page 30) and Chocolate Sorbet (page 197), and garnish with Cocoa Nib Biscotti (page 193).

MAKE AHEAD/STORAGE The figs can be stored in the refrigerator, covered, up to 2 weeks, or frozen for 3 months.

4 cups sugar

2 cups water

Grated zest and juice of 1 lemon

1 cinnamon stick, about 2 inches long

½ vanilla bean, split lengthwise

2½ to 3 pounds green or black figs, stemmed

1 Place the sugar, water, lemon juice and zest, and cinnamon in a medium saucepan, and scrape in the seeds from the vanilla bean half (save the pod for another use). Bring to a simmer over medium heat, stirring. Add the figs and reduce the heat to a slow simmer.

2 Gently poach the figs for 2 hours, until the poaching liquid has reduced and the figs are thick and similar to marmalade. Transfer the figs with a slotted spoon to a 1-quart container. Reserve the poaching liquid separately for vinaigrettes, wine reductions, or topping frozen desserts.

Chocolate Opera Torte
with Chocolate Ganache

P ■ *Serves 12*

This dessert is all about chocolate, so use the best-quality chocolate you can find (I prefer Valrhona or Callebaut). It's elegant, very rich, and impressive—a real show-stopper for very special occasions. I've made it for birthdays and for Shabbat dinners when I wanted to wow my guests. It looks like a lot of work, but it is pretty simple when taken in steps. Each component can be done in advance, and even the whole cake can be made ahead. For a stunning presentation, serve cake slices with Raspberry Coulis (page 29) or Champagne Sabayon (page 30).

MAKE AHEAD/STORAGE The roulades can be stored at room temperature, covered, up to 3 days, or frozen for 1 month. The ganache can be stored in the refrigerator, tightly covered, up to 5 days, or frozen for 1 month. The meringue layers can be stored at room temperature, tightly covered, up to 3 days. The completed cake can be stored in the refrigerator, covered, up to 3 days.

For the Roulades

6 ounces bittersweet chocolate, chopped

2 ounces unsweetened chocolate, chopped

⅓ cup brewed coffee, leftover Champagne or sparkling wine, or water

1 tablespoon vanilla extract

8 large eggs, separated, at room temperature

1 cup sugar

For the Ganache

28 ounces (1¾ pounds) highest-quality bittersweet chocolate, chopped

2 cups brewed espresso or strong coffee

4 large egg yolks

2 teaspoons vanilla extract

For the Meringue Layers

5 ounces hazelnuts or your favorite nut (about 1 cup), toasted, skins rubbed off, and finely chopped

4 large egg whites, at room temperature

1 teaspoon fresh lemon juice

½ cup sugar

¼ cup all-purpose flour

1 Make the Roulades Preheat the oven to 400°F. Line three 11½ × 17¼ × 1–inch baking sheets with parchment paper.

2 Melt the chocolates with the coffee in a small saucepan over medium-low heat,

Fall

stirring. Transfer the chocolate mixture to a bowl and whisk in the vanilla and egg yolks.

3 Whip the whites to soft peaks (you may need to do this in batches). Add the sugar and continue beating until the eggs are stiff and glossy. Stir one-third of the egg whites into the chocolate mixture until well combined. Gently fold in the remaining whites in two additions, and spread the batter in the prepared pans. Bake for 8 to 9 minutes, until the tops of the roulades are springy to the touch. Cool the roulades in their pans on a cooling rack.

4 **Make the Ganache** Melt the chocolate with the espresso in a medium saucepan over very low heat, stirring. (Watch the pan very closely, as the chocolate can scorch).

5 Place the egg yolks in bowl of a stand mixer fitted with a whisk. Turn on the motor to medium-low, and slowly pour a small amount of the chocolate mixture into the egg yolks to raise their temperature slowly. Slowly add the remaining chocolate, mixing at medium speed, and continue to mix until the ganache has cooled, about 5 minutes. Occasionally turn off the motor and scrape down the sides and the bottom of the bowl. Transfer the ganache to a large container with a tight-fitting lid.

6 **Make the Meringue Layers** Lower oven temperature to 375°F for the meringues and line two 11½ × 17¼ × 1–inch baking sheets with parchment paper.

7 Place the egg whites in a mixing bowl fitted with a whisk and add the lemon juice. Begin mixing the whites at low speed until

they are quite foamy, about 3 minutes. Increase the speed to high and continue whipping until the whites form medium peaks. Slowly add the sugar and continue whipping until stiff peaks form. Fold in the nuts and flour. Spread the meringue in the prepared baking sheets. Bake until the meringue layers are golden brown and no longer sticky, about 15 minutes. Remove the meringue layers on their parchment paper to racks to cool thoroughly.

8 Place 2 cups of the cold ganache in the bowl of a stand mixer fitted with a paddle. Whip the ganache until it is light and fluffy, about 5 minutes.

9 To assemble the cake, invert a roulade layer onto a cutting board or large platter. Peel off the parchment paper and generously spread on a layer of ganache. Place a meringue layer on the ganache, peel off the parchment (don't worry if the meringue cracks), and spread on another layer of ganache. Invert another roulade layer on top of the cake and continue to layer the ganache, meringue, ganache, and the final cake layer. Cut the cake in half to form 2 smaller rectangles. Top one half with another layer of ganache and place the other half on top.

10 Transfer remaining ganache to a small saucepan and heat gently, stirring, until melted. Pour the melted ganache over the top of the cake. (Do not try to spread it with a spatula, as it will become dull and smear.) Chill the cake, uncovered, for 1 hour. Trim off the sides to expose the layers before serving.

11 To serve, cut the cake into diamond shapes and serve.

Chocolate Sorbet

P ■ *Makes about 1½ pints*

I love this sorbet as the flavor of really good chocolate comes through. Sometimes I don't want heavy-textured chocolate ice cream, even when I am not eating meat. I just want chocolate! This recipe is all about satisfying that craving for pure chocolate decadence. Feel free to stir in more chopped chocolate (or toasted nuts, chopped dried fruit, or crushed cookies) after processing. Pass Chocolate Sauce (page 28) and Cocoa Nib Biscotti (page 193) to complete the experience.

MAKE AHEAD/STORAGE This sorbet can be made up to 4 days ahead and kept frozen. (See page 81 for more information on sorbets and granitas.)

- 2 cups water (bottled water yields a tastier sorbet)
- 1½ cups sugar
- 2 tablespoons light corn syrup
- ¼ cup cocoa powder
- 8 ounces best-quality bittersweet chocolate, such as Callebaut, chopped fine

1 Heat the water, sugar, corn syrup, and cocoa powder in a small saucepan over low heat, stirring until the sugar is dissolved and the cocoa powder is incorporated. (The cocoa powder will float on top of the water at first, until it becomes saturated.)

2 Place the chopped chocolate into a deep bowl and pour the hot cocoa syrup over it. Allow the mixture to sit for 10 minutes before stirring, to melt the chocolate. Combine thoroughly with an immersion blender or process in a blender. Cool completely.

3 Process the sorbet mixture in your ice cream machine, following the manufacturer's instructions. Transfer the sorbet to a covered container and freeze until hard, at least 4 hours or overnight, before serving.

WINTER

Announced by all the trumpets of the sky,
Arrives the snow.

RALPH WALDO EMERSON

ALTHOUGH EACH SEASON BRINGS ITS own rewards, winter is probably my favorite time of the year. For someone who loves fresh fruit and vegetables as much as I do, this may be surprising, but I actually find it an inspiring time to be a cook. Although produce is scarce, especially toward the end of the season, I look forward to the challenge of cooking with winter foods.

What I love most about winter is that everyone is actually hungry. I don't need to tempt overheated diners with delicate salads and cooling soups. When the weather is treacherous, we seek out real comfort—and real food. Snowstorms force us inside to our fuzzy slippers, roaring fires, and to big, flavorful meals shared with friends and family. Winter is a time to hibernate and enjoy each other's company. This is my chance to cook stick-to-your-ribs stews, like Braised Veal Shanks with Moroccan Spices and Mango "Gremolata"

(page 241) and slow-baked dishes like Cassoulet with Beef Short Ribs, Duck Confit, White Beans, and Mustard Crust (page 236). They're the kind of dishes that can cook for hours on their own, and all I need to do is give an occasional stir and an appreciative sniff to the aromas coming from my stove.

The beginning of winter always starts off with a bang. I love the squashes and root vegetables that can still be found in the market. The first frost gives me an excuse to make chestnuts, one of my favorite cold-weather treats. A classic American delicacy, chestnuts present a culinary puzzle to many home cooks: How do you pry them out of their smooth, glossy shells? Although they require a bit of extra effort, the end result is a sweet, slightly starchy bite, with a nutty flavor unlike any other. Chestnuts appear in the market late in the fall and stick around for only about a month, so it's wise to stock up while you can; then use them in a delicious side dish of Caramelized Cipollini Onions, Chestnuts, and Savoy Cabbage (page 210). (Turn to page 166 for another chestnut recipe—Braised Chestnuts, Fennel, Leeks, and Golden Raisins—and instructions on peeling.)

I love to use parsnips in winter soups. This ivory-hued root vegetable sweetens after the frost. It's similar to a carrot but even sweeter when cooked, and earthier in flavor. It purees to a smooth and silky texture that's popular with adults and kids alike. I like to make a big batch of Parsnip and Roasted Garlic Bisque (page 205) to serve on a chilly Shabbat eve or Shabbat lunch. I also roast parsnips along with other root vegetables to make Vegetable "Chips" (page 223) that are even more addictive than french fries. The technique works with any root, so give it a try.

When produce becomes too meager and the subzero weather keeps me indoors, I like to compensate with grains, which are a terrific accompaniment to many dishes. There are so many grains, rices and other starches to try—farro, barley, wild and brown rice, even cornmeal for creamy polenta—I can keep tasting and experimenting with them all winter long. Some warming results are Wild Rice Soup with Porcini Mushrooms (page 203), Polenta Fries (page 218), and Arancini di Farro (page 207).

Wintertime does not have to mean no fruits when tropical and citrus fruits are still plentiful and versatile. Nothing makes the house smell as good as pineapple roasting (page 243), its natural juices mingling with the vanilla bean and brown sugar: exotic, luscious, and familiar all at once. I rely on citrus juice and zests for adding bursts of flavor and still appreciate light-textured sorbets, like tangy Grapefruit Sorbet (page 251) for a quick and refreshing finish to a hearty dinner. And wintertime is when I always say bring on the chocolate! Although I'm a year-round chocolate lover, there's something wonderful about indulging in deep, bittersweet chocolate delights when it's bitterly cold outside.

SOUPS AND STARTERS

Wild Rice Soup with Porcini Mushrooms

Parsnip and Roasted Garlic Bisque

Arancini di Farro

Braised Duck Ravioli

Creamy Polenta with Mushroom and
Rosemary Ragout

MAIN DISHES

Macaroni and Cheese Casserole

Pasta Puttanesca

Chicken Cacciatore

Braised Chicken with Mushrooms,
Leeks, and Red Pearl Onions

Crispy Cod with Lemon Vinaigrette
and Vegetable "Chips"

Red Snapper in Romesco Sauce

Roasted Red Snapper with Charmoula
and Red Lentils

Tuna Confit with Winter Grilled Salad
and Mixed Olive Tapenade

Horseradish-Potato Crusted Grouper
and Remoulade

Roasted Grouper with Yukon Gold Potatoes
and Garlicky Eggplant-Tomato Sauce

Pan Seared Rib-Eye Steaks

Cassoulet with Beef Short Ribs,
Duck Confit, White Beans,
and Mustard Crust

Slow-Roasted Short Ribs

Braised Veal Shanks with Moroccan
Spices and Mango "Gremolata"

DESSERTS

Roasted Pineapple
with Pineapple Sorbet

S'mores Cake

Sticky Toffee Pudding

Devil's Food Cake

Pistachio Sorbet

Grapefruit Sorbet

Peanut Butter and Jelly Sorbet

Wild Rice Soup with Porcini Mushrooms

M ▪ *Serves 6*

This soup is pure comfort. If you just mention "wild rice soup" people get warm and cozy thoughts. I love to eat this as a light dinner or with a more hearty winter meal. The porcini mushrooms add a touch of richness. I have made this soup with turkey stock and even added chunks of leftover turkey to the soup for a kind of chowder. Feel free to improvise and make this winter dish your own.

MAKE AHEAD/STORAGE The soup can be stored in the refrigerator, covered, up to 3 days, or frozen for 1 month

½ cup wild rice

Olive oil

1 large onion, diced small

2 medium carrots, peeled and diced small

2 celery stalks, small diced small

1 cup thinly sliced cremini mushrooms

½ cup dried porcini mushrooms (about 2 ounces)

1 cup dry white wine, such as Sauvignon Blanc

4 cups Chicken Stock (page 15) or water

Kosher salt and freshly ground black pepper

3 tablespoons chicken fat or olive oil

3 tablespoons all-purpose flour

Porcini Oil (page 148, optional), for serving

1 Put the rice and water to cover in a large saucepan and place the pan over medium heat. Cook the rice until it has split and is tender, 30 to 40 minutes. Drain the rice of any excess liquid and set aside.

2 Place a large sauté pan over medium heat. Lightly coat the bottom of the pan with olive oil. Sauté the onion, carrots, celery, and cremini mushrooms until lightly browned and fragrant, 5 to 7 minutes.

3 Combine the rice, sautéed vegetables, and dried mushrooms in a large saucepan or stockpot. Add the wine and broth and season to taste with salt and pepper. (You may need to add more liquid to cover the mixture.) Bring to a simmer and cook for 30 minutes.

4 In a sauté pan over medium heat, place the chicken fat. Add the flour and whisk until the roux is smooth and creamy. Continue to cook until the roux has darkened to a golden brown, about 10 minutes. Spoon the roux into the soup and stir to combine. This will thicken the soup and make it creamier. Adjust seasoning to taste with salt and pepper.

5 Serve the soup in large bowls, drizzled with Porcini Oil, if desired.

Parsnip and Roasted Garlic Bisque

M and P ▪ *Serves 6 generously*

I don't know why my mother never made parsnips for me when I was a child. They are everything she likes in a vegetable: beautiful ivory color, sweet earthy flavor, and they pair nicely with other foods. This soup has a velvety texture. Try it at home; your kids will like it, too!

MAKE AHEAD/STORAGE This soup can be stored in the refrigerator, covered, up to 2 days.

- 8 medium parsnips, peeled and cut into 1-inch pieces
- Olive oil
- Kosher salt and freshly ground black pepper
- 1 head of garlic
- 2 large leeks, light green parts only (save the dark green tops for stock and the white parts for other uses), thinly sliced
- 2 teaspoons fresh thyme leaves
- 2 tablespoons fresh lemon juice
- ½ cup dry white wine, such as Sauvignon Blanc
- 4 to 5 cups Chicken Stock (page 15)
- Crunchy Herbed Croutons (recipe follows)
- Thyme sprigs

1 Preheat the oven to 300°F. Lightly toss the parsnips with olive oil and salt and pepper to taste and lay them on a baking sheet. Roast the parsnips until they are caramelized and soft, about 45 minutes depending upon thickness.

2 Turn the oven up to 400°F. Cut ½ inch off the nonroot end of the head of garlic to expose the cloves. Place the garlic in a small baking dish or ovenproof ramekin and lightly sprinkle with salt and pepper. Lightly drizzle with olive oil and add enough water to come about 1 inch up the side of garlic. Cover the dish with foil, and roast until the garlic is lightly browned and soft enough to squeeze out of the skins, about 1 hour. Set aside to let the garlic cool.

3 Heat a large sauté pan over medium heat, and lightly coat the bottom of the pan with olive oil. Cook the leeks until they are very soft and translucent, about 20 minutes.

4 Squeeze out the individual cloves of garlic from the roasted head.

5 Puree the roasted parsnips, garlic, leeks, thyme, lemon juice, wine, 4 cups stock, and salt and pepper to taste in batches in a blender or food processor. Place the soup in a large saucepan and simmer for 30 minutes. (Thin with more stock if necessary.)

6 Serve soup in large bowls, garnished with the croutons and thyme sprigs.

Crunchy Herbed Croutons

P ▪ *Makes about 1 cup*

Homemade croutons are wonderful to have around—you can toss them into soups, salads, and stews for an extra bit of garlicky crunch.

MAKE AHEAD/STORAGE The croutons can be stored at room temperature, covered, up to 5 days.

2 garlic cloves

Kosher salt

2 slices of bread, crusts trimmed off (leftover challah works well for this)

Extra-virgin olive oil

¼ cup chopped mixed fresh herbs such as thyme, parsley, chives, or rosemary

Freshly ground black pepper

1 Place the garlic cloves and 1 teaspoon salt in a mortar and pound to a paste; or use a cutting board and the side of your knife to smash and scrape the garlic with the salt. Set aside.

2 Cut the bread into tiny cubes. Place a medium sauté pan over medium hat. Lightly coat the bottom of the pan with olive oil. Sauté the bread cubs until they are lightly browned, about 5 minutes. Add the herbs, garlic, and more olive oil. Continue to cook the croutons until they are crispy and golden. Season with salt and pepper.

Arancini di Farro

D ▪ *Serves 8*

When cooked, farro, an ancient grain, is creamy and starchy like risotto, but it has the flavor and texture of barley. *Arancini* are a southern Italian specialty meaning "little oranges," a reference to the small, round shape of these croquettes. I like the idea of using farro for this twist on fried foods for Hanukkah. Using an ancient grain helps us to recall the culinary traditions of our past.

MAKE AHEAD/STORAGE The arancini will stay crispy for 4 hours at room temperature, uncovered. Reheat on a baking sheet, uncovered at 300°F for about 5 minutes just before serving.

½ pound farro* (about 2 cups)

4 to 6 cups water or Vegetable Stock (page 17)

Kosher salt and freshly ground black pepper

½ cup freshly grated Parmesan cheese

½ cup ricotta cheese

2 tablespoons chopped fresh flat-leaf parsley, plus extra for sprinkling, if desired

1 teaspoon chopped fresh thyme

3 large eggs

2 cups fresh, untoasted bread crumbs

Extra-virgin olive oil

*Farro can be purchased online or at specialty markets. (See Sources, page 257.)

1 Rinse the farro under running water to remove any loose husks. Place the farro in a large saucepan over medium heat. Add 4 cups water and a teaspoon salt and boil for 15 minutes. Lower the heat, cover the pan and cook the farro until tender, thick and creamy (a wooden spoon should almost stand up in it), about 45 minutes. Season with salt and pepper. If the farro seems too hard, add the remaining water and continue cooking until done.

2 Remove the pan from the heat. Place the farro in a shallow dish and stir in the Parmesan cheese. Cover the dish and refrigerate the farro until completely cold.

3 Place the ricotta cheese in a bowl, add the parsley and thyme, and season with salt and pepper.

4 Scoop the farro with a tablespoon and roll into a small ball. With your finger, push a small indentation into the ball. Spoon a small amount of the ricotta cheese mixture into the farro, and close the opening by rolling the ball between your palms. Set aside and continue until all the farro is used.

5 Beat the eggs in a large, shallow plate. Place the bread crumbs, seasoned with salt and pepper, in another shallow plate. Place a medium saucepan over medium-high heat and heat about 2 inches oil to approximately 350°F.

6 Dip a farro ball into the eggs, then roll it into the breadcrumbs. Place the ball on a separate plate. When you have coated 6 to 8 balls, place them in the hot oil and fry until golden brown. Remove the balls to a plate lined with paper towels. Continue coating and frying the rest of the balls.

7 Sprinkle arancini with more chopped parsley, if desired, before serving warm or at room temperature.

Braised Duck Ravioli

M ■ *Serves 4*

This ravioli is a twist on the classic. The ravioli are not sealed, but rather the filling is piled on top of the pasta. You can use the pasta recipe (page 20) or use store-bought wonton skins for a shortcut. The pasta sauce is simply the braising liquid from the duck, reduced to enhance its richness. Adding the Caramelized Cipollini Onions, Chestnuts, and Savoy Cabbage (recipe follows) makes this a beautifully wintry first course or lunch.

MAKE AHEAD/STORAGE The duck and braising liquid can be prepared through Step 4 and stored in the refrigerator, covered, up to 2 days. Reheat sauce before serving.

- 4 whole duck legs
- 1 bottle (750 ml) sweet white wine, such as Riesling
- 1 medium Spanish onion, coarsely chopped
- 1 medium carrot, peeled and coarsely chopped
- 1 celery stalk, coarsely chopped
- Bouquet garni (several stems of fresh thyme, 1 bay leaf, and 6 parsley stems, tied together with kitchen twine)
- 1 cup Chicken Stock (page 15)
- Kosher salt and freshly ground black pepper
- About ½ recipe Pasta Dough (page 20), rolled and cut into twelve 2-inch squares (make extra in case they tear) or 8 store-bought wonton skins
- Caramelized Cipollini Onions, Chestnuts, and Savoy Cabbage (recipe follows)

1 Heat a large sauté pan over medium heat. Cook the duck legs, skin side down, until the skin is browned and most of the fat has rendered off, about 25 minutes. Keep draining the fat from the pan into a small bowl. (Reserved duck fat can be stored, if desired, and used for sautéing.)

2 Transfer the browned duck legs to a large nonreactive saucepan or Dutch oven and add the wine, onion, carrot, celery, bouquet garni, and stock. Cover the pan and place over medium-low heat. Braise the legs until they are very tender and the meat falls from the bone, about 2 hours.

3 Remove the legs from the pan. Strain the liquid (discard the solids) and return the liquid to the pan to cool. Pull off and discard the duck skin, and pull out and discard the bones. Shred the meat from the legs into a bowl and set aside.

4 Skim the fat from the braising liquid and return to the heat. Simmer the liquid until it is reduced to about 1½ cups and is deeply flavorful and slightly thickened, about 30 minutes.

5 Bring a large pot of lightly salted water to a boil. Lightly toss the caramelized onion mixture in a sauté pan over medium to reheat. Add the shredded duck to the onion mixture and adjust seasoning with salt and pepper.

6 Cook the pasta until it is al dente, 3 to 4 minutes, and drain. (Cook wonton skins, if using, in same manner.)

7 To serve, place a pasta square in a shallow bowl. Spoon a generous mound of duck mixture on top of the pasta. Top with another pasta square and lightly spoon reduced duck juices around the ravioli.

Caramelized Cipollini Onions, Chestnuts, and Savoy Cabbage

P ▪ *Makes 3 cups*

Chestnuts require a bit of work to peel, but the method described on page 167 seems to always work well. The season for fresh chestnuts lasts into the winter months and perfectly coincides with the times that I like to prepare my favorite, full-flavored duck dishes. I consider duck and chestnuts an ideal pairing.

MAKE AHEAD/STORAGE The caramelized onion mixture can be prepared through step 2 three days ahead. Rewarm onion mixture while cooking the cabbage.

6 golden cipollini onions, peeled and halved

12 chestnuts, peeled (see page 167)

1 Granny Smith apple, cored, peeled, and diced

¼ cup golden raisins

½ cup light brown sugar

¼ cup sweet white wine, such as Riesling

Olive oil

1 small head of savoy cabbage (about 1½ pounds), quartered, cored, and thinly sliced (you should have about 3 cups)

Kosher salt and freshly ground black pepper

1 Combine the onions, chestnuts, apple, and raisins in a large bowl. Stir in the brown sugar and wine.

2 Cook the onion mixture in a medium saucepan over medium-low heat, occasionally stirring, until the onions and chestnuts are deeply browned, caramelized and "gooey," about 45 minutes.

3 Place a medium sauté pan over medium-high heat and lightly coat the bottom of the pan with olive oil. Add the cabbage and season with salt and pepper. Stir frequently until the cabbage has wilted and has given off most of its water (about 10 minutes). Stir the cabbage into the onion mixture and adjust seasoning.

Duck

Duck is probably my favorite food—I enjoy it so much that I cook with it year-round, matching it with the best ingredients of each season. If you're hesitant to cook duck at home, fear not! Start off by preparing duck breasts. You can simply order the duck breasts, already deboned, from your butcher. Later, when you become more confident, you can order a whole duck with the breasts deboned and save all the other parts in your freezer: Then you can use the legs, the trimmed fat, and any fat drained from cooking for other recipes like Cassoulet with Beef Short Ribs, Duck Confit, White Beans, and Mustard Crust (page 236). (I've tried making stock from kosher duck carcasses and wingtips, but unfortunately it turns out unacceptably salty.)

Over the years, I've learned a lot about cooking duck, especially kosher duck, which I find far superior to the nonkosher "gourmet" brands. Kosher ducks are smaller and tastier. They do have a lot of salt, so season them with care, adding salt sparingly or not at all. Ducks are very fatty, so it's important to always prick or score the skin and fat layer before cooking to allow the fat to escape from under the skin. A small, sharp paring knife is the best tool for this.

The method I like most for cooking duck breasts is to start them in a cold pan; a heated pan would cause the skin to darken too quickly before the fat has rendered off. There are many techniques for cooking duck breast; I have found that this method yields crispy skin without all the fat. This renders off the most fat and crisps the skin. When it comes to roasting a whole duck, I find that it helps to boil it first, to drive out all the fat.

Making duck does require some effort, but it's certainly worth it for the rich, succulent meat and the crispy skin. You won't regret it!

If you're a duck fanatic like me, try these recipes:

Braised Duck Ravioli (page 209)

Crispy Roasted Duck with Balsamic Pan Sauce (page 165)

Duck Breast Salad with Peppered Strawberry Vinaigrette (page 53)

Duck Breast Schnitzel with Maple Mashed Sweet Potatoes and Braised Swiss Chard (page 162)

Roasted Duck Breast with Cherry—Red Wine Reduction (page 118)

Creamy Polenta with Mushroom and Rosemary Ragout

D ▪ *Serves 4 as a starter or side*

I am real fan of creamy comfort foods and winter is the perfect time of year to indulge. I love the texture of polenta and the way that it complements so many dishes. Polenta is really Italian cornmeal. It can be prepared in a creamy style, such as in this recipe, or firm and then fried as in the Polenta Fries (page 218). The nutty, earthy mushrooms combined with the herbs make a hearty, meatless topping. This dish makes a great opener for a dairy meal—or for the rare occasion when I'm eating solo, I love to just curl up on the couch with a bowlful.

For the Ragout

Extra-virgin olive oil

2 medium shallots, thinly sliced

½ cup stemmed, halved cremini mushrooms

½ cup halved button mushrooms

¼ cup dried porcini mushrooms (about 1 ounce)

¼ cup dry white wine, such as Sauvignon Blanc

¼ cup heavy cream

3 tablespoons unsalted butter (optional)

2 tablespoons chopped fresh flat-leaf parsley

1 teaspoon chopped fresh thyme

2 tablespoons chopped fresh rosemary

2 tablespoons fresh lemon juice

Kosher salt and freshly ground black pepper

For the Polenta

1 cup Italian coarse cornmeal or yellow cornmeal

4 cups water

½ teaspoon kosher salt

½ cup mascarpone cheese

¼ cup freshly grated Parmesan cheese

Freshly ground black pepper

Chopped fresh flat-leaf parsley (optional)

1 Make the Ragout Place a medium sauté pan over medium heat. Lightly oil the pan. Sauté the shallots until lightly browned, about 3 minutes. Add the mushrooms and sauté until golden brown, about 7 minutes. Add the wine and simmer until reduced by half, about 3 minutes. Add the cream and simmer gently until reduced by half, about 3 minutes more. Add the butter, if using, the parsley, thyme, rosemary, and lemon juice, season with salt and pepper, and turn down the heat to medium-low. Simmer the mushroom mixture about 15 minutes to allow the flavors to combine.

2 **Make the Polenta** While the mushrooms are simmering, stir together the water, cornmeal, and salt in a large, high-sided saucepan, and place over medium heat. Cook the polenta stirring with a wooden spoon, vigorously at first, until it is very thick and fairly dry, 15 to 20 minutes. Turn the heat down slightly when the polenta begins to thicken and sputter. (Be careful, as the polenta can sputter out of the pan and cause quite a burn.) Remove the pan from the heat, and stir in the mascarpone and Parmesan cheeses. Adjust the seasoning with salt and pepper. If necessary, keep the polenta warm, covered, on very low heat.

3 To serve, pour the polenta into large shallow bowls or a serving platter. Spoon the mushroom ragout over the top. Sprinkle with additional parsley if desired.

Macaroni and Cheese Casserole

D ▪ *Serves 6 generously*

My oldest son Zachary is a champion for this dish. He is always happy when I serve it. One time, he came home desperate for a copy of the recipe, as he was going to a friend's house for a card game. He needed the recipe and made sure that I sat down and typed it out so that his friends would be able to follow it. After assuring him that I knew how to write a recipe, I asked why he needed it. He never really said. I sometimes flatter myself that the recipe was part of the "pot" at the card game that evening! Needless to say it is family favorite and a real comfort dish.

MAKE AHEAD/STORAGE This casserole can be assembled (through Step 5) up to 1 day ahead and stored in the refrigerator, covered. Bring to room temperature before baking.

Unsalted butter, for greasing the casserole

1 pound macaroni or favorite pasta shape

1 cup sour cream

5 tablespoons unsalted butter

3 tablespoons all-purpose flour

1 medium shallot, finely chopped

2 garlic cloves, finely chopped

2 cups milk (preferably whole milk)

3 cups grated Cheddar cheese (¾ pound)

½ cup dry bread crumbs (panko is perfect for this)*

Kosher salt and freshly ground black pepper to taste

*Panko is a Japanese bread crumb with a coarse flake. It is very light and becomes very crispy when fried. It makes a superb crust for many items. Panko is available with a *hechsher* online or at specialty markets. (See Sources, page 257.)

1 Preheat the oven to 350°F. Lightly grease an ovenproof casserole or baking dish.

2 Bring a large saucepan with salted water to a boil. Cook the pasta until al dente (about 10 minutes depending upon size of

214

pasta; follow package directions). Drain pasta and transfer to a large bowl. Stir in the sour cream and set aside.

3 Meanwhile, melt 3 tablespoons butter in a large sauté pan over medium heat.. Add the shallot and garlic and cook until light golden brown, about 3 minutes. Add flour and stir together. Cook the roux for several minutes to remove the raw flour flavor.

4 While shallot mixture is cooking, in a small saucepan, heat the milk until simmering. Add

milk all at once to flour mixture, whisking to prevent lumps. Cook until thickened, 3 to 5 minutes. Remove from the heat. Add the cheese and stir until melted and incorporated. Season the cheese sauce with salt and pepper and stir into the pasta. Transfer the pasta to the greased casserole.

5 Melt the remaining 2 tablespoons butter. Stir in the bread crumbs and sprinkle on top of casserole. Bake until bubbly and golden, about 30 minutes.

Pasta Puttanesca

D or P ■ *Serves 4 to 6*

This Neopolitan classic is a specialty of my friend and co-chef of many years, Dennis. He threw this together one night when we were looking for something to eat that was not on the menu. This certainly fit the bill and has since become a late-night staff favorite. We also eat this pasta so often in our house that it's scary to calculate just how much we consume in a month. All of my kids love it. Jonah (my youngest) was a holdout and would not even look at it for a long time. He now requests it and gobbles up large bowls of it.

Note that the anchovies don't make this fishy; keep 'em! They "melt" in the olive oil, become nutty-flavored, and add depth. This is a pantry dish. You can have everything on hand (except the parsley) in your cabinets and whip it together in less than thirty minutes.

1 pound long pasta (we love perciatelli or bucatini, long, hollow strands with grooves to hold the sauce)

Extra-virgin olive oil

5 garlic cloves, thinly sliced

8 anchovy fillets (packed in olive oil), lightly chopped

½ teaspoon chili flakes (or to taste)

1 cup diced tomatoes

½ cup canned tomato sauce

¼ cup capers, drained

½ cup pitted, sliced kalamata olives

¼ cup chopped fresh flat-leaf parsley, plus extra for garnish

Kosher salt and freshly ground black pepper

¼ cup grated Parmesan cheese (optional)

1 Bring a large pot of salted water to a boil. Cook the pasta until it is al dente, 7 to 9 minutes or according to package directions (we like it very toothy in our house!), and drain.

2 Meanwhile, place a large sauté pan over medium heat. Lightly coat the bottom of the pan with extra-virgin olive oil. Add the garlic, anchovies, and chili flakes. Stir until the anchovies break up and almost melt, about 2 minutes. Be careful not to brown the garlic. Add the tomatoes and sauce. Stir to combine. Add the capers and olives. Cook for 5 minutes to combine the flavors. Add the parsley and salt and pepper to taste.

3 Just before serving add the cooked pasta to the hot sauce and toss together over low heat for a minute. Transfer pasta to a large warmed serving bowl, and serve garnished with additional chopped parsley, tasty extra-virgin olive oil, and grated Parmesan cheese, if desired.

Chicken Cacciatore

M ■ *Serves 6 to 8*

This Italian-American dish refers to the Italian term *alla cacciatora*, which means "hunter-style." It is a tasty concoction that doesn't really follow any rules. Cacciatore generally includes tomatoes, mushrooms, wine, herbs, and usually chicken. It is fairly easy to prepare and reheats well. It feeds a crowd when you double or triple it. Serve it with Polenta Fries (recipe follows), cooked fresh pasta (see page 20), or cooked dried pasta.

MAKE AHEAD/STORAGE This dish can be cooked and stored in the refrigerator, covered, up to 2 days.

Extra-virgin olive oil

2 chickens, (each about 4 pounds), each cut into 6 pieces (see page 220)

2 cups sliced mushrooms such as cremini or button

2 medium onions, diced

1 medium fennel bulb, thinly sliced

6 garlic cloves, thinly sliced

2 cups canned whole peeled plum tomatoes, broken up into small pieces with your hands

¾ cup dry red wine (ideally Italian, such as Chianti)

½ cup Chicken Stock (page 15)

1 bay leaf

Kosher salt and freshly ground black pepper

¼ cup capers, drained and rinsed

¼ cup pitted kalamata olives

½ cup chopped fresh flat-leaf parsley

1 Heat a large covered ovenproof sauté pan or Dutch oven over medium heat, and lightly coat the pan with oil. Brown the chicken in batches (to prevent crowding) until each piece is golden brown and the skin is crispy. Set aside on a platter.

2 Drain most of the fat from the pan, leaving a small amount in the bottom. Add the mushrooms and sauté until golden and crispy, about 3 minutes. Add the onions and fennel, and sauté until golden brown and quite limp, about 15 minutes. Add the garlic, the tomatoes and their juices, the wine, stock, and bay leaf. Reduce the heat and simmer the mixture until it reduces and has thickened, about 30 minutes.

3 While the sauce is cooking, preheat the oven to 325°F.

4 Season the sauce with salt and pepper. Add the chicken and any collected juices back to the pan. Cover the pan and place it in the oven. Braise the chicken until it is cooked through and the juices run clear when a thigh is pricked, about 45 minutes.

5 Sprinkle the capers, olives, and parsley on top of the chicken.

Polenta Fries

P ■ *Serves 8*

These tasty little fries are addictive. Their outer crusts are crunchy and fragrant with toasty corn flavor, and the insides are creamy and gooey. Basically, you can't miss with this dish. It's perfect for sopping up garlicky braising juices, as in the Chicken Cacciatore (page 217).

MAKE AHEAD/STORAGE The polenta can be prepared through Step 2 and can be stored in the refrigerator, covered, up to 5 days. You can also store the cooked fries in the refrigerator, covered, up to 1 day and recrisp them in a 300°F oven.

4 to 5 cups cold water

1½ cups Italian coarse cornmeal or coarse yellow cornmeal

1 tablespoon kosher salt

½ cup chopped fresh mixed herbs, such as rosemary, thyme, parsley, chives, and basil (optional)

Extra-virgin olive oil

Coarse sea salt and freshly ground black pepper

1 Stir together the water, cornmeal, and salt in a large, high-sided saucepan and heat over medium heat, stirring with a wooden spoon. Continuously stir the polenta until it is very thick and fairly dry, 15 to 20 minutes. Turn the heat down slightly when the polenta begins to thicken and sputter. (Be careful, as the polenta can sputter out of the pan and cause quite a burn.) Stir in the herbs, if using.

2 Generously coat the bottom of a jelly roll pan or shallow casserole with olive oil. Scrape the polenta into the prepared pan, and smooth it with a spatula. Chill the polenta completely.

3 Place a large nonstick sauté pan over medium heat, and pour in olive oil to a depth of 1 inch. Heat oil until it reaches approximately 350°F.

4 Cut the polenta with a knife or pizza cutter into short, thick fries, about 1 by 3 inches. (They are easier to handle when cut short and thick). Fry the polenta in batches (to prevent crowding) until it is golden brown and crispy, about 5 to 7 minutes per side. Try not to move the fries too much before they are browned, as they can stick to the pan and leave a mess that will burn. Remove the fries with a slotted spoon to a paper towel—lined plate. Sprinkle with coarse salt and a few grinds of fresh pepper.

Braised Chicken with Mushrooms, Leeks, and Red Pearl Onions

M ■ *Serves 4 to 6*

This is a warm, comforting chicken dish. The flavors of the vegetables lightly perfume the chicken and the sauce that the dish makes by itself. I like to serve this with roasted and lightly fried potatoes. Feel free to pile it on mashed potatoes or pasta instead.

MAKE AHEAD/STORAGE The chicken and vegetables can be braised and the braising liquid reduced (through Step 4) and stored separately in the refrigerator, covered, up to 3 days. The onions can be peeled and sautéed and stored in the refrigerator, covered, up to 3 days. Reheat the chicken, vegetables, and onions in the reduced braising liquid.

Olive oil

¼ cup all-purpose flour

¼ cup Herbes de Provence (page 27)

2 chickens (each about 4 pounds), each cut into 6 or 8 pieces (see page 220)

Freshly ground black pepper and kosher salt

2 leeks, white and light green parts only (save the dark green tops for stock), thinly sliced

6 garlic cloves, finely chopped

3 medium carrots, peeled and thinly sliced

1 pound cremini mushrooms, stemmed and sliced

1 pound shiitake mushrooms, stemmed and sliced

3 tablespoons tomato paste

1 bottle (750 ml) dry red wine, such as Cabernet Sauvignon or Merlot

2 cups Chicken Stock (page 15)

¼ cup dried porcini mushrooms (about 1 ounce)

1 cup red pearl onions

Pan-Fried Smashed Potatoes (page 186)

¼ cup finely chopped fresh flat-leaf parsley (optional)

1 Preheat the oven to 325°F. Place a large Dutch oven or covered sauté pan over medium heat. Lightly coat the bottom of the pan with olive oil.

2 Mix the flour with the Herbes de Provence in large shallow plate. Season the chicken with freshly ground black pepper and lightly with salt (kosher chicken can be very salty). Dredge the chicken pieces in the flour mixture. Immediately place the pieces into the hot pan. Brown the pieces in batches (to prevent crowding). Set the chicken aside as each batch is browned.

3 Add more oil to the pan if needed, and sauté the leeks and garlic until lightly browned, about 10 minutes. Add the carrots and continue sautéing until the carrots are browned, about 10 minutes. Add the sliced mushrooms and sauté until browned, adding more oil if needed, about 10 minutes more. Push the vegetables aside and add a small spoonful of olive oil to the pan. Sear the tomato paste in the oil until visibly darkened, about 2 minutes. Add the wine and stir to combine. Add the stock and porcini mushrooms, and return the chicken pieces to the pan. Cover and place in the preheated oven. Braise until the chicken is cooked through, about 1½ hours.

4 Remove the chicken and vegetables from the pan with a slotted spoon and set aside on a warm ovenproof platter. Cover the platter with foil and keep chicken warm in a 250°F oven. Place the pan over medium-high heat and reduce the cooking liquids by about half, until the flavors are concentrated and the liquid is slightly thickened, about 20 minutes.

5 Meanwhile, fill a small saucepan with water and bring to a boil over medium-high heat. Prepare a bowl of ice water with a strainer that fits in the bowl. Add the pearl onions to the boiling water and blanch them for 5 minutes. Drain them through the strainer and place the strainer in the ice water to cool the onions completely. (See page 41 for more information on blanching and shocking vegetables.) Remove the onions, cut the root end off, and peel off the loosened skin.

6 Place a small sauté pan over medium-high heat and add a small amount of olive oil. Sauté the onions until browned. Season with salt and pepper.

7 To serve, scatter the onions on top of the chicken and vegetables and ladle on some of the wine sauce. Garnish with chopped parsley if desired. Serve with potatoes and pass extra sauce in a gravy boat.

Chicken

Many chefs have a "love-hate" relationship with chicken. A piece of chicken is a blank canvas for the adventurous chef. It's one of the most versatile ingredients, and it partners so well with such a range of flavors, from luxurious exotic mushrooms to toasty spice mixtures. On the other hand, everyone knows that chicken is the most popular answer to "what's for dinner, Mom?"—and who wants to compete with that?

I really do love chicken, though, and that's probably because I only use kosher chicken. Even if I didn't have kosher kitchens, I'd still only use kosher chicken. It just tastes more "chicken-y" than the meat I remember from my pre-kosher days. Part of this is just a result of the koshering process. Since the salt has a chance to fully permeate the flesh, the meat is already wonderfully seasoned even before any other ingredients are added.

Chicken is my playground—it gives me so many creative opportunities in the kitchen. On a wintry day, I know that I'll want to braise it in a rich, deep wine sauce. A crisp fall day is the perfect time to stew it with end-of-season tomatoes and plump cloves of garlic. A summer picnic isn't complete without a batch of my special fried chicken (page 116). I try to make an interesting variation every day.

Another reason that my chicken is so delicious is that I always cut it myself. If you're used to buying precut pieces, you'll be surprised at how much nicer a chicken looks and tastes when you do it yourself. With a whole bird, the world is your kosher oyster! You can start saving all the bones and scraps that are the base of a wonderful stock. Toss the back and wings into a resealable heavy-duty plastic bag and freeze. Keep adding to the bag and soon you'll have plenty to make the tastiest stock you can imagine. Stock is essential in every kitchen—neither bouillon cubes nor canned broth come close. My partner, Beth, is so picky about her chicken stock for soup that she has to make it herself *every week* for her family. She feels that freezing it, even for one week, changes the flavor. (I say freezing is fine; I do it all the time!)

I prefer to cut a chicken into six or eight pieces (kosher chickens tend to have scrawny wings, so I just save them for stock). Here's how: Place the bird on a cutting board with the legs pointing at you. Be brave, this is easy! A line of fat is visible between the leg and the body of the chicken. Cut along that line with your favorite chef's or santoku knife. You may have to wiggle the leg free from the body. Turn the leg and thigh piece skin side down and look for a fat line separating the drumstick from the thigh. Cut along that line and repeat steps on other side. To remove the breasts, feel along the top of the chicken to find the breastbone. Cut from the back to the front of the breastbone along one side. With your knife, follow along the contours of the body to release the meat from the ribs. Separate the wing from the breast by finding the joint and cutting through it. Repeat with the remaining breast. If the breast pieces seem particularly large, you can halve them crosswise (right where the rib bones get thin) to make eight pieces. Use a cleaver or a large chef's knife, since you need to cut through the rib bones.

Chicken deserves as much respect and attention as even the most exotic ingredients. Try it in the following recipes:

Braised Chicken with Mushrooms, Leeks, and Red Pearl Onions (page 219)

Chicken Cacciatore (page 217)

Herbed Roasted Chicken with Quinoa-Mushroom Pilaf (page 61)

Shallots Fried Chicken (page 116)

Crispy Cod with Lemon Vinaigrette and Vegetable "Chips"

P ▪ *Serves 4*

I admit to being a fan of crispy and fattening treats. In the cold weather there is nothing more enjoyable than an afternoon meal of fish and chips. Unfortunately, I can't eat it that often without the guilt, so I came up with a modern take on the classic pub grub. Using an egg-white fish batter and serving oven-baked veggie chips instead of fries, makes this an affordable splurge.

MAKE AHEAD/STORAGE The dressing can be stored in the refrigerator, covered, up to 5 days.

For the Vinaigrette

½ cup unseasoned rice vinegar

¼ cup chopped fresh chives

¼ cup chopped fresh flat-leaf parsley

2 tablespoons fresh lemon juice

1 medium shallot, finely minced

⅓ cup extra-virgin olive oil

Kosher salt and freshly ground black pepper

1 cup rice flour

1 egg white

¼ cup water

Pinch of cayenne pepper (optional)

Olive oil

4 skinless, boneless 6-ounce cod fillets or other meaty, lean fish

Kosher salt and freshly ground black pepper

Vegetable "Chips" (recipe follows)

1 Make the Vinaigrette Whisk together the vinegar, chives, parsley, lemon juice, shallot, and olive oil in a small bowl. Season with salt and pepper.

2 Whisk together the rice flour, egg white, water, and cayenne, if using, in a large bowl until smooth and free of any lumps.

3 Place a large sauté pan over medium heat. Fill the pan with enough olive oil to come to a depth of ½ inch. Heat the oil to 350°F.

4 Season the fillets with salt and pepper. Lightly coat the fish with the batter. Place the fish in the oil and pan fry until lightly browned and crispy, about 5 minutes. Turn the fish over and fry on the other side, about 3 minutes longer, until golden. Remove the fish from the oil and drain on paper towels.

5 To serve, place a generous mound of chips on individual plates or a serving platter. Place the fillets next to the chips and drizzle with the vinaigrette.

Vegetable "Chips"

P ▪ *Serves 4*

Actually much tastier than french fries, these chips are crispy, colorful, and healthy, too.

MAKE AHEAD/STORAGE The roasted vegetables can be stored in the refrigerator, covered, up to 3 days. Reheat on a baking sheet in a 350°F oven until warm and recrisped.

- 1 medium parsnip, peeled and cut into sticks about 3 inches long and ½ inch wide
- 1 medium carrot, peeled and cut into sticks about 3 inches long and ½ inch wide
- 2 large sweet potatoes, peeled and cut into sticks about 3 inches long and ½ inch wide
- 1 large celery root (celeriac), peeled and cut into sticks about 3 inches long and ½ inch wide

Olive oil

Kosher salt and freshly ground black pepper

1 Preheat the oven to 350°F. Place all the vegetables in a large bowl. Lightly coat the vegetables with olive oil. Season with salt and pepper.

2 Scatter the vegetables on a baking sheet in one layer. Roast the vegetables, without stirring, until caramelized and lightly browned, about 1 hour.

Red Snapper in Romesco Sauce

P ▪ *Serves 4*

This version of the Spanish classic is great any time of the year. The fillets make it easy for a weeknight meal; a whole red snapper (see Variation) on a platter makes a dramatic presentation and is fun at the table for your family or guests to "dig" into! The sauce is equally delicious with grouper or other mild-flavored fishes. Serve with Saffron Rice with Almonds, Raisins, and Caramelized Onions (recipe follows).

MAKE AHEAD/STORAGE The sauce can be stored in the refrigerator, covered, up to 2 days. The sauce actually gets better if made the day before serving.

For the Sauce

    2 medium red bell peppers

    1 medium Spanish onion, cut in half

    ½ cup extra-virgin olive oil (use your best-quality oil)

    1 ancho chile*

    ½ cup blanched almonds

    4 garlic cloves, sliced

    1 slice of soft bread, cubed (leftover challah works well)

    3 tablespoons red wine vinegar

    1 teaspoon pimenton**

    Kosher salt and freshly ground black pepper

    Olive oil

For the Fish

    4 skin-on 6-ounce red snapper fillets

*Dried ancho chiles can be found in most Latin-American markets, and many neighborhood grocery stores now carry them. Anchos can range from mildly sweet to slightly spicy. Generally, I find, they are fruity in flavor with a slight "kick" on the palate. In this dish this amount of chile is not too spicy for the amount of other ingredients.

**Pimenton is Spanish smoked paprika. It is really not comparable to the paprika found in most grocery stores. It has a wonderful sweet smokiness essential to paellas, chorizo, and other Spanish delicacies. Pimenton can be found readily online or at specialty markets. The Spice House (see Sources, page 257) has a kosher-certified product that is excellent and easily shipped to your home.

1 **Make the Sauce** Preheat the oven to 375°F. Place the bell peppers and onion in an ovenproof casserole. Toss with 2 tablespoons extra-virgin olive oil. Roast the vegetables, occasionally turning, until golden brown and soft, about 1 hour. Remove from the oven and set aside. Raise the oven temperature to 400°F.

2 Heat 1 tablespoon extra-virgin olive oil in a small saucepan over medium-high heat. Fry the ancho chile until it is slightly darkened in color and puffs up, about 1 minute. Remove the chile and place it in a bowl of water to soak. Add the garlic to the same pan and sauté until it is golden brown, 1 to 2 minutes. Set aside.

3 Peel the cooled bell peppers. Drain, stem, and seed the ancho chile. Toast the almonds and bread in a dry pan until fragrant and slightly browned, about 3 minutes. Place the onion, garlic, peeled peppers, ancho chile, almonds, bread, vinegar, and pimenton in a blender, and process until mixture resembles a coarse paste. You may need to add up to 3 tablespoons extra-virgin olive oil. Season with salt and pepper.

4 **Make the Fish** Place a large sauté pan over medium heat. Lightly coat the bottom of the pan with olive oil. Salt and pepper the fillets. Place the fillets skin side down in the pan, and cook them until the skin is browned and crispy, about 5 minutes; try not to turn the fillets before they are ready, as the skin will stick to the pan. Remove the fillets and place them in an ovenproof dish, skin side up. Roast the fish until it is cooked through but not dry, about 6 minutes.

5 To serve, gently warm the romesco sauce in a saucepan over low heat. Place the fillets on a platter or individual plates. Spoon the sauce over the fillets. Serve saffron rice.

VARIATION

Whole Red Snapper (P) Use a 4- to 5-pound whole red snapper in place of the fillets. Lightly rub fish with extra-virgin olive oil and season with salt and pepper. Roast on a baking sheet lined with parchment paper at 400°F until firm to the touch or a thermometer registers 130°F when inserted in the thickest part of the fish, 35 to 40 minutes. Carefully transfer the fish to a serving platter and generously spoon the sauce over the fish.

Saffron Rice with Almonds, Raisins, and Caramelized Onions

P ▪ *Serves 4*

I like to use brown rice for this dish as often as possible. It has a nutty flavor and slightly chewy texture. White rice or basmati would be good substitutes.

MAKE AHEAD/STORAGE This pilaf can be stored in the refrigerator, covered, up to 3 days. Add a spoonful of stock or water when reheating.

Extra-virgin olive oil

2 large Spanish onions, thinly sliced

1 garlic clove, chopped

2 cups brown rice or long-grain white rice

4 cups water

½ teaspoon saffron threads

Kosher salt and freshly ground black pepper

½ cup slivered or sliced almonds, toasted

½ cup golden raisins

1 Place a large saucepan over medium-low heat. Lightly coat the bottom of the pan with olive oil. Slowly caramelize the onions and garlic until they are very soft and browned, about 30 minutes.

2 Add the rice, water, and saffron. Season with salt and pepper. Increase the heat to medium and cover. Cook the rice until it is cooked through and all the water is absorbed, about 45 minutes for brown rice and 25 for white rice. Do not stir rice yet. Set pan aside, covered, for 10 minutes, to allow the rice to finish cooking. Uncover pan and gently fluff rice with a fork.

3 Transfer the rice to a serving bowl and toss with the toasted almonds and raisins.

Roasted Red Snapper
with Charmoula and Red Lentils

P ■ *Serves 4*

Charmoula is one of the most versatile recipes. This brilliant sauce from Morocco is typically served with fish. It also works well as a vinaigrette and marinade. The flavor is piquant with a little kick from the chili flakes. I love the richly flavored condiment, Charmoula, with this fish recipe as well as drizzled over a platter of grilled vegetables.

MAKE AHEAD/STORAGE The Charmoula can be stored covered in the refrigerator for up to 5 days. The fish can be marinated a day ahead, covered, in the refrigerator.

For the Charmoula

5 garlic cloves

Kosher salt

½ cup fresh lemon juice

⅓ cup high-quality extra-virgin olive oil

½ teaspoon chili flakes

½ teaspoon paprika

½ teaspoon ground cumin

½ cup finely chopped fresh flat-leaf parsley

½ cup finely chopped fresh cilantro

Freshly ground black pepper

4 skin-on 7-ounce red snapper fillets

Olive oil

Kosher salt and freshly ground black pepper

Red Lentils (recipe follows)

Suggested Garnishes thinly sliced Preserved Lemons (page 21), finely chopped fresh flat-leaf parsley, finely chopped fresh cilantro

1 Make the Charmoula Place the garlic and 1 teaspoon salt in a mortar and pound it to a paste; or on a cutting board smash and scrape the garlic and 1 teaspoon salt with the side of your knife. Transfer the garlic paste to a small bowl and whisk in the lemon juice, olive oil, chili flakes, paprika, cumin, parsley, and cilantro. Season with salt and pepper.

2 Place the fish fillets in a shallow container and cover with charmoula, reserving about 1 cup for garnish. Marinate for 1 hour at room temperature or covered overnight in the refrigerator.

3 Preheat the oven to 450°F and lightly oil a baking dish.

4 Place a medium sauté pan over medium-high heat. Lightly coat the bottom of the pan with olive oil. Remove fillets from marinade and pat dry (discard marinade). Season both sides of each fillet with salt and pepper and place in the sauté pan, skin side down. Cook the fish until the skin is browned and crispy, about 2 minutes. Transfer the fish to the baking dish, skin side up. Roast for 10 to 12 minutes, or until fish is cooked through and flakes easily when pressed with a fork.

5 To serve, remove the fish from the pan and place atop a bed of lentils. Drizzle with reserved Charmoula and top with your choice of garnish.

Red Lentils

P ■ *Serves 4*

Lentils come in hues ranging from ivory to yellow, red, green, and black. The red lentil is one of the most delicate and quick-cooking. It will turn to mush if overcooked, so keep an eye on the pot and drain the lentils right away.

MAKE AHEAD/STORAGE These lentils can be stored in the refrigerator, covered, up to 3 days. Reheat lentils over low heat, stirring once or twice only so they don't break apart, until warmed through.

Olive oil

1 small onion, finely diced

1 garlic clove, finely diced

1 medium carrot, peeled and diced small

1½ cups red lentils (sort through the lentils to make sure there are no pebbles or debris)

2 cups water

Kosher salt and freshly ground black pepper

¼ cup chopped fresh flat-leaf parsley

2 tablespoons extra-virgin olive oil

1 Heat a medium saucepan over medium-high heat and lightly coat the pan with olive oil. Add the onion and sauté until lightly browned, about 5 minutes.

2 Add the garlic and carrot and sauté until lightly browned, about 5 minutes.

3 Add the lentils and water, and season to taste with salt and pepper. Cover the pan and simmer the lentils over medium-low heat until they are al dente, about 20 minutes. Remove pan from the heat and drain off any excess water.

4 Toss lentils with the parsley and extra-virgin olive oil, and adjust the seasoning to taste with salt and pepper.

Tuna Confit with Winter Grilled Salad and Mixed Olive Tapenade

P ■ *Serves 4 to 6*

Tuna is kind of like the "steak of the sea" and the less you do to it, the better. Generally I don't like to cook tuna above a sear or, if pushed, to medium rare. This preparation is the exception. The fruitiness of the olive oil infuses the meat, gently cooking it through. The result is a glorious mélange of tuna and oil that will never be mistaken for the canned variety. The oil can be used once again for "confit"-ing tuna or other fish.

MAKE AHEAD/STORAGE The cooked tuna can be stored in the refrigerator, covered, up to 2 days. Bring to room temperature before slicing and serving. The vinaigrette can be stored in the refrigerator, covered, up to 2 weeks. Remove vinaigrette from the refrigerator 30 minutes before using; shake well just before using. The confit oil can be saved and used again. Strain it through a fine-mesh sieve and store in the refrigerator, covered, up to 2 weeks; discard the oil after the second use.

1 to 2 pounds center-cut tuna steak in one large piece, skin and any dark brown spots removed by your fishmonger

1 bottle (750 ml) fruity extra-virgin olive oil (use your best-tasting oil)

For the Salad

¼ cup Slow-Roasted Tomatoes (page 23) or drained oil-packed sun-dried tomatoes

1 tablespoon balsamic vinegar

½ cup extra-virgin olive oil, plus more for grilling

Kosher salt and freshly ground black pepper

2 heads of firm lettuce, such as radicchio, romaine, or Bibb, cut in half lengthwise

Mixed Olive Tapenade (recipe follows)

Suggested Garnishes chopped olives, chopped fresh flat-leaf parsley, chopped Slow-Roasted Tomatoes (page 23)

1 Place the tuna in a large shallow roasting pan or saucepan. Cover the tuna with enough extra-virgin olive oil so it is completely submerged. Place the pan over low heat. Slowly cook the tuna (a thermometer should read 180°F for the oil temperature; do not allow the oil to boil) until cooked through, about 1 hour, depending upon the size of your pan. The tuna is cooked through when a knife tip poked in the center of the tuna piece comes out hot. The tuna should feel firm and will not yield when lightly pressed.

Remove the pan from the heat and let the tuna cool in the oil until the oil reaches a warm room temperature.

2 **Make the Salad** while the tuna is cooling. Place the tomatoes, vinegar, and olive oil in a food processor or blender and process until smooth. Season vinaigrette with salt and pepper. Transfer the vinaigrette to a container and set aside.

3 Place a grill pan over medium-high heat or preheat the grill to medium. Generously sprinkle lettuce halves with olive oil, salt, and pepper.

4 Grill the lettuces, cut sides down, until they are slightly caramelized and wilted, 5 to 7 minutes.

5 To serve, place the lettuces decoratively on a large serving platter and lightly drizzle with some of the vinaigrette. Remove cooled tuna from olive oil with two slotted spatulas and break it into big chunks with a fork. Transfer the tuna to the platter and generously dollop the tapenade over the tuna. Drizzle some of the remaining vinaigrette over the tuna and top with your choice of garnishes.

Mixed Olive Tapenade

P ■ *Makes about 1 cup*

A must for any olive lover, this mixture can be used as a spread or a dip or dolloped onto fish as a sauce.

MAKE AHEAD/STORAGE Tapenade can be stored in the refrigerator, covered, up to 3 weeks.

½ cup pitted kalamata olive

½ cup pitted cracked green olives

Juice and grated zest of 1 lemon

1 garlic clove

2 anchovy filets (optional)

Extra-virgin olive oil

¼ cup finely chopped red onion

¼ cup chopped fresh flat-leaf parsley

Kosher salt and freshly ground black pepper

Pinch of chili flakes (optional)

Place the olives, lemon juice and zest, garlic, and anchovy filets (if using) in a food processor. Pulse the mixture until it resembles a chunky paste, adding olive oil, a spoonful at a time, if needed. Transfer the mixture to a small bowl and stir in the onion, parsley, salt and pepper to taste, and chili flakes if desired.

Horseradish-Potato Crusted Grouper and Remoulade

P ■ *Serves 4*

This recipe is adapted from the classic French technique of crusting fish with blanched potatoes. The result is a lovely crunchy crust that dresses up the fish. I served this in the late winter and my kids loved it. You can leave out the horseradish if your family doesn't like the heat. This fish recipe works for Shabbat, as the fish is kept moist by the potato crust. The crust will recrisp when reheated because of the olive oil tossed with the potatoes. I have even served this dish during Passover, using whatever fish is available.

MAKE AHEAD/STORAGE The fish can be cooked ahead and stored in the refrigerator, covered, up to 4 hours. Reheat at 400°F for 8 to 10 minutes. The crust may soften in the refrigerator, but it will crisp up again in the oven.

1 large russet potato (about 1 pound)

Olive oil

2 tablespoons prepared horseradish

1 tablespoon chopped fresh flat-leaf parsley

1 tablespoon chopped fresh chives

½ teaspoon kosher salt and ¼ teaspoon freshly ground black pepper

4 skinless, boneless 6-ounce grouper or halibut fillets

Remoulade (recipe follows)

1 Preheat the oven to 400°F and bring a small saucepan of salted water to a boil.

2 Peel and grate the potato into fine strands using a box grater, a mandoline, or Asian slicer fitted with a julienne blade. Boil the potato for 2 to 3 minutes, just until it turns soft and opaque, and drain. Toss the blanched potato strands with a spoonful of olive oil, the horseradish, parsley, and chives, and season with salt and pepper.

3 Divide the potato mixture among the four fillets, piling it on the nonskin side, and pressing firmly to help it to stick. Heat a large sauté pan over medium heat and lightly coat the bottom of the pan with olive oil. Using a spatula, carefully transfer the fillet to the pan, potato-crusted side down, and cook 5 minutes. (Do not try to move, turn or peek at the fish, as the crust will fall off or stick to the pan. The crust takes 5 minutes to become crispy and brown. It will begin to stick to the fish as the starch forms a crust from the heat). Carefully transfer the fillets to a baking sheet or ovenproof casserole, crusted side up, and bake about 8 minutes, until fish is cooked through.

4 Serve fish with Remoulade.

Remoulade

P ■ *Makes about ⅔ cup*

This tasty classic piquant and creamy sauce is a snap to make and goes perfectly with the crusted grouper. I also serve it with tuna tartare. I enjoy it so much that I have even been known to smear it on bread for a remoulade sandwich!

MAKE AHEAD/STORAGE Remoulade can be stored in the refrigerator, covered, up to 5 days.

½ cup Garlicky Aioli (page 26) or best-quality store-bought mayonnaise

1 tablespoon capers, roughly chopped

2 tablespoons chopped sweet gherkins or cornichons

1 tablespoon prepared horseradish

1 tablespoon chopped fresh flat-leaf parsley

1 tablespoon chopped fresh chives

1 tablespoon anchovy paste (optional)

Kosher salt and freshly ground black pepper

Place the ingredients in a small bowl and whisk together. Season with salt and pepper to taste.

Roasted Grouper with Yukon Gold Potatoes and Garlicky Eggplant-Tomato Sauce

P ■ *Serves 4*

This method of preparing fish is a bit unusual. I based it on Mediterranean recipes in which foods such as eggs and fish are gently simmered directly in a sauce. The food absorbs the flavors of the sauce, becoming very tender and delicious in the meantime. A version of this dish is a staple on our menu at the restaurant and is always popular with fish lovers.

MAKE AHEAD/STORAGE Sauce can be made ahead and stored, covered and chilled, up to 5 days, or frozen for 1 month. When cooking fish in cold sauce, increase roasting time to 30 to 40 minutes.

1 large eggplant, peeled and sliced into ½-inch rounds

Kosher salt

2 large Yukon gold potatoes, unpeeled

Olive oil

One 28-ounce can tomato puree

½ cup kalamata olives, pitted and cut in half

1 head of garlic, cloves separated, peeled, and thinly sliced (not chopped)

¼ cup capers, drained and rinsed

1 teaspoon chili flakes (optional)

Kosher salt and freshly ground black pepper

1 large bunch of flat-leaf parsley, washed well and leaves and tender stems chopped

4 skinless, boneless 6- to 7-ounce grouper fillets

Extra-virgin olive oil (use your best-tasting oil)

1 Preheat the oven to 350°F.

2 Lay the eggplant slices on a rack set over a baking sheet. Generously sprinkle the eggplant with kosher salt. Turn the eggplant over and repeat. (The salt helps to draw out any bitter juices that are in eggplant.) Set aside for 1 hour.

3 Meanwhile, rub the potatoes with olive oil and place on a baking sheet. Lightly prick the skin of the potatoes. Roast until tender, about 40 minutes, then set aside to cool. Turn the oven down to 300°F.

4 Rinse the eggplant, pat dry with paper towels, and cut into large dice. Heat a large sauté pan over medium-high heat and generously coat the pan with olive oil. Add the eggplant and brown on all sides, stirring occasionally. Turn the heat down and stir in the tomato puree, olives, garlic, capers, chili flakes, if using, and salt and pepper to taste. Simmer sauce for 15 minutes.

5 Tranfer about one-third of the eggplant sauce to a blender or food processor and process until smooth (be careful when processing hot items, as steam can build up and cause burns.) Return the puree to the sauce in the pan and stir in the parsley. Remove the pan from the heat and set aside to cool slightly.

6 Lightly coat a large, deep, ovenproof casserole with olive oil. Slice the potatoes into thick slices and place them in the casserole in a single layer, completely covering the bottom of the dish. Place the fish, seasoned with salt and pepper, on top of the potatoes. Spoon the eggplant sauce over the fish, covering it completely. Generously drizzle with extra-virgin olive oil. Roast the fish for about 15 minutes, or until the fish is cooked through, and the sauce is bubbling.

7 Serve the fish, potatoes, and eggplant sauce directly from the casserole, drizzling each serving with more olive oil if desired.

Pan-Seared Rib-Eye Steaks

M ▪ *Serves 4*

Sometimes the simplest way to prepare something is also the best way. I believe that steak is a classic example. You can go all out with your fancy grill, but the humble sauté pan is really all you need. I love this method because the juices stay in the pan. They don't drip down and flare up at my steak. I also like the ability to control the heat more efficiently. I can get a really nice crust (a key to good flavor) and keep the inside very juicy and tender. All those great pan juices make a tasty little sauce as well.

Olive oil

Kosher salt and freshly ground black pepper

4 rib-eye steaks, each about 14 ounces and ¾ to 1 inch thick

For the Sauce

2 medium shallots, finely chopped

1 garlic clove, very finely chopped

½ cup dry red wine, such as Cabernet Sauvignon (try Baron Herzog)

1 cup Chicken Stock (page 15)

¼ cup chopped fresh herbs, such as parsley, thyme, rosemary, or chives

1 tablespoon Dijon mustard

1 Heat a large sauté pan (not nonstick) over medium-high heat for about 3 minutes and lightly coat the pan with olive oil. Season the steaks on both sides with salt and pepper, and cook the steaks (in two batches if needed to avoid crowding your pan) until a dark brown crust has formed on the bottom, about 7 minutes. Turn the steaks over with tongs (to avoid piercing the meat) and brown the other side about 5 minutes for rare meat or
7 minutes for medium-rare. Transfer the steaks to a platter and cover loosely with foil to keep warm and to let the meat rest while you make the pan sauce.

2 Make the Sauce Drain the fat from the pan, leaving the browned bits. Add a small amount of fresh olive oil if needed to the pan, and sauté the shallots until they are golden brown, about 3 minutes. Add the garlic and the wine and bring to a boil, stirring and scraping the bottom of the pan to incorporate any browned bits. Reduce the wine by half, add the stock, and reduce by half again. Stir in the herbs, mustard, and any accumulated juices from the resting steaks.

3 Serve the steaks with the sauce spooned over.

VARIATION

Peppercorn Steaks (M) First, generously rub the steaks with the peppercorn mixture in the Venison Loin Poivrade (see page 183).

Winter

Cassoulet with Beef Short Ribs, Duck Confit, White Beans, and Mustard Crust

M ▪ *Serves 8*

At first glance this dish looks a bit like the classic long-cooking stew cholent, but it's actually a classic French farmhouse dish. It's a delicious choice when you're looking for a recipe that you can assemble well ahead of time, then leave to bubble and bake all day long. Cassoulet is a great dinner to eat while watching a football game, along with great beer or red wine.

MAKE AHEAD/STORAGE The bean can be soaked up to 2 days ahead.

1 pound dried white beans (preferably Great Northern)

8 to 10 cups water

2 cups Chicken Stock (page 15)

¼ cup tomato paste

3 medium Spanish onions, chopped

6 garlic cloves, chopped

1 medium fennel bulb, trimmed and chopped

3 ribs celery, chopped

1 bay leaf

6 fresh parsley sprigs

One 14-ounce can whole peeled plum tomatoes

2 pounds beef short ribs, cut into 3-inch rib pieces

Kosher salt and freshly ground black pepper

Olive oil

4 legs of Duck Confit (recipe follows) or braised duck from Braised Duck Ravioli (see page 209; through Step 2)

1 pound garlic sausage or favorite sausage, diced

2 cups fresh, untoasted bread crumbs

1 cup chopped fresh flat-leaf parsley

¼ cup Dijon mustard

1 Place beans in a large container and add enough water to cover beans by 2 inches. Soak beans for 8 hours or overnight.

2 Drain the beans and place them in a large stockpot or Dutch oven. Add 8 cups water, stock, and tomato paste. Wrap the onions, garlic, fennel, celery, bay leaf, and parsley sprigs in a large piece of cheesecloth. Draw the corners together and tie with kitchen twine. Add the herb package to the beans. Bring the beans to a boil over medium-high heat. Reduce heat to a simmer and cook the beans, partly covered, for 1 hour.

3 Crush the tomatoes with your hands and add to the beans with their juices. Continue simmering the beans while preparing the short ribs.

4 Rinse the short ribs to remove any bone fragments and debris. Pat the ribs dry. Heat a large sauté pan over medium heat and lightly coat pan with oil. Brown the short ribs on all sides, about 15 minutes. Add the ribs to the beans, adding more water if the beans are not covered with liquid, and cook, partly covered, until ribs are tender, about 1 hour. Season with salt and pepper

5 Preheat oven to 375°F.

6 Meanwhile, remove and reserve the skin and fat from the duck. Remove the meat from the bones. Lightly shred the duck meat and set aside. Using the sauté pan from the short ribs, crisp the duck skin in the fat over medium heat until crispy and browned. Set aside.

7 Brown the sausage in the fat. Remove the sausage from the pan and set aside. Add the breadcrumbs to the pan and toast them until lightly browned. Remove the breadcrumbs and place in a medium bowl. Toss the bread crumbs with the chopped parsley and mustard and set aside.

8 Remove the herb package from the beans. Add the duck meat and sausage, and adjust seasoning to taste with salt and pepper. Sprinkle the breadcrumbs over the top of the casserole. Crumble the duck skin over the top. Bake the cassoulet in the oven until the mustard crust has browned and the cassoulet is bubbly, about 15 minutes.

Duck Confit

M ▪ *Makes 6 duck legs*

In the depths of winter, when I don't have fresh fruits to turn into jams, jellies, and preserves, I prepare duck confit instead. Not quite for spreading on breakfast toast, but it gives me equal satisfaction whenever I spot my container filled with these tender and flavorful legs tucked in the back of the refrigerator.

MAKE AHEAD/STORAGE Store the confit in the duck fat in the refrigerator, covered, up to 1 month. The fat can be used several times again for confit.

    6 whole duck legs

    3 tablespoon Herbes de Provence (page 27)

    Kosher salt and freshly ground black pepper

    About 3 cups rendered duck fat, or enough to cover the legs

1 Rub the duck legs with the herbs. Place them in a covered container to marinate overnight in the refrigerator.

2 The next day, wipe off the herbs with a cloth and pat the legs dry. Heat the fat with the legs in a Dutch oven over very low heat, making sure the legs are completely submerged in the fat. Cook the legs below a simmer about 2 hours (the fat should never bubble, and a thermometer inserted in the liquid fat should read about 165°F), until the meat is tender enough to fall off the bone when pierced with a fork.

3 Remove the pan from the heat and allow the duck and fat to cool completely to room temperature. Carefully transfer the legs to a container and pour fat over to seal, making sure the legs are completely covered in fat. Cover the container and refrigerate at least overnight before using the legs.

Slow-Roasted Short Ribs

M ▪ *Serves 6 to 8*

Nice and easy is the phrase that fits the method for this recipe. The rib meat becomes soft and fragrant if they are not rushed. They also take on deep rich flavors from the spices, aromatic vegetables, and the slow cooking. I like to roast the ribs on a bed of vegetables, so they don't sit in the fat that renders out from them. This way they maintain their moisture and flavor without the heaviness of a typical braising method. Serve with Barley Pilaf (recipe follows).

MAKE AHEAD/STORAGE The ribs can be made 3 days ahead and stored in the refrigerator, covered. Reheat ribs, covered, at 300°F for about 30 minutes, or until hot but not dried out.

10 pounds short ribs on the bone, cut into 3-inch rib pieces

3 large onions, roughly chopped

6 garlic cloves, roughly chopped

3 celery stalks, roughly chopped

2 large carrots, peeled and roughly chopped

1 teaspoon ground cumin

1 teaspoon ground coriander

½ teaspoon ground fennel seeds

2 tablespoons dried shallots or salt-free onion powder

1 tablespoon salt-free dried garlic

1 tablespoon sweet paprika

½ teaspoon pimenton*

Kosher salt and freshly ground black pepper

*Pimenton, Spanish smoked paprika, can't really be compared to the paprika found in most grocery stores. It has a wonderful sweet smokiness essential to paella, chorizo, and other Spanish delicacies. It can be found online or at specialty markets. The Spice House (see Sources, page 257) has a kosher-certified product that is excellent and easily shipped to your home.

1 Preheat the oven to 275°F.

2 Rinse the short ribs to remove any bone fragments and debris. Pat the ribs dry. Scatter the onions, garlic, celery, and carrots in a large roasting pan (you may need 2 pans to avoid crowding the pan).

3 Stir together the cumin, coriander, fennel seeds, dried shallots, dried garlic, paprika, and pimenton, and liberally rub the ribs with the spice mix. (Any remaining spice mix can be stored covered in a cabinet for 1 month.) Place the ribs on top of the vegetables. Sprinkle with salt and pepper.

4 Roast the ribs for 2½ hours or until the meat is tender and easily pierced. Discard the vegetables.

5 To serve, heap the ribs on a platter and serve hot.

Winter

Barley Pilaf

M ■ *Serves 6 to 8*

Barley has a rich and somewhat sticky consistency when cooked, almost like risotto. It's the perfect accompaniment to rich and meaty dishes, like the slow-cooked short ribs, with their tender, falling-apart texture. It's also wonderful to serve with stews since the barley soaks up all the braising juices.

MAKE AHEAD/STORAGE The barley can be stored in the refrigerator, covered, up to 3 days.

Olive oil

1 large Spanish onion, chopped

1 medium carrot, peeled and diced

1 medium fennel bulb, trimmed and chopped

2 garlic cloves, chopped

Kosher salt and freshly ground black pepper

2 cups medium pearled barley

4 to 5 cups Chicken Stock (page 15)

1 Heat a large saucepan over medium-high heat, and coat the bottom of the pan with olive oil. Sauté the onion, carrot, fennel, garlic, and salt and pepper to taste, until the vegetables are lightly browned and caramelized, about 10 minutes.

2 Add the barley and 4 cups Chicken Stock to the pan. Boil the barley, uncovered, until it is chewy, about 35 minutes. If all the liquid has been absorbed and the barley is not cooked through, add remaining cup stock and continue to boil until cooked through. Remove the pan from the heat and let the barley stand, uncovered, for an additional 5 minutes so that any excess liquid can be absorbed.

Pomegranate-Glazed Chicken (Page 159) with Bulgur Pilaf with Golden Raisins and Pine Nuts (Page 160) ■ FALL

Baked Apples with Dates and Apricots (Page 189) *with*
Apple, Honey, and Walnut Sorbet (Page 192) ▪ FALL

Chocolate Opera Torte with Chocolate Ganache (Page 195)
and Raspberry Coulis (Page 29) ▪ FALL

Braised Veal Shanks with Moroccan Spices
and Mango "Gremolata" (Page 241) ▪ WINTER

Whole Red Snapper in Romesco Sauce (Page 224) ■ WINTER

Arancini di Farro (Page 207) ▪ WINTER

Roasted Pineapple with Pineapple Sorbet (Page 243) ■ WINTER

Braised Veal Shanks with Moroccan Spices and Mango "Gremolata"

M ▪ *Serves 6*

This dish is an example of fusion cooking, without too much eccentricity; the flavor changes make sense. It came about when I was making osso buco, but instead of using typical Italian ingredients, I found myself heading in the direction of a rich and exotically flavored Moroccan tagine. It was a fun way to mix two types of cuisine that I love. Make sure your butcher cuts the shanks neatly, leaving the whole piece intact. This will make a nice looking dish. I like to pile this stew on a big platter and let everyone serve themselves. Serve with bulgar. Or, if you own a tagine, serve this dish in it and pass some couscous with it.

MAKE AHEAD/STORAGE This is a great dish to make ahead, as it seems to get better overnight. The cooked tagine can be stored in the refrigerator, covered, up to 5 days.

One 2-inch cinnamon stick

1 whole clove

1 tablespoon coriander seed

2 tablespoons fennel seed

1 tablespoon cumin seed

½ teaspoon chili flakes

¼ cup all-purpose flour

6 meaty veal shanks (about 6 pounds total), have your butcher tie them for you

Kosher salt and freshly ground black pepper

2 medium leeks, white and light green parts only (save the dark green tops for stock)

2 medium carrots, peeled and cut on the bias into 1-inch pieces

1 large fennel bulb, trimmed

6 garlic cloves, finely chopped

3 tablespoons tomato paste

1 cup pitted kalamata olives

One 14- to 15-ounce can chopped tomatoes

1 cup dry white wine, such as Sauvignon Blanc

2 cups Dark Chicken Stock (page 16) or Veal Stock (page 18)

Kosher salt and freshly ground black pepper

For the "Gremolata"

Grated zest of 1 lemon, cut into strips

¼ cup chopped fresh cilantro

¼ cup chopped fresh flat-leaf parsley

3 garlic cloves

2 tablespoons extra-virgin olive oil

¼ cup finely diced ripe mango

Kosher salt and freshly ground black pepper

1 Preheat the oven to 275°F.

2 Grind the cinnamon, clove, coriander, fennel, cumin, and chili flakes in a spice grinder, and mix with the flour. Season the veal shanks with salt and pepper.

3 Heat a large Dutch oven or large, deep, covered ovenproof sauté pan over medium heat. Lightly coat the bottom of the pan with olive oil. Dredge the flat sides of the veal shanks in the flour mixture. Sear the meat on all sides until golden brown and caramelized, about 10 minutes. Remove the veal and set aside.

4 Brown the leeks, carrots, fennel, and garlic in batches (adding more oil if necessary) until all the vegetables are browned (be careful not to overbrown the garlic).

5 Add a spoonful of oil to the pan and add the tomato paste, stirring and scraping the pan until the tomato paste is fragrant and visibly darkened, about 3 minutes. Stir in the olives, chopped tomatoes, wine, and stock, and season with salt and pepper. Return the veal and vegetables to the pan.

6 Cover the pan and transfer it to the oven. Braise the veal until the meat is very soft (about 2 hours).

7 **Make the "Gremolata"** Place the grated lemon zest, cilantro, parsley, garlic, and olive oil in a food processor or blender. Process until the mixture resembles a coarse paste. Transfer to a small bowl, toss with the diced mango, and season with salt and pepper.

8 To serve, spoon one shank on each plate and top with a spoonful of vegetables and sauce. Sprinkle with gremolata and serve with bulgur.

Roasted Pineapple with Pineapple Sorbet

P ▪ *Serves 4*

In the winter, fresh pineapple is a real treat. I love the candylike sweetness and vibrant yellow color.

Seeds scraped from 1 split vanilla bean

½ cup dark brown sugar

½ cup granulated sugar

1 cup light rum or apple juice

1 whole large pineapple, peeled

Pineapple Sorbet (recipe follows)

1 Preheat the oven to 300°F.

2 Heat the vanilla bean seeds, sugars, and rum in a large, ovenproof sauté pan over medium-low heat, stirring, until the sugars are completely dissolved. Add the pineapple to the pan and cook the pineapple, gently turning it several times, until thoroughly coated with the rum mixture. When the pineapple has become fragrant and is starting to give off its natural juices, about 15 minutes, transfer the pan to the oven.

3 Roast the pineapple, basting it frequently with the pan juices, until it is a deep golden brown and very fragrant, about 30 minutes.

4 Carefully remove the pineapple from pan and set it aside to cool slightly. Return the pan to a low burner and simmer the roasting juices until they are thick and syrupy.

5 When the pineapple is cool enough to handle, cut it into 4 wedges and cut out the tough core from each piece. Serve with Pineapple Sorbet (recipe follows), and drizzle with the reduced syrup.

Pineapple Sorbet

P ▪ *Makes about 1½ pints*

This sorbet is a snap to make if you use quality precut fruit. It pairs well with roasted pineapple.

MAKE AHEAD/STORAGE The sorbet can be made up to 4 days ahead and kept frozen. If the sorbet begins to separate, simply melt it and reprocess it in your machine. (See page 81 for more information on sorbets and granitas.)

4 cups cubed fresh pineapple or drained unsweetened canned pineapple

½ cup dark brown sugar

Seeds scraped from ½ a vanilla bean or ½ teaspoon vanilla extract

1 Puree the pineapple, sugar, and vanilla in a food processor or blender. Let the mixture stand for several minutes to allow the sugar to dissolve. Chill completely.

2 Process the sorbet mixture in your ice cream machine, following the manufacturer's instructions. Transfer the sorbet to a covered container and freeze until hard, at least 4 hours or overnight.

S'mores Cake

D ▪ *Serves 8 to 10*

My children and I love to toast s'mores on summer evenings, and when the weather is bad we often make them in the oven or microwave. However, s'mores have a much longer history in my family. Family lore attributes this recipe to my great-grandmother, who had this cake from her childhood. I certainly remember it from mine, since it seemed like the only cake my mother ever baked for our birthdays. I sometimes bake my slightly fancied- up version for my boys and have even served it at the restaurant.

MAKE AHEAD/STORAGE The cakes can be baked 1 day ahead and kept, tightly wrapped in plastic, at room temperature or frozen for up to 2 weeks. The marshmallows can be stored at room temperature, covered, up to 1 week.

4 tablespoons unsalted butter at room temperature, plus additional for greasing the pans

1 cup sugar

3 large eggs, separated

1 teaspoon vanilla extract

2¼ cups graham cracker crumbs

2 teaspoon baking powder

½ teaspoon kosher salt

¾ cup milk

For the Marshmallows

Confectioner's sugar

2 tablespoons plus 2½ teaspoons kosher gelatin

½ cup cold water

2 cups granulated sugar

½ cup light corn syrup

½ cup hot water

1 teaspoon vanilla extract or seeds scraped from 1 split vanilla bean

2 large egg whites

Chocolate Sauce (page 28)

Chocolate Sorbet (page 197; optional)

1 Preheat the oven to 350°F and grease two 9-inch cake pans.

2 Using a hand-held or standing mixer, beat the butter with the sugar on medium speed until light and fluffy, about 5 minutes. With mixer running, add the egg yolks one at a time, beating well after each addition until incorporated. Beat in the vanilla.

3 Stir together the crumbs, baking powder, and salt. Turn the mixer to low speed and alternately beat in the dry ingredients and the milk, in batches, beginning and ending with crumb mixture. In a clean dry bowl with clean beaters whip the egg whites to medium peaks and fold the whites into the batter. Divide the batter between the pans. Bake the layers until they lightly spring back, 20 to 25 minutes. Cool the cakes in their pans, on racks, for 15 minutes. Run a thin-bladed knife around the side of the pan to loosen and turn out the cakes onto the racks to cool completely.

4 Make the Marshmallows While the cake is baking, generously coat the bottom of a jelly roll pan with confectioner's sugar and set aside. Place the gelatin in the bowl of a stand mixer fitted with a whisk. Add the cold water and set aside until the gelatin has softened and "bloomed," about 20 minutes.

5 In a medium saucepan, boil the granulated sugar, corn syrup, and water until it reaches 240°F on a candy thermometer. Turn the mixer to low and gradually pour the hot sugar mixture into the gelatin. Continue beating until the mixture has doubled in volume and the outside of the bowl feels barely warm, about 10 minutes. Beat in the vanilla and set aside.

6 in a clean dry bowl with clean beaters beat the egg whites to stiff peaks and fold into the sugar mixture. Spread the marshmallows in the prepared jelly-roll pan and generously dust the top with confectioner's sugar. Set the marshmallow aside to firm up, uncovered, at least 4 hours at room temperature.

7 To assemble the cake, halve the cake rounds horizontally, to make 4 layers, and place the bottom of a cake, cut side up, on a cake plate. Use a pizza cutter to slice the marshmallows into 1-inch squares. Place some marshmallow pieces on the cake layer. If you have a propane torch, you can use it to toast the marshmallows slightly, just until golden. Drizzle with chocolate sauce. and cover with the top cake layer, cut side down. Continue layering with the remaining marshmallows, cake halves, and chocolate sauce, ending with top cake layer, cut side down, drizzled with Chocolate Sauce. For extra decadence, serve cake slices with scoops of Chocolate Sorbet.

Sticky Toffee Pudding

D ▪ *Serves 8*

My version of the classic British dessert has an extra helping of dried fruit folded in to it before baking. The fruit gives the pudding a very moist texture. Serve the cake with the Toffee Sauce for a dairy treat; or spoon it into a tumbler and top with a big spoonful of Champagne Sabayon (page 3) for a pareve dessert.

MAKE AHEAD/STORAGE This pudding can be stored in the refrigerator, covered, up to 1 day. Reheat pudding, covered, at 275°F just until warmed through, about 20 minutes.

Nonstick vegetable oil spray

1 cup chopped, pitted dates

1 cup water

1 teaspoon baking soda

1 teaspoon vanilla extract

2 cups all-purpose flour

1 teaspoon baking powder

¼ cup canola oil

¾ cup sugar

2 large eggs

2 tablespoons dried cherries or cranberries, chopped

2 tablespoons chopped dried apricots

For the Toffee Sauce (optional)

3 tablespoons butter

½ cup dark brown sugar

2 tablespoons heavy cream

1 Preheat the oven to 350°F. Lightly grease an 11 x 7–inch baking pan.

2 Bring the dates, water, and baking soda to a boil in a small saucepan. Remove pan from the heat, stir in the vanilla extract and set aside.

3 Whisk the flour and baking powder together in a small bowl.

4 Beat together the oil and sugar in the bowl of a stander mixer fitted with a paddle attachment, set on medium speed. Add the eggs one at a time, beating thoroughly after each addition. Add the flour mixture and stir in by hand. Add the date mixture and stir to combine. Fold in the dried fruit.

5 Spread the batter in the prepared pan and bake for 40 minutes, until a wooden skewer inserted comes out with moist crumbs clinging to it. (You do not want this to be too dry.) Remove pan from oven and put on a rack to cool slightly, about 10 minutes.

6 **Make the Toffee Sauce,** if desired, while the pudding is cooling. Combine all the ingredients in a small saucepan and simmer for 5 minutes.

7 To serve, scoop pudding into bowls and drizzle with Toffee Sauce.

Winter

Devil's Food Cake

P ■ *Serves 10*

This recipe is pure genius! There are no eggs, and yet the cake puffs up dramatically in the oven—then levels off, seemingly magically, as it cools. This is a perfect cake for birthdays or anytime you're serving a meat meal and need a real showstopper of a dessert. All the parts are free of dairy—the cake layers, the filling, and the glaze—but it's so rich and chocolatey, with such a lovely and delicate texture. My friend, the great French pastry chef Jacquy Pfeiffer, gave me this recipe. The cake is a signature item at the restaurant and in my home (we seem to have lots of celebrations). It is so versatile and delicious that I know you will love it as well.

MAKE AHEAD/STORAGE The cake layers can be baked one day ahead and stored, tightly covered in plastic wrap, in the refrigerator. Let layers come to room temperature before assembling the cake. The cake can be filled and frosted 1 day ahead and kept, covered with a cake dome, at cool room temperature.

2½ cups sugar

¾ cup neutral-flavored vegetable oil, such as canola

3½ cups all-purpose flour

¾ cup best-quality cocoa powder, such as Valrhona, plus extra for assembly

1 teaspoon fine sea salt

2 teaspoons baking soda

2¾ cups water

⅓ cup cider vinegar

2 teaspoons vanilla extract

Chocolate Mousse Filling (recipe follows)

Champagne Glaze (page 30), warmed

1 Preheat the oven to 350°F. Line three 9-inch cake pans with parchment paper.

2 In the bowl of a stand mixer fitted with a paddle attachment beat the sugar and the oil on medium speed to combine.

3 Sift together the flour, cocoa, salt, and baking soda. In a large measuring cup combine the water, vinegar, and vanilla extract.

4 On low speed alternately, add a third each of dry and wet ingredients to the sugar mixture, beating after each addition and stopping to scrape down the sides of the bowl if needed. Continue to beat just until all traces of the flour are absorbed into the batter; do not overmix the cake, or it may be tough.

5 Pour the batter immediately into the prepared pans, and bake the layers until they lightly spring back, about 25 minutes.

6 Transfer the cake pans to a cooling rack and let the layers cool completely to room temperature in the pans. Run a thin-bladed knife around the cake edges to loosen the layers. Dust the tops of the cakes lightly with cocoa powder to prevent sticking and carefully turn out the cakes, one at a time, onto a rack lined with a paper towel. Gently remove parchment paper.

7 To assemble the cake, place one cake layer on a 9-inch cardboard cake circle, top side up, and spread on half of Chocolate Mousse Filling. Top mousse with a second cake layer, top side up, then spread on remaining mousse filling. Top with the final cake layer, top side up, and transfer cake to the refrigerator to firm up, about 1 hour.

8 Place the cake on a wire rack set over parchment paper or a baking sheet to catch drippings. Slowly pour the glaze over the top of the cake, and let it drip down the sides. (Glaze may not completely cover all of cake, but don't try to spread the glaze with a spatula or knife, or it won't be smooth and glossy.) Chill the cake briefly, about 30 minutes, to set the glaze, before serving.

Chocolate Mousse Filling

P ■ *Makes about 3 cups*

I usually make this ultra rich chocolatey concoction to fill Devil's Food Cake layers, but any leftovers are pretty great on their own! If you prefer your cake with thin layers of filling, spoon the remaining

mousse into ramekins and serve with fresh raspberries or strawberries or simply dolloped with whipped cream.

MAKE AHEAD/STORAGE Make this filling at least 2 hours ahead, as it needs time in the refrigerator to set. Mousse may be made 1 day ahead and chilled in the refrigerator, covered.

> 6 ounces best-quality bittersweet chocolate, such as Valrhona or Callebaut, chopped (about 2 cups)
>
> 2 large egg yolks
>
> 5 large egg whites
>
> ½ cup sugar

1 Melt the chocolate in a large bowl set over (but not touching) a pan of barely simmering water. Remove bowl from heat and whisk the yolks into the melted chocolate, one at a time. Set chocolate mixture aside to cool slightly.

2 While chocolate is cooling, beat the whites in a clean large bowl until they form soft peaks. Slowly add the sugar, beating constantly and continue beating until the whites are stiff and glossy. Stir ⅓ of the whites into the chocolate mixture to lighten. Gently fold in the remaining whites in two additions, turning the bowl and scooping the chocolate over the whites just until most traces of white are absorbed. Cover the mousse with plastic wrap and chill it in the refrigerator until thickened enough to spread.

249

Pistachio Sorbet

P ▪ *Makes about 1½ pints*

I am a real pushover when it comes to pistachios. Their sweet flavor and subtle nuttiness gets me every time. You'll have extra pistachio paste left over from making this; I always try to keep some extra in the freezer so I can whip this sorbet up any time. I love the fact that I get pure pistachio flavor without having to deal with the shells. This recipe is fantastic paired with the Devil's Food Cake (page 248) or Chocolate Sauce (page 28), or both.

MAKE AHEAD/STORAGE Store the pistachio paste in the refrigerator, covered, up to 1 week, or freeze for 3 months. The sorbet can be made up to 4 days ahead and kept frozen. (See page 81 for more information on sorbets and granitas.)

250

For the Paste

2 cups unsalted shelled pistachios (about 12 ounces)

1½ cups sugar (about 10 ounces)

1½ cups Simple Syrup (page 31)

5 cups water (bottled water yields a tastier sorbet)

2¼ cups sugar

4 tablespoons light corn syrup

1 Make the Paste Place the pistachios and sugar in a food processor and process until the mixture is sandy with no large pieces of nuts remaining. Add Simple Syrup and continue to process until the mixture comes together and forms a paste.

2 Bring the water, sugar, and corn syrup to a boil in a medium saucepan. Remove from the heat and cool completely. Transfer to a blender, add ½ cup of the pistachio paste, and process until completely combined, or add the pistachio paste to the mixture and use an immersion blender to process it in the pan. Chill completely.

3 Process the sorbet mixture in your ice cream machine, following the manufacturer's instructions. Transfer the sorbet to a covered container and freeze until hard, at least 4 hours or overnight.

Grapefruit Sorbet

P ■ *Makes about 1½ pints*

This sorbet is very refreshing! The difference between this recipe and other sorbet recipes in this book (and at the restaurant) is the addition of an egg white. Because the grapefruit juice has very little fruit solids and the home ice cream machine doesn't spin very quickly, I add an egg white to help pull the sorbet together. The result is a sorbet that is almost like a sherbet in texture and mouth feel—this sorbet has an almost creamy texture and a bright citrus flavor.

MAKE AHEAD/STORAGE This sorbet can be made up to 4 days ahead and kept frozen. If the sorbet begins to separate, simply melt it and reprocess it in your machine. (See page 81 for more information on sorbets and granitas.)

4 cups water (bottled water yields a tastier sorbet)

2½ cups sugar

1 cup fresh grapefruit juice, preferably ruby red variety for better color

2 tablespoons fresh lemon juice

Finely grated zest of 2 grapefruits

1 egg white

Pinch of kosher salt

1 Place water and sugar in a medium saucepan, and cook over low heat until the sugar has dissolved completely. Remove from the heat and add the grapefruit and lemon juices and zest. Mix thoroughly and cool completely.

2 Whisk the egg white in a small bowl just until foamy and whisk in the salt. Add the egg white to the cold juice mixture. Process the sorbet mixture in your ice cream machine, following the manufacturer's instructions. Transfer the sorbet to a covered container and freeze until hard, at least 4 hours or overnight.

VARIATION

Caramelized Grapefruit Sundaes (P)

Peel 2 grapefruits and cut between the sections, leaving the membranes behind (see page 152). Place the sections in a flameproof baking dish or in 4 individual flameproof ramekins and sprinkle with raw sugar to cover. Caramelize the sections with a propane torch or under the broiler. Top with a scoop of grapefruit sorbet.

Peanut Butter and Jelly Sorbet

P ▪ *Makes about 1½ pints*

Peanut butter is not just for kids any more! When the last of the fruit is gone from the markets shelves and winter has really settled in, there is a bright spot—a fun rendition of the childhood treat. I make this all year long and serve it for dessert and snacks. I even served it at the restaurant when I was looking for a bit of whimsy on the dessert menu.

MAKE AHEAD/STORAGE This sorbet can be made up to 4 days ahead and kept frozen. (See page 81 for more information on sorbets and granitas.)

1 cup of favorite preserves or jelly (I use strawberry preserves)

2⅔ cups peanut butter

2¼ cups sugar

3 tablespoons honey

5 cups water (bottled water yields a tastier sorbet)

½ cup chopped roasted, unsalted peanuts (optional)

½ cup chocolate chunks (optional)

1 Spread the jelly on a silicone mat or parchment paper on a baking sheet. Spread 1 cup of the peanut butter on a silicone mat or parchment paper on another baking sheet. Freeze both overnight. (The jelly won't freeze hard because of the sugar content, but it will be very cold and help set the sorbet).

2 Stir the sugar, honey, and water in a medium saucepan over medium heat, until the sugar has dissolved. Transfer to a blender or food processor, add the remaining 1⅔ cups of peanut butter and blend until combined well. Chill completely.

3 Process the peanut butter sorbet mixture in your ice cream machine, following the manufacturer's instructions. When the sorbet is ready to be removed from the machine, stir in the frozen jelly and peanut butter and the chopped chocolate and peanuts, if using. Freeze until hard, at least 4 hours or overnight.

RECIPES BY CATEGORY

FIRST COURSES

STARTERS

SOUPS

SALADS

PASTA

MAIN DISHES

ESSENTIAL RECIPES AND SEASONINGS

SOURCES

KOSHER COOKS HAVE EVEN MORE OF A CHALLENGE than most to find ingredients. Here are some sources I've used and found to be helpful. Some of these sources are specifically for kosher products, while others have a mix of kosher and nonkosher items but are wonderful stores that are terrific for any cook. This list isn't comprehensive, but it gives you a good start in locating some unusual ingredients and kitchen equipment if you can't find them in a store near you.

Bridge Kitchenware
711 Third Avenue
New York, NY 10017
212-688-4220
www.bridgekitchenware.com
Knives, cookware, and bakeware

Chef's Catalog
3215 Commercial Avenue
Northbrook, Illinois 60062
800-338-3232
www.chefscatalog.com
Knives, cookware, and bakeware

Chef Shop
877-337-2491
www.chefshop.com
Many specialty products, grains, lentils, and rice

ChocoSphere
877-992-4626
www.chocosphere.com
High-quality specialty chocolates and chocolate products; many have kosher certification. They carry cocoa nibs.

Far Away Foods
650-344-1013
www.farawayfoods.com
Many specialty products, grains, lentils, and rice

King Arthur Flour Company
The Baker's Catalogue
P.O. Box 876
Norwich, VT 05055
800-827-6836
www.kingarthurflour.com
www.bakerscatalogue.com
Their flour is wonderful.

KosherBison.com
www.kosherbison.com
Certified kosher bison.

Musicon Farms
385 Scotchtown Road
Goshen, New York 10924
845-294-6378
www.koshervenison.com
Venison certified kosher under the Orthodox Union.

Oh! Nuts
www.ohnuts.com
Specialty dried fruits, nuts, and bulk items that are certified kosher by the OK Laboratories.

Sadaf
www.sadaf.com
Pomegranate molasses and paste, and other Middle Eastern products.

The Spice House
www.thespicehouse.com
Specialty whole spices, dried mushrooms, and vanilla beans and extracts. They also carry pimenton, Spanish smoked paprika. Most products have a kosher certificate on file. This company will send you a copy of the kosher certificate with your order.

Sur la Table, Catalogue Division
410 Terry Avenue North
Seattle, WA 98109
800-243-0852
www.surlatable.com
Fine cookware and bakeware, and hard to find items such as tagines.

INDEX

258

Index

259

Index

Index

270